OUTBACK COP

Evan McHugh is a journalist who has written for newspapers, television and radio. His previous books include *The Stockmen: The Making of an Australian Legend, Outback Stations, Bushrangers, The Drovers, Birdsville, Outback Pioneers, Outback Heroes* and *Shipwrecks: Australia's Greatest Maritime Disasters.* Evan's book about true crime in the outback, *Red Centre, Dark Heart*, won the Ned Kelly Award for best non-fiction in 2008. He lives with his wife in the Hunter Valley, New South Wales.

OUTBACK COP

THE COLOURFUL LIFE AND TIMES OF THE BIRDSVILLE POLICEMAN

NEALE McSHANE
with EVAN McHUGH

MICHAEL JOSEPH
an imprint of
PENGUIN BOOKS

MICHAEL JOSEPH

UK | USA | Canada | Ireland | Australia
India | New Zealand | South Africa | China

Penguin Books is part of the Penguin Random House group of companies
whose addresses can be found at global.penguinrandomhouse.com.

Penguin
Random House
Australia

First published by Penguin Random House Australia Pty Ltd, 2016

Cover design by Alex Ross © Penguin Random House Australia Pty Ltd
Text design by Louisa Maggio © Penguin Random House Australia Pty Ltd
Maps by Michelle Havenstein
Cover photograph by Hugh Brown
Every effort has been made to identify the owners of the uncredited photographs in the
image section and the publisher welcomes hearing from anyone in this regard.
Typeset in Sabon by Louisa Maggio © Penguin Random House Australia Pty Ltd
Colour separation by Splitting Image Colour Studio, Clayton, Victoria
Printed and bound in Australia by Griffin Press, an accredited ISO AS/NZS 14001
Environmental Management Systems printer.

National Library of Australia
Cataloguing-in-Publication data:

McShane, Neale, author
Outback cop : the colourful life and times of the
Birdsville policeman / Neale McShane, Evan McHugh
9780143797302 (paperback)

McShane, Neale
Police, Rural–Queensland–Birdsville–Biography
Police–Queensland–Birdsville–Biography

Other Creators/Contributors:
McHugh, Evan, author

363.2092

penguin.com.au

For Sandra,
Andrew, Lauren and Robbie

Contents

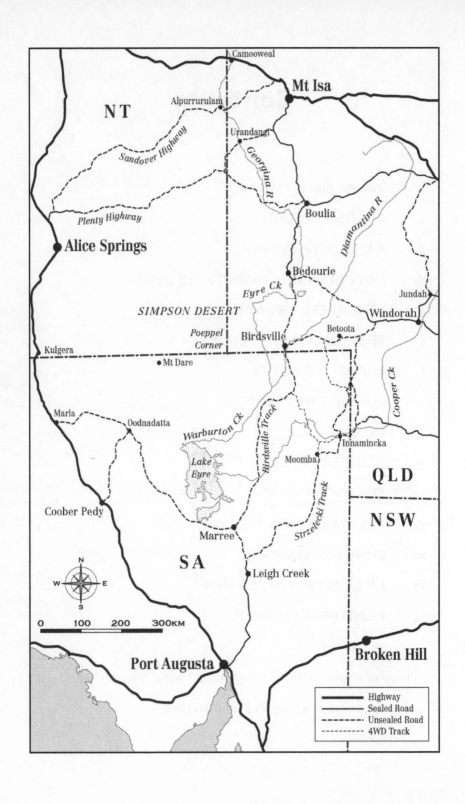

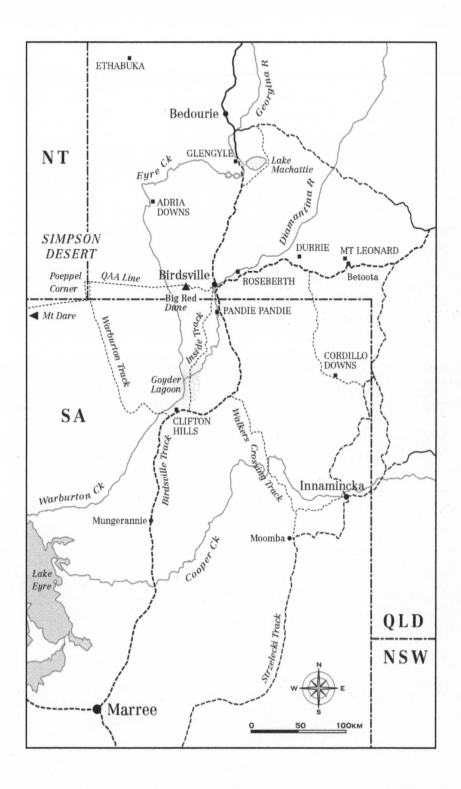

INTRODUCTION

by Evan McHugh

In November 2015, I returned to Birdsville, the town I'd lived in and written about in *Birdsville: My Year In the Back of Beyond*. I made the trip for the retirement of Senior Constable Neale McShane, who'd been the Birdsville cop since 2006. Neale was one of the many Birdsville residents who took me and my wife, Michelle, under their wing and showed us how special the outback could be. Neale was also one of the people who ensured we maintained our connection with Birdsville and its community after we'd left. Every now and then, he'd ring to share his latest adventure with me.

'You'll never believe what just happened,' he'd say, then launch into an epic tale of dust and danger or flood and mud.

From an initial reserve that's understandable when a writer and police officer first meet, our acquaintance quickly grew into a lasting friendship. Perhaps the key was an aspect of Neale's character that came as a surprise in someone who has made policing a career. Rather than having a jaded view of his fellow man, the result of years of dealing with the worst of human nature, Neale tends to look for the best in people.

There's also an element of trust involved in a friendship where anything Neale says and does could turn up in print. Before my Birdsville book was published, I gave Neale the opportunity to review what I'd written about him. There was one observation he'd made that he thought might cause problems. Then he said, 'You know what? I said it. I'll stand by it.' In the end it caused him no problems at all.

A friend of Neale's suggested other qualities that were also unexpected in the Birdsville cop. Sergeant Major Ian Haycock (retired) said, 'He's got a big heart.' Everyone who has spent any time with Neale would have to agree. He doesn't just do his duty as a police officer, he actually cares about people and tries to help them. Rather than get them out of trouble then point them to the caravan park, he's put them up in the police barracks or the courthouse. Rather than tear strips off someone when they didn't report in when they said they would, he'd say, 'Evan, I'm just checking that you made it back safe.' Or when Mount Isa Police rang him on holidays to say I'd been reported missing (while I was trying to get through to them to say I wasn't) he replied, 'Nah, we couldn't get that lucky.'

When the chance came up to do a book on Neale's experiences, I couldn't wait to get started. That said, we were worried that the stroke he'd suffered just months before may have affected his memory. We also wondered if he would have the stamina to get through hours of recording his experiences over nearly ten years as the Birdsville cop.

In the end, no worries. From the moment we sat down on the verandah of the old courthouse in Birdsville, the stories flowed. The process continued at the apartment in Brisbane where he stayed courtesy of the Police Helping Hand Fund during his continuing rehabilitation. We put the finishing touches on the project on the verandah of his beautifully renovated Queenslander in Charleville.

As much as possible, in the text I've sought to retain the mood of two blokes having a yarn in the shade of a classic old outback building, the kind of rambling conversation you might overhear anywhere from the back of Bourke to Broome. So when Neale occasionally says 'you' he means me, and his references to experiences he and I have shared are mostly self-explanatory. Where they're not, I've added notes and comments in brackets. Neale's humour is also integral to much of his storytelling, and in places I've noted where one or both of us were laughing, especially where it might not be obvious that he's being ironic.

It shouldn't be hard to imagine you're on the courthouse verandah with us, even though I've deleted most of the flies. The wide expanse of the Birdsville airstrip is in front of where we're sitting, with the pub shimmering in the heat on the other side. The dark green foliage that lines the Diamantina River is away to the right, while a long low sand hill on our left marks the edge of the desert. Appropriately, this is where the story of the Birdsville cop begins and ends.

CHAPTER 1

BAPTISM OF FIRE

Looking for a challenge both in your lifestyle and working environment?

Desirous of living/working in one of the remotest Western Queensland Police Divisions?

Looking for the opportunity to maybe set yourself and your family up financially?

Then seriously consider the following position that is now being readvertised.

Vacancy 334/06 in Qld Police Gazette dated 16 June 2006 advertises a position of Senior Constable, Officer In Charge, Birdsville Police Station. There are numerous career and financial advantages associated with this position. These include:

- The position has a department residence and a fully equipped barracks.
- $310.30 per fortnight family locality allowance = $8067.80 per year extra.
- 35% Operational Shift Allowance (OSA).
- Potential for approved secondary employment in Division.

- Potential employment for spouse/partner through Q-Gap at Police Station.
- Five (5) days per year isolation leave.
- Ability to accumulate paid days off.
- Higher rate of accrual of recreation leave (250.8 hours per year).
- Two (2) annual return air fares for Officer and family. Ability also to take cash in lieu of airfares.
- Cross border (QLD/NT) policing opportunities.
- This is a dedicated Officer In Charge position.
- Work at major events, including Birdsville Races.
- Too many other advantages to mention e.g. fishing, hunting, camping, remote-area policing and four-wheel driving.

Birdsville Police Station is within the Mount Isa Police District and is located approximately 1592 kilometres west from Brisbane and 670 kilometres south from Mount Isa.

If you are up to a challenge and looking to gain an advantage in the promotional and financial stakes, then:

- do your research;
- speak with the current acting officer-in-charge;
- consider your personal circumstances; and
- submit your application.

And yes, be aware that living and working in Birdsville can be difficult, challenging and at times isolated.

It was hot. Four days after I took up my new post as OIC, officer-in-charge, at Birdsville Police Station, in November 2006, the town set the record for the hottest day in Australia that year: 48.7 degrees Celsius. That's 120 degrees Fahrenheit. So I noticed the heat.

We had box air conditioners back then. Not the split-system air conditioning we have now. They really struggled to keep you cool.

It was dusty. There were a lot of dust storms that year because it was very dry. It was the middle of a drought. The breezeway beside the barracks and the garage were both full of dust and I thought, Gee, the copper before me must have been a bludger. So I cleaned it all out, hosed it all out. Beautiful. And then a dust storm came, and four or five days later it was like I'd never cleaned it.

You can guarantee you'll get a dust storm just after you've cleaned the place, too. Nevertheless, sweeping dust is part of the job. You clean the house. You clean the police station. Then you do it all again.

And there were flies. You couldn't go out for a walk during the day without being covered. You could drive out into the middle of nowhere, nothing and no-one for hundreds of kilometres, and within seconds you'd have hundreds of them trying to be your best friend. It made me wonder what they all did before I came along.

My first experience of Birdsville was a fair shock to the system. I thought Charleville, where I was a prosecuting sergeant with the Queensland Police Service, was hot because it's in the middle of Queensland. It's regularly 40 degrees. I thought it might be a couple of degrees warmer in Birdsville but you don't realise how much hotter it is until you actually get there. It's just oppressive.

But everyone knows Birdsville. I'd been here once because I'd brought a house out here. Not bought, brought. Out here they transport houses from place to place and I was escorting one of those. They load them onto huge semitrailers, sometimes they cut them in half, but they can be so wide they need a police escort to warn oncoming traffic, supervise removing and replacing road signs and to ensure that nothing gets damaged along the way.

The town is on the eastern edge of the Simpson Desert, in the south-west corner of Queensland, near the borders of South Australia and the Northern Territory, and it really is the land of plenty: plenty of heat, plenty of dust, plenty of flies.

The population is seventy to a hundred permanent residents during the cooler months, when tourism is a major part of the town's activities. Over summer, that can drop as low as forty as things wind down and people take holidays to escape the heat. The town is also surrounded by cattle stations that measure in the thousands of square kilometres. For much of the year, it's a sleepy little outback town like any other. However, it's also famous for its iconic outback pub, the Birdsville Hotel, and for its annual horse races, which see the population increase a hundred-fold for two days at the beginning of September. Being on the edge of the Simpson Desert, it's also the starting point or destination for four-wheel drive and off-road motorbike adventurers hoping to tackle the hundreds of kilometres of sand hills that surround the town and extend far to the west, south and north.

I initially thought being the Birdsville cop wasn't for me. The job was advertised three times before I put in an application. The position was for a senior constable and I was a sergeant (a rank above) at the time, so I thought, Nah. I didn't even think about putting in for it.

Then, a month later, it got advertised again and the superintendent from the Mount Isa District put a spiel out: come to Birdsville, this is what we offer you. And it's got all these perks. Then I considered it, but I thought, What about my family? We'd been separated a few times before because of work, and by this stage my daughter, Lauren, was finishing her final year at school. Anyway, for a second time I thought, Nah, I'm not putting in for it.

Then it was advertised for a third time, with another spiel: come to Birdsville. And I thought, I'm gonna put in for it. I was fifty years old and I had nine years to go with the Queensland Police Service before I had to retire (the compulsory retirement age in the QPS is sixty). I thought, That would be a good way to finish my career. I'd never been an officer-in-charge of a police station.

So I spoke to my wife, Sandra, and we came out and had a look at the place. The whole town was dry and dusty and practically deserted, as it was getting into the hotter months and the tourists were few and far between. When there aren't many people around, it feels more remote than ever.

We went through the house, which was carpeted at that stage. The carpet was full of dust and crushed-in dirt. Sandra went around to look at something and I came out and the copper who was there, who was relieving at the time, he said, 'She doesn't like it, does she?'

I said, 'Yes, she does.'

He said, 'Nah. I can tell she doesn't like it.'

And he was right. Police are pretty good at that.

Nevertheless, the job had lots of attractions. I looked at the crime figures: virtually none. Traffic accidents? Probably four or five a year. A good community. You had the races. Obviously the hotel. You had the house, which was free. They gave you extra money for being here.

So, I had nine years to go with the police, and it was either Birdsville or go up to senior sergeant. And I'd done that, relieving at Cunnamulla, a town about 200 kilometres south of Charleville, but you've got all the issues that go along with being senior sergeant: people management, budget, blah blah blah.

And I didn't want to do that again.

I wanted a change from prosecuting, too. I'd spent ten years representing the Queensland Police Service in court for everything from traffic tickets to serious crime. Sometimes you get a case, like a murder committal, and you're up against the best barristers in the state so you've got to really prepare, you've got to listen to every word. Or you can run into trouble when witnesses don't turn up and you've got to try and find them. It's just stressful. Nothing runs smoothly. Honestly, in prosecutions, nothing runs smoothly.

If you win, it's because the police officers involved put together a good brief. If you lose, it's the prosecutor's fault. One or the other. Then you'd have a win and you'd get the police you were representing saying, 'Well how come he didn't get jail?' They don't realise that if you negotiate a plea they have to get a discount. Sometimes you have an aggrieved, a victim, who doesn't want to give evidence, so you try to get a successful outcome where they don't have to. The deal might be that you don't ask for a term of imprisonment or something like that. And any plea you negotiate has to be approved by the inspector anyway. That didn't stop me getting nicknamed Do-a-deal-Neale.

In hindsight I'd probably had enough of prosecutions. It's a desk job or you're in court, negotiating with police, lawyers and magistrates. There's not much opportunity to engage with the rest of the community. When I'd done some relieving as officer-in-charge at the famous little opal town of Quilpie (population 570, compared to Charleville's 3000 and Birdsville's 70) I'd found that working in a small community was much more appealing. Something happens, you've got to deal with it. It can be people having to land a damaged plane, which thankfully in most cases is just a landing-gear light not working. You know what that's like.

You can have people die. That's life, people have accidents. And you can bet your bottom dollar, in ten years, there are going to be two or three deaths in town. You've got to deal with all that. If there's a fire, you've got to deal with it. Missing persons. You've got to go with what you got.

Sandra and I spent quite a while talking about it, and eventually we struck a deal. I would come out, then our daughter Lauren would join me once she finished high school and take the QGAP job. QGAP is a one-stop State Government shop that provides a suite of government services such as car registrations, applying for housing, and so on. Lauren wanted to have a gap year so she could come out and work with me, doing the QGAP job for sixteen hours a week, and I'd look after her, being her dad. Sandra would stay in Charleville with our youngest son, Robbie, while he finished school. He still had a couple of years of high school to go and didn't want to go to boarding school. We didn't want him to go either. It was far from being an easy decision: effectively splitting up the family and having to spend long periods apart. Sandra and I both loved family life and each other. The job in Birdsville wouldn't mean the end of that but it would involve some major changes in all our lives.

There were other considerations, too. We'd bought a Queenslander in Charleville a few years earlier and Sandra could finish doing it up, get it painted. She was also working as a probation parole officer part-time and working at the Cosmos Centre as a guide. Our oldest son, Andrew, was already doing a carpentry apprenticeship in Brisbane after returning from three years in the UK.

Lauren coming out here was probably the clincher. She didn't want to go straight from school to uni. I didn't think she was ready to leave the nest but that may say more about me than it does about her. So if Lauren came here, she'd be with me. And Sandra had a job in Charleville, and Robbie. Lots of people have long-distance relationships: miners, pilots, whatever. So Sandra could fly out when she was on holidays or for big events. It was probably $300 return in those days, which wasn't a large amount of money. Robbie could come out all the time, too, and I'd go home whenever I could. We'd see each other on a semi-regular basis. It would work out.

I said, 'We'll take the job but the carpet has to go.' (Laughter) There were a few other things that I requested before I agreed to move in, and they did all those. They put the lino in and I took the job.

Heading out to Birdsville in late 2006, I said goodbye to my family and headed off from Charleville in my trusty 1996 Toyota Land Cruiser. I drove 220 kilometres to Quilpie, then 245 kilometres to an even smaller town, Windorah. I dropped into the police station at Windorah and introduced myself to the officer, then Senior Constable Jim Beck. I had a cuppa and yarn with Jim, as Windorah was going to be my neighbouring station when I got to Birdsville, albeit 400 kilometres away. I had a feeling we would have a lot to do with each other, and I was right: overdue tourists, accidents, criminals, joint patrols, you name it.

I filled my car, checked it and headed off. I had just shy of 400 kilometres to travel, the first 100 kilometres single-lane bitumen then the rest gravel roads. I travelled for hours without seeing another vehicle. Finally, I spotted dust coming towards me. I laughed when I saw it was the furniture removalists who had taken my furniture out to Birdsville on their return leg. I stopped and had a yarn to them. It was good to talk to someone. I said goodbye, headed off again and six hours after leaving Windorah I went over a sand hill and saw the famous Birdsville Race Course on the right-hand side. Ah, made it.

By this time it was late afternoon. It was very hot and dusty. The whole town was brown with no green. Even the trees were brown from the dust. There was no-one about. One four-wheel drive was parked outside the pub. I went to my house. Fortunately, Inspector Trevor Kidd had arranged for it to be thoroughly cleaned before I arrived, as no-one had lived in it for almost eight months. The fridge was on and all the furniture was in place. There were still heaps of boxes to unpack. There was no police officer to welcome me. There hadn't been one in Birdsville for weeks and weeks. The keys to the police station and vehicle were on the kitchen bench.

Prior to going to Birdsville my plan was to stay till retirement, a decade in the future. I thought, Well, I'm here now. I unpacked the vehicle, turned on the air conditioner, cracked open a beer and wondered what the next ten years would bring.

I came in after the previous policeman had had a few problems. He had an incident with cattle wandering onto the airstrip and he solved that problem by shooting them. Mind you, he *was* in charge of the security of the airstrip at the time. Queensland Police lost the security job after that. Those two incidents were related. They were very much related.

People have got their opinions on the shooting. I wouldn't have done it myself. However, you imagine you're in a plane, or your family is in a plane, and you hit a beast. What's going to be the outcome? The beast is probably going to die, but people are going to die as well.

So he solved that problem and it kicked the Diamantina Shire Council into gear, because they fixed the fence. You'd be surprised to know that since then there's never been a beast on the airstrip. Not since I've been here, in nine-and-a-half years. There was a lot of publicity about that incident, but the person who owned the cattle, Geoff Morton from Roseberth Station, was one of the first to invite me out for a cup of tea at his place.

Not long after, the new assistant commissioner came to town, and Geoff was a councillor with the local council. I invited the locals up to meet him; all the movers and shakers in town: the Gaffneys, the Brooks, Don and Lyn Rowlands. I warned the assistant commissioner, 'Geoff might jam you about the cattle because it's only a few months since it happened.' I think the police department had refused to pay for the cattle, so I thought he could do with some warning. And he said, 'Thanks for that.'

But Geoff never mentioned it to him, to his credit. Just came in, shook his hand, had a cup of tea with him, talked about many things, issues, the drought, the land, isolation, but never mentioned his cattle. I thought a lot of Geoff for that. I really thought he might say something and he didn't.

That was one of the first things I noticed about Birdsville: how welcoming the community was. People from all walks of life went out of their way to introduce themselves to me, from the Aboriginal community to the townspeople to business people, kids, everybody. They all made a real effort to welcome me to their town.

I was invited out for cups of tea at Roseberth; Sandra, Lauren, Robbie and I were invited down for dinner with David and Jane Morton at Pandie Pandie Station. David and Nell Brook, who own five cattle stations in the area and a share in the Birdsville Hotel, introduced themselves. Whenever people from Bedourie – a small town north of Birdsville – came down, they made it their business to come up and introduce themselves. I found it so pleasing that people made a point of making me feel welcome.

Dusty the Baker rang me up a couple of days after I got here.

He said, 'Come down for a cup of tea. I'd love to meet you.'

So I went down and met Dusty and that was the start of a friendship with him.

I didn't know it when I took the job, although I'd heard whispers, but after I got here I realised you've got some really good people in Birdsville. People who will help you out at any time of the day or night.

I formed a good relationship with Don the ranger; he's a good mate of mine. He knows the desert like the back of his hand. I've got Peter Barnes, and Theo Nel before him, brilliant mechanics who could do anything. Then you've got people like Dusty who are electrical people. So you look around the town, probably any town, and you find people with a vast array of skills who can help you do things. Here, you know they'll help you without a second thought.

So I wasn't lonely when I arrived, even though at first I was here by myself. I found it a very welcoming, very friendly, very hot town.

One of my first jobs, early in December 2006, was a call from the pub that someone was overdue on his way from Innamincka to Birdsville. Innamincka is about 300 kilometres as the panting crow flies, 412 kilometres by dirt road, to the south-east of Birdsville. Given the huge distances between towns, on dirt roads or remote tracks that may see no other vehicles for days, it's recommended that people log their travel plans with a friend, relative, local police or their next accommodation in case something happens to them. If you're a couple of hours overdue, you can be reasonably confident that help will be on the way. If you stay with your vehicle, on the route you intended to take, you can be sure help will come. The Birdsville Police Station logs dozens of such calls a year. The only inconvenience is when people like Evan forget to let me know when they've arrived safely.

First thing I did with that was record it. It should have taken five or six hours to drive to Birdsville but the person was already much later than that. You learn pretty quickly to start a log of these sorts of calls, because you don't want any of them to slip through the cracks. If you forget about it, the next thing someone's dead, especially when the temperature is in the high forties.

I contacted the inspector and let him know that I had a possible search happening. Then I contacted Cordillo Downs Station, which the road from Innamincka passes through, to see if they'd seen or heard anything. I asked that if they were going for a fly in the station's plane that day, could they fly down the road and try and find the missing person. I also contacted South Australia Police to let them know what was going on, because the area where the person was missing is actually in South Australia.

The South Australian Border is only 12 kilometres south of Birdsville but at the time of this search, the closest SA police station was at Leigh Creek, 630 kilometres further south, as the police officer's position at Marree, 518 kilometres south, was vacant. That's too far to be any help, but I got in touch anyway because there was a chance the Leigh Creek cops'd be at Innamincka on a job. Unfortunately, in all my time in Birdsville they never were. Not when a search was on, anyway.

Then I started getting ready to go out there and try to locate the missing car. It helps if you can get a rough idea of where they are. In this case, it was 116 kilometres from Birdsville to the Cordillo Downs Road turn-off. Then, how far down to Cordillo? About 160 kilometres. So nearly 300 kilometres each way. Assuming this bloke had at least made it past Cordillo, that's still a long way to drive to pick him up. That's where, if someone nearby can go and find them for you, it can save you an entire day. If you can get the support of property people or other community members, it's so good. And a lot of times they can nip things in the bud.

Which is what happened with this search. Anthony Brook, David Brook's son, hadn't seen any vehicles on the road that goes past the homestead, so he went for a drive down towards Innamincka and found the vehicle not far from the station. Flat tyre. Instead of driving 550 kilometres, all I had to do was ring the inspector and say, 'We've found him. They've taken him back to Cordillo and fixed the tyre. He's going to report to me when he gets to Birdsville.' I continued to monitor the person as an ongoing job until he reported. Then I crossed it off the log and waited for the next one.

All of that and it's just a flat tyre. It's a lot of effort for something that, in the city, wouldn't usually matter. Out here, if you get a flat you could die. It's hot. People panic. They may not have sufficient water. They might try and walk somewhere, and then it's a major problem. So it's really important that you get onto that sort of stuff quickly out here and get it sorted before they start doing silly things.

Often, the best thing for people to do when they get stuck in the outback is nothing. Just stay in the car until someone comes along. If you've got a flat tyre, the motor will still work. So you've still got an air conditioner. Unfortunately, people think they've got to do something, like try and walk to help or whatever. And that's where things go from bad to worse very quickly. Especially if it's 300 kilometres to the nearest place. You're not going to walk there. No way.

In mid-December, only a few weeks after I arrived, I went on holidays. Seven weeks in school holidays. I'd got that approved before I knew I had the Birdsville job. At the time the job was advertised, we'd just bought a house in Byron Bay. That was another plus of the move west: it meant there'd be extra money coming in, and if we rented our house in Byron Bay we'd be well on our way to paying it off, which was the long-term goal. Before it was rented, though, we went there for a big long holiday.

My connection with Byron Bay goes back to my childhood, and even earlier. My grandparents lived there. A lot of itinerant people have different places they think of as 'home' and Byron Bay is one of mine.

I was born in South Australia in 1955 but when I was eighteen months old my father was transferred to England. He worked for the Australian dairy industry back when Australia did a lot of exporting to Britain. My older brother, Paul, and I went to England with my parents and over the next five years my three younger brothers, Michael, Simon and Philip, were born there. My mother always wanted a girl but she gave up after five boys.

We lived in a beautiful home in England, at Seven Oaks in Kent, with about a hectare of gardens. We even had a nanny.

In 1961 or '62 we moved back to Australia, first to Byron Bay. That's where I started school in Australia. Byron was a small town then, a little sleepy fishing village.

Then my father bought a house in Aspley, in Brisbane, in about 1963. My mother went from a beautiful home in England with a nanny to a three-bedroom home in Brisbane where she had to do everything. It was a three-bedroom home with five boys. In Brisbane there were trams and trolleybuses, and my oldest brother, Paul, and I walked from Aspley to Chermside to catch a tram into town and watch the latest movies.

On 14 February 1966, the day Australia went from pounds, shillings and pence to decimal currency, we moved to Melbourne. When we got there, it was freezing cold and raining – in February! – and I was disappointed because I really liked Brisbane. I liked going down to Byron Bay, seeing my grandparents. But that was how it was with my father's job: he moved. Fortunately, with five boys, you soon adapt to any new place, because you've got four friends to play with straightaway. Cricket, footy . . . I was never lonely.

In Melbourne I did my final two years of primary school, then went to Box Hill High. When I started at Box Hill, you had to have short back and sides and wear a suit. When I left, in 1972, it was all long hair and virtually no uniform. The teachers, instead of wearing those black gowns, were wearing shorts and shirts. This is after the 1960s with the Vietnam War demonstrations and everything that went along with that. People realised they could have a bit of freedom in their life if they wanted it.

Every year we used to drive up to Byron Bay in an old EH Wagon; my mother and father and five boys crammed in. And the dog. This was in the days prior to seat belts. And air conditioning, unfortunately. We'd stop at a pub if it got too hot. Mum and Dad would have a drink. We boys would play pool and have a soft drink. When it cooled down a bit, we'd get back in the car and get going. Once, we left the dog behind and had to go back about 60 kilometres to get him. He was still there outside the pub, just waiting for us.

When I finished school I didn't want to work in an office so I got a job in a cordial factory in Melbourne and made $70 a week, which was pretty good money in those days. That was in 1973, the year after Gough Whitlam came to power. I worked for Cottee's for a while and then my mother said, 'You've got to get a proper job.'

So I became a bank teller. I didn't like it. I got paid about $35 a week, so I had dropped half my pay. Then I noticed ads in the paper for Victoria Police. I thought that was probably better than working in a bank or a cordial factory. So I applied and I got a letter asking me to come in for testing. In those days you just went into a room and they gave you some general knowledge questions, which weren't that hard: what's the population of Melbourne, who's the prime minister, who's the premier? Then you did an eyesight test, a hearing test and as you went from room to room, the numbers dwindled off.

I got to the stage where they said, 'Yeah, you passed all that. Come back tomorrow for an interview.'

I went before three senior police officers who asked the normal questions you get when you go for a job interview: why do you want to be a police officer, what can you offer the service? Then I got a letter saying I'd been accepted.

I started at the Police Academy on 15 September 1975. I graduated on 6 February 1976. I remember Gough Whitlam being dismissed while I was in the Academy. It was big news in there. After I graduated, I went to Ringwood Police Station for three months of on-the-job training.

About that time I went with a friend to South Molle Island in the Whitsundays for a holiday. That's where I met Sandra. She was an airline hostess, as flight attendants were called then, for TAA, Trans Australia Airlines, which was later absorbed into Qantas. It was love at first sight. She was quite beautiful, reserved at first, but we got on really well together. I was supposed to be there for a week, but we ended up extending our visit another week because of Sandra. Sandra also came from Melbourne, so we kept seeing each other after the holiday ended.

After Ringwood, I went to Hawthorn for two-and-a-bit years. Sandra and I got married in 1978 and bought a house in Bundoora, which was convenient for Sandra because it was close to the airport. Sandra and I had similar goals in life, but back then I never thought that a Victorian policeman and a TAA flight attendant would end up living and working in Birdsville. Come to think of it, neither did she.

In 1980 I was transferred to Broadmeadows, a western suburb of Melbourne near where we lived. I was a senior constable, but was quickly promoted to acting sergeant, because it's hard to attract police there because it's quite rough.

In February 1983 I'd worked the night shift and was on a day off when Sandra and I went for a walk. We got home and there were burnt gum leaves landing on the front lawn. This is in suburbia. Later on, the phone rang and they said, 'We need you back at work.'

There was a bad fire out at Macedon. So I went in and we went up to Macedon in the morning. Most of the town had been destroyed. They saved the children by putting them all in a child care centre or a kindergarten, and the fireys just surrounded it and doused the roof.

A lot of fireys had been brought in to the medical centre from the firefronts, burnt. Their eyes had been burnt from the heat and so on.

Mount Macedon, up the hill, was even worse. What became known as the Ash Wednesday fires were still going at that stage. And I was there for the best part of a week: watching out for looters, helping people, taking them back to their houses because they had to return under police escort.

It wasn't just Macedon that was affected, it was the whole of Victoria and parts of South Australia. The fires burned right from Adelaide, the Adelaide Hills, the Great Ocean Road, to Melbourne and Macedon and east to the Dandenong Ranges. In Melbourne, no matter what direction you looked, there was fire. The entire state was dry after years of drought. It had only been the week before, when I was on night shift, there was that big dust storm that came through Melbourne.

It was terrible going through something that traumatic. People had lost everything. Houses had become piles of rubble. If the family unit was still intact, if they'd hadn't lost someone in the fires, they were happy because they were all together. You can always get another house. And all the local businesses came together and handed out clothes and found people accommodation. They gave them money and helped them get started. There was a lot of support for people who were affected by the fires.

During the fires, I had to deal with fatalities. And in other situations as well. It's sad, sad if it's a young kid and you've got to tell the parents. It's a parent's worst nightmare. Half the time they know. If it's the police knocking on the door, they've got a rough idea why you're there. So sometimes you try and get a neighbour or a friend or someone. Sometimes you try and leave it till later in the morning. Not go round straightaway so they can function during the day. If you do it at one in the morning, you've woken them up, so you might leave it until five or something like that. Now you can't because of Facebook and all that. It gets on Facebook and off it goes.

In 1985, I used to do a bit of prosecuting at Broadmeadows, so I transferred to the prosecutions section full-time. I got promoted to sergeant in 1987 at Victoria Dock. That was a plain-clothes position regarding crime on the waterfront. In those days the Painters and Dockers, a Union whose members were widely believed to have organised crime connections, were in full swing. Crime was rampant.

I remember once climbing up a tower overlooking an area where containers were being broken into, to do covert surveillance with other police. We went up early every morning, freezing cold, stayed up there all day, pissing into a cordial bottle. Several of us did that for a week, then this bloke we were secretly watching said, 'How long are you coppers going to stay in that tower for?'

I remember pulling up a van that was full of barbeques, all in packets. And I said to the bloke, 'Where have you got those barbeques from?'

And he said, 'What barbeques?'

They'd never admit to anything. They'd go to trial on everything. Even though we found the barbeques loaded in his car, this bloke denied it. He still got convicted.

In 1987 I transferred to Preston because I knew the senior sergeant there; I used to work with him at Broadmeadows. Preston was a western suburb of Melbourne, too. The same sort of area. Working-class. Fair few criminal elements there as well.

In August 1987 I was working a night shift. I got to work early and there was a call about a shooting in Hoddle Street. Preston was probably 5 kilometres from Hoddle Street, so we went down there. As a police officer you're taught command, control, contain, isolate, evacuate. Well everyone was running around not knowing what was going on because we didn't know how many people were shooting.

We knew a lot of people had been shot and killed (the eventual toll was seven dead and nineteen injured). The helicopter had come along and a gunman had shot at the helicopter. So we had no helicopter in the sky. It did come back later but a lot higher up. Then we got word that one gunman had been caught. But you had all these stories about different gunmen. So our job was mainly containing the place until eventually police got a handle on what was happening.

I remember going to houses around Northcote just after it happened and people were lying on the floor. It was a Sunday night and a lot of people were visiting friends and family. You'd go to a house and they'd open it up and you'd see their fingers on the bottom of the door. They were all lying on the floor. People were terrified.

We said to people, 'Just stay here. Don't go home. Just stay the night.'

We weren't sure if there weren't more shooters. So we spent the entire shift going around the area just answering calls from people, containing (restricting access in and out of the area) and so on. We were there until probably nine in the morning when we were relieved by other police. By that time, they knew there was one shooter because they had him in custody.

The event became known as the Hoddle Street Massacre, in

which a lone gunman armed with a Ruger rifle, a Mossberg shot-gun, and an M14 semi-automatic military rifle, embarked on a 15-minute shooting rampage, firing at passing cars and pedes-trians on Hoddle Street, in central Melbourne. After killing or fatally wounding seven, and injuring seventeen, he started hunt-ing the forty police who had arrived at the scene within minutes of the first emergency call. The police helicopter had a fuel tank punctured by a bullet fired by the gunman. He was eventually arrested, after using his remaining ammunition firing at police, forty-five minutes after he started shooting.

I got promoted to senior sergeant in 1991, in the city, so I used to catch a train to work. By then we were living at a place called Romsey, which was a little country town about a forty-minute drive north of Melbourne Airport. Romsey is a beautiful town. We liked it there. We had a block that went down to a little creek, so the kids (Andrew, born in 1985, Lauren, 1989, and Robbie, 1991) used to play down there. Hardly any crime. Just a little country town of about 1000 or 1500 people. Very cold in winter.

I used to go to Clarkfield, about 15 kilometres away, to catch the train. It was so cold you stayed in the car until you saw the light of the train coming. And you'd get out with a ski jacket on and gloves and a beanie and get on the train. Then you came home and it would be dark when you got home. So you left home in the dark in winter and came home in the dark. And Sandra was working, we had to get the kids to child care, so we used to do different shifts, to save on babysitting. So we didn't see that much of each other.

In 1994 I saw an ad recruiting for police in Queensland. I got thinking about that and I mentioned it to Sandra because I was sort of over policing in Melbourne. I was in an office, driving a desk. The office that I had didn't have any windows. It was just the same old, same old, every day. I needed a change. And in 1994, I was thirty-nine.

So I moved to Queensland. I went to the Academy in February 1995. Sandra stayed in Melbourne with the kids. We got a girl in, a German girl called Sybilla, as an au pair, and she looked after the kids, who loved her. I'd come home on the weekends because Sandra had access to discount flights through her work.

I graduated as a Queensland police officer in June 1995, came home and then drove up the coast with Sandra and the kids. We dropped the kids off at the parents' because they were still pretty young, and travelled up to Cairns. I started work, Sandra stayed for a few days and then flew home. I was going to look for a house for us in Cairns and Sandra said she wanted to have a nice block overlooking the water, with a pool and close to good schools. I drove around with the copper who was training me for half the day looking at suburbs. Eventually we bought a block and built a house in Redlynch, a northern suburb of Cairns with views over the city and out to Green Island.

In Queensland I went from general duties to prosecutions. So I was prosecuting at Cooktown, Mossman, Thursday Island, Cape York, all around there. Sandra went part-time and was still commuting to Melbourne, flying down to Melbourne and living with my parents and working there.

In 2000 Sandra retired from flying, with what was then Qantas. In December 2001 I got offered a job as prosecuting sergeant in Charleville. Prior to that we drove out there and the kids loved it. Andrew didn't come; he was at high school. Lauren and Robbie loved it. We ummed and aahed, and the inspector rang up and said, 'If you come out here, we'll really look after you. We're keen to get you.'

And the job came with a house, so that was good. The kids were keen to go so we moved there and had this tiny little house compared to what we lived in. We called it a pigeon coop on stilts but the kids enjoyed it because it was a country town. They could ride their bikes around till almost dark, like I did when I was a kid. Sandra started being a guide at the Cosmos Centre, which she loved. She had other jobs as well, and ended up becoming a fully qualified probation parole officer.

We'd been there five years when I saw the job in Birdsville.

It was a hell of a culture shock going from Byron Bay back to Birdsville after our seven-week holiday. One moment we were watching TV with all those channels. You could go down the street and buy whatever you wanted, whatever food you wanted. You come back here and you've got a general store that's open two hours in the morning and two hours in the afternoon. And a pub. And the Blue Poles Gallery and Cafe was open then.

Still, you've just got to deal with what you've got. Like, I remember growing up in Byron Bay, and it was so expensive to ring interstate, someone had to die or you had to have won the Tatts sweep or whatever. Here, it's remote but now you've got phones, email, internet. So you're not remote like it was years ago.

When I left to go on holidays, there had been dust storms. When I came back with Lauren, it was flooded. We had to fly in. Birdsville was effectively an island. You're isolated. Yet people take it in their stride when that happens. Supplies are flown in. People stock up on spaghetti bolognaise and rice and stuff like that.

Everyone goes down to the river and checks out the river levels. It's a bit of a social event. They go down there, have a talk about it. You go out in the floodboat for a bit of a drive, have a look around.

You do feel a bit trapped because even though you probably wouldn't go anywhere, you can't. So you always go and check the levels, see if it's rising, staying the same or dropping. You have a big powwow with everyone else down at the river.

Lauren took three weeks to unpack her bags when she first arrived. She missed her mother, obviously. These were the days prior to mobile phones, the internet and Facebook in Birdsville. Well, internet was there, but people couldn't get it in their homes.

After about three weeks, Lauren got to love the place. She used to go around to Wolfie's place (artist Wolfgang John's Blue Poles Gallery and Cafe) and use the internet there. And Wolfie's family took her under their wing. She used to work for them on her days off from the police job. She made friends with young people who worked at the pub and the roadhouse. Theo Nel, the mechanic who leased the roadhouse, offered her a job, so she worked there too. And then the schoolteacher offered her a job as a teacher's aide (Lauren wanted to study teaching at uni), so she took that as well. Then they needed a cleaner, so she took that. So she had all these jobs and in the end, she loved Birdsville.

People spoiled her. She was the policeman's daughter. They all looked out for her. She spent a couple of years here before she applied for and went to uni. She was the youngest Queensland Police employee because she joined at seventeen. Even though the QGAP job is advertised to the public, it's a job that traditionally goes to the police officer's wife. It's sort of a carrot to get them here. So Lauren got the job without an interview. She saved a bit of money and I got her to buy some shares, which came in handy when she used them to put a deposit on a house, down the track.

She went off to uni but she used to come home on semester breaks to Birdsville with her boyfriend, Damien, who is now her husband. They used to work in the bakery. That was another job Lauren had, when it was busy. I think everyone has worked at the bakery at one time or another, including you, Evan. And me.

Sandra regularly came out in those early years and Robbie used to come out and ride his bike around. There're heaps of areas where you can ride bikes around here: sand hills and so on. And Robbie used to work for Theo too, at the roadhouse, and later for Barnesy. He used to love coming out here. And they used to always come out for the races.

My first major rescue happened in February 2007. It had been pouring rain. Two guys from the Bureau of Meteorology – nice blokes, but I'd describe them as eggheads, very smart with computers and so on – came out and were doing the servicing on the weather station and the instruments at the police station.

When they were done, their next destination was Thargomindah, 800 kilometres south-east. The quickest way there was east towards Windorah for 220 kilometres, then south on the Arrabury Road, which hugs the Queensland–South Australian border and goes past Haddon Corner (at the turn-off you're 15 kilometres from Haddons). You go down there, then you head east again, on the Adventure Way, to Thargomindah.

These two guys asked me about the road and I said, 'The road's closed due to wet weather, very wet weather, but come in in the morning and I'll make some phone calls just on the off-chance that it's open.'

They didn't come in.

About two or three o'clock in the afternoon, I got a phone call. It was one of the weather guys in a state of panic. I've got from him that they're stuck in the middle of a creek, please help, and then the phone went dead.

I was able to ascertain, by putting two and two together, that these two had gone down the Arrabury Road and got stuck in a creek. It was probably Deep Creek. So named because, well, normally it's bone dry and it's just a big dip in the road, but when it rains, like most outback creeks, it goes from nothing to flood in a very short space of time.

I got hold of Theo Nel from the roadhouse and by the time we organised everything it was on dusk. Out we go. I follow Theo. He's an excellent driver so I followed his tracks. It was really hard going. Pouring rain. Wet. Muddy. Car slipping. And there were also cattle on the road, which we had to look out for.

It took us ages to get up to the Arrabury Road. Then we went down there. It's about 120 kilometres to Deep Creek. Theo was ahead of me and got on the radio and said, 'Yeah, they're here.'

I got there and the four-wheel drive, a Toyota Land Cruiser like yours, Evan, was in the middle of the creek with water up to the headrests. All their stuff was floating in the back of the car. The two weather guys were on the other side of the creek. They'd taken some of their gear out of the car and put it on the other side as well. Wouldn't you have put it on the side your rescuers are coming in from? They also had silver foil blankets on.

I said, 'What have you got those on for?'

They said, 'Oh, it's to keep us warm.'

This is in February in the outback. I was in shirtsleeves.

Anyway, they had to get all their gear and carry it back through the creek to our side. Theo pulled the car out and put it on the trailer. I had food to give the guys because they hadn't had any since they left Birdsville.

We drove back to Birdsville, which was a long, long trip back.

I took them to the pub, which I'd rung before and asked to hold a room for them, although at that time of the year, they're not likely to be booked out. I did that so we didn't have to knock anyone up, as it was now late at night. The guys could just go to the room and let themselves in.

I found out later they'd got bogged at Betoota. They'd been stuck there for one or two hours before someone pulled them out. Then off they went again. It was keep going, hell or high water. It was high water, actually. They were determined to make it to Thargomindah but they'd never have got there. The creek was just too deep.

I spoke to their boss and he went ballistic because the car was wrecked and it had only 17000 kilometres on it. Brand-new $60000 Land Cruiser. All the computer gear, which would have been worth tens of thousands of dollars, was ruined. It had been sitting in water for the best part of twelve hours.

They almost drowned. They had managed to speak to me for fifteen seconds before their satphone went dead. If they hadn't got that phone call out, no-one would have known they were there. It probably would have been days before a search started. They didn't have any food. Plenty of water, though.

Then, would they have tried to walk out? The road was closed. They'd have had no hope. There's no properties near; no homesteads to drop into.

A couple of days later, they were flown out. They were a bit sore and sorry. I think they knew they were going to be facing the music when they got back. Lovely guys, though.

There were a few lessons there: make sure your communications are right, make sure you don't travel down a closed road, make sure someone knows where you're going, carry food, and when the sign says 'Deep Creek', believe it.

They told me they just drove into it. They didn't even check the flood height.

The story didn't end there. It was probably a year or two later when the same two came out again. This time it was the middle of summer but dry, whereas the last time they came out it was soaking wet. They got a flat tyre. They changed that. Then they got another flat tyre, which often happens in outback areas, on dirt roads, which is why it's wise to carry two spare tyres. Anyway, these two thought they had only one spare, so they put a call out for Theo to go down and collect them again, which he did.

It took Theo only a moment to realise they had two spares. They had one on the back door, which they used. However, there was another spare tyre under the vehicle at the back of the car. They didn't know about that one, even though it's not hard to see. Theo changed the tyre but that probably cost the weather bureau a bit of extra money. They'd have to sell quite a few calendars to pay for that rescue as well.

Birdsville is isolated but there are some very powerful and influential people in it. David and Nell Brook are the ninth biggest landowners in Australia, size-wise. They own the pub, they own the roadhouse, they own a lot of property in town. They own a fair slice of grazing land in Queensland and South Australia as well.

They're really good people. You go to the pub and David's there and you talk about the same things in the pub that you talk to anyone about: the footy, the drought, the flood. He's just like any other person. He's the Chairman of the Stockman's Hall of Fame, he's got the Order of Australia, he mixes in very influential circles. The Brooks have got friends like Dick Smith, they've had prime ministers and premiers stay at their place and yet they talk to people, they go to all the community events, they mix with people who are working for the council, the police, the clinic, and they're very proud of their community.

I remember with Nell once, there was a social club event on the oval. It was like egg and spoon races and such. It was a stinking hot day and I thought, Nah, I'm not goin'. So I never went and Nell chided me. She said, 'You've got to go to community events. That's what you're expected to do.'

And she's right. You should. When you're the police officer, you need to be there to support the community and talk to people. So after that I said, 'Yeah.' I took it onboard and never missed a community event if I was in town.

Even before I got here, I was warned by the inspector. He gave me the drum: 'Watch those cattle people. They're from the old National Party days. They've all got the local politician on quick dial.'

After I'd been in town a while, I went to Geoff Morton, from Roseberth, and asked him. I said, 'Is it true? Have you guys got the local politician on quick dial?'

And he said, 'Nah. I've got the CJC on quick dial.'

Which is the Criminal Justice Commission. Complaints against police.

He may have been joking, but at the time, the Federal Member for Maranoa was Bruce Scott. He always comes and stays with David and Nell.

I remember with Nell once, the twice-weekly passenger flight by MacAir was late. They were always late, or they just wouldn't come. We'd just say, 'If they're not comin' in, they're not comin' in.'

But Nell said, 'Oh, I've spoken to Vaughan, I've spoken to Peter.'

I knew Vaughan Johnson was the state member for the electorate of Gregory (now retired). But I said, 'Who's Peter?' It might have been Tony, or whatever.

She said, 'Oh, that's the Transport Minister.'

And back when Bob Atkinson was the Commissioner of Police, I'm driving him around Birdsville, and he said to me, 'Are David and Nell in town?'

I said, 'Nah, they're away.'

And he said, 'Well when you see them, give 'em my regards.'

And I thought, Gee, you know.

So they were very well connected but at the same time they're very down to earth, hard-working people like everyone else. Their kids have all got jobs. They've got a nice home but nothing compared to homes you see in Sydney. They've got a car that's probably fourteen years old. Their second car is probably twenty-four years old. Or thirty-four years old. With no air conditioning. They could live in Toorak, they could live in Double Bay. With internet and email they could run everything remotely these days, but they don't. They choose to live in Birdsville. They're in their late sixties but they're still here. They love the town. They love the outback. They love the people and they'll probably be here for a lot longer to come.

CHAPTER 2

A LINE IN THE DUST

As the Birdsville cop, it's your job to enforce the laws of Queensland. At the same time, you want the community to give you their respect and trust. The community expects that if someone has done the wrong thing, you'll charge them, whether it's assault or stealing or whatever. And that's what I've had to do from time to time. You're not living in a utopia. There's going to be trouble now and then.

By the same token, you don't want a situation where the community is scared of you, too scared to come and see you. So you have to exercise discretion. Otherwise people will go, 'Oh we're going to get pulled up for a crack in the windscreen or crack in the taillight or something minor.' Obviously you don't let drink-driving or people not wearing seatbelts go because it's so important to wear your seatbelt in the bush. The only accidents we get are rollovers and if you don't have a seatbelt on, you'll die or get very seriously injured. Wearing a seatbelt is the law for a very good reason.

Then there's things like, every tourist parks around the pub to get their photo taken and you aren't supposed to park within 9 metres of an intersection. So if I went up there every time I saw someone parked outside the pub and gave them a serve or a parking ticket, I'm not going to do much for tourism or public relations for the police service. So you see people up there having their photo taken and you just wave to them or you might stop and they'll take your photo. You don't worry about it because this is Birdsville and you've got that discretion.

Minor matters like that you don't worry about. Sometimes you get young kids who do silly things and the best thing to do is talk to them and talk to their parents, letting them know they've got to be responsible for their actions and the consequences. If you can resolve it that way, you resolve it.

That was the case with one of my first jobs in Birdsville. This local fella from one of the stations stole two bar mats from the pub. When the barman walked out the back, this bloke took one mat and put it down the back of his pants. Then he took the other another one a couple of minutes later. I got called up there, checked the security camera vision, then went round and saw him.

I said, 'I'm here to talk to you about those two bar mats you stole from the pub.'

He said, 'I didn't steal any bar mats.'

I said, 'Well you did. You took one at 10.11 p.m. and the second one you took at 10.16 p.m. when the barman went out.'

He goes, 'Oh.'

So he came up with them and what are your options? Do you charge him with stealing, which is a serious offence? You know when it goes to court he's only going to get a good behaviour bond or a small fine or something but you've still got to go through the process of fingerprinting, collecting DNA, taking photographs and all that stuff. Plus he'd have a record. Even if there's no conviction recorded, he's still got a record for stealing. This young fella was eighteen. So he'd have to go before the Magistrate's Court, instead of the Childrens' Court.

So I got him to take the mats back and apologise. Everyone in the community knew he'd taken them and he copped a three-month ban from the hotel. I think that's a lot better than charging him and putting him before a court. Even though those mats are worth $30 each, it was still a relatively minor matter or a prank.

Another time, when I first got here, a woman called me up. This bloke was throwing rocks on her roof. It was about two in the morning. So I went up there, but with the lights of the police car they can see you coming a mile away. I spoke to her. She was really scared, a woman living by herself. I went back home but got another call about half an hour later. I'd just got back to bed.

She said, 'They're rockin' the roof again.'

So I walked up there this time and I hid in the shed at the back of her place. I was bitten by a zillion sandflies because it had been raining. He came back and rocked the roof again and I got him.

He said, 'Can't you give me a warning?'

I said, 'No way mate. You got me out of bed twice.'

He was probably the first person I charged when I was here.

There's a school of thought in policing: you go to a new town and if someone does the wrong thing, you charge them. Then everyone says, 'Oh, he's a tough copper,' and they behave themselves. Whereas, if you let it go, they take it as a sign of weakness. So you charge 'em and it gets around.

In this case, it was justified. This woman is in bed and the roof's getting rocked. And he did it three times. So he got charged. I think he got fined $100 or $150. But, if you charge him, then you can ease off and people say, 'That bloke did that and he got charged, so I'll watch what I do.' So the moral of the story is, new police officer comes to town, don't be the first to break the law. (Laughter)

This bloke had his reasons for rocking the woman's roof and they're part and parcel of the politics of small country towns. When it comes to the various groups in town, the different alliances, likes and dislikes, as a police officer, you don't get involved in town disputes or gossip. You've got to be like Switzerland. You've got to be neutral. I work on the principle that I talk to who I want to, socialise with who I want to. If someone doesn't like it, that's their problem. You don't listen to gossip and you certainly don't cart gossip because then you're part of it.

I invite people around and if they don't get on with other people that's their problem. It's not my problem. I've had turns like your send-off, where we invited virtually the whole town. People who didn't like each other came but they just danced around the food and different things. Someone was getting meat so they'd go get salad, then someone got salad so they'd go get meat. They sat in their areas. It wasn't uncomfortable or awkward; that's just how it is. Some people haven't liked each other for probably the best part of thirty or forty years, so I don't think that's going to change any time soon. Some of those disputes are part of the local folklore. Everyone in town knows who doesn't like who. It's part of Birdsville, like the heat, the dust and the flies.

I knew that before I got here. I'd done some due diligence when I applied. I rang the National Parks' ranger, Don Rowlands, and spoke to him for a while.

He said, 'Don't get involved in town politics.'

And Don'd know.

If you're smart, when you go to places, you align yourself with people who are good at their job and know the country. I didn't know the country. I'd never been to the desert and hadn't done much four-wheel driving in sand. I'd done a bit of four-wheel driving up at Cooktown but that was mainly rainforest. It wasn't desert. It was very muddy, so it was different driving.

One time, just after we'd bought our car, the one we've got now, the 80 Series Land Cruiser, we went up the Daintree. We put the car into four-wheel drive and negotiated about four creeks. At the fifth we stopped and the kids got out and had a swim. There I was, feeling proud of meself, having got through all these four creeks, and then this Datsun 180B with four Murris came flying down and through the creek and off they went. So much for my four-wheel driving skills.

Anyway, when I got to Birdsville, I got to know Don and his wife Lyn. Lyn was doing the weather reports at the police station when I got here. She taught me how to do the weather.

Both of them know the country so well. I've said it many times about Don: he knows the country better than any person living on planet earth. Lyn's not far behind him. She was born here. She went to school here. There's a black-and-white photo of Don and Lyn at the school here, years ago. Barry Gaffney's got that. They were young kids, pre-teens, back in the fifties, with their teacher, a male in shorts, long socks and a short-sleeved shirt. There's nothing in the background because it's Birdsville. Apart from the trees along the river, there's generally nothing between you and the horizon.

Don took me out in the desert and taught me how to drive in

sand. He gave me advice, told me what I was doing wrong. And I just felt so comfortable with him because I could tell he knew what he was doing. It's like going to see a top specialist in Sydney. You know you're safe in their hands. They know their job. If you had a heart problem years ago, you saw Victor Chang. Well, Don's like the Victor Chang of the Birdsville desert. He knows it so well.

Don's a great person to sit round a fire with and talk to, telling stories of his life. He could be bitter about the way he was treated when he was younger, when the racism he was subjected to was sometimes subtle and sometimes overt. He tells some of the stories of when he went to school and worked on properties and was treated very poorly but he doesn't hold grudges at all.

Well, almost. Don might say, 'We'll stop here for smoko.'

And you'd go, 'Yeah that's a good spot.'

Then you'd go out and say, 'We might stop here.'

And he'd say, 'Yeah, no worries. That's a good spot.'

But one time Don and I took this bloke from the caravan park out into the desert, for some reason, I can't remember why.

Don said, 'Oh, we might camp here.'

This bloke said, 'Oh, let's camp over there; it looks a bit better.'

That got Don really cranky, ay. So I learned: if Don says it's a good spot, it is a good spot. Because Don knows. He knows where's out of the wind, he knows where there's plenty of firewood nearby (in areas outside the National Park). It's like if Victor Chang says you need a heart operation, you listen. When that bloke questioned Don's choice, you could tell. Don wasn't happy one little bit. You could cut the air with a knife. I don't think that bloke ever went out with Don again. (Laughter)

We didn't go out on patrols right from the beginning because everything was flooded. You're talking summer: January and

36

February. But Don took me out a couple of times just to give me a bit of a run, probably a month into when I was back here, in 2007. Once things got a bit drier, we started doing patrols regularly into the desert to check on conditions at creek crossings and camp sites and to remind people out there that law and order and national park regulations didn't end where the wilderness began.

As useful as it is for me having Don around, it's good for Don, too. When I go out on patrols with him, he's got someone to talk to. On patrols where we took the police car and the ranger's car if he got stuck, I could snatch him off (attach a snatch strap from his vehicle to my vehicle to pull him out). Though that never happened. It was always him snatchin' me off, never the other way around.

People say, you know, 'You do all these rescues, it's good,' but every rescue's a team effort. It's not just me going out and getting someone and bringing them back. It's Don, Barnesy or Theo (the roadhouse mechanics and recovery specialists), the nurse if someone's injured, and normally another community member, too. Like Padraic O'Neill, or Sam Barnes, someone you can rely on, sometimes to drive the ambulance. Everyone contributes.

When I first arrived, there were no tourists. None. At that stage, the desert was open during the summer but it was too hot for most people. A few years later we started closing the desert, stopping people driving across it from December to mid-March. At that time of year, it was just too dangerous, for them and for anyone who might have to go and rescue them.

Back when the roads were open, you'd only occasionally see a car come into town in the middle of summer. You'd go talk to them and if they'd come across the desert, more often than not it would be a German couple. You'd think, Gee, they were lucky. If they got stuck there, they'd be completely on their own. Emergency Position Indicating Radio Beacons (EPIRBs) were around when I first got to Birdsville, but not like they are now. It was the same with satphones, you can easily hire them now but that hasn't always been the case. If people got into trouble out in the desert in the middle of summer without an EPIRB or a satphone, it could be big problems for them.

As it turned out, one of my early rescues was initiated when an EPIRB got set off out there. I got a call from the Australian Maritime Safety Authority (AMSA) in Canberra, which monitors the satellites that pick up EPIRBs on land and sea in Australia's area of search and rescue (SAR) responsibility. The AMSA covers about a tenth of the earth's surface. My patch is the size of the UK or Victoria, roughly 500 kilometres by 500 kilometres, but it's only a small part of SAR Canberra's coverage. On the main roads, I can drive my area from north to south in about five hours. To the east it's a couple of hours but to the west, in the desert, you can be driving for eight to twelve hours to get to someone who's in trouble.

Theo Nel, Lauren and I went out and found a German couple in a BRITZ camper. They didn't have any water (they'd run out) and they were bogged in the sand. The tyre pressure on the van was 45 psi – in each tyre.

To avoid getting bogged in the sand your tyre pressure should be around the mid-twenties, or even lower depending on your vehicle and tyres. Lower pressure means the tyres spread out more, distributing the vehicle's weight over a larger area. So Theo just dropped the tyre pressure, went backward and forward, then drove right out.

If that couple didn't have an EPIRB, they'd have been in big trouble. If they'd known the basics of driving in the outback, they wouldn't have had any trouble at all.

There are a lot of other jobs that I do in Birdsville apart from policing. The main one's the weather. Queensland ABC-TV's weather presenter, Jenny Woodward, often reports Birdsville as the hottest location in the state. Jenny's the longest-serving weather reporter in the world and she frequently gives Birdsville a mention, whether it's been the hottest town or not. When I did my last weather recording before retiring, the ABC actually had a segment about it on the TV news. They showed the tiny room in the Birdsville Police Station where the weather terminal is.

If I was ever away, Sandra (after she moved to Birdsville) would do the weather. If Sandra was away, Lyn would do it or you'd get a responsible community member to do it. If you ran out of them, you'd get Evan to do it. (Laughter/miffed silence)

Any time I was away, I'd watch the evening news and think, Thank goodness they've done the weather.

It's important because people are interested to see what's happening in Birdsville. If it's really hot, they need to know. Flooding, they need to know. With people flying in, they need to know if there's a dust storm because once you drop below a certain visibility the airport's closed.

I also empty the cash out of the phone boxes in town. That was a very important job prior to mobile phones, but not as much now. I also check the locust tank, which is an early warning system for the southern states if a locust plague is travelling down, that can have a devastating impact on agriculture if farmers and land-management authorities are unprepared. It's been that way since Egypt got eaten out in the Bible. There wasn't a plague during my time but occasionally you get locusts in there, normally after it rains.

There's also a setup out the back of the police station yard with painted panels and roofing material. I don't handle that. A scientist rings Sandra every now and again and she collects paint samples or bits of Colorbond and sends them off to him. That's how they measure how well things last in the hot Queensland sun out at Birdsville.

Then there're a couple of dust monitors measuring dust in the air. I do a monthly calibration of those. And there's an instrument that measures the earth's crust. I can't remember how because I'm not that smart. I've occasionally got to do things there. And just over there is a CSIRO instrument, on a tripod, that measures the ozone layer – I regularly calibrate that.

All that's involved is listening on the end of the phone as the the scientist in Canberra says, 'Push the yellow button, push the red button, push the white button, now push the green button, now push the yellow button again.'

I've got no scientific expertise but I know my colours and when you say 'push a button', I push that corresponding button.

You don't get paid for that but they used to say, 'Thanks very much for doing that.'

Normally you'd be covered in flies and it'd be 47 degrees, blowing a gale, and they'd just say thanks.

I'd say, 'Yeah, and thanks for the Christmas card you send me every year.'

I think they finally felt guilty after about six years because they sent me a CSIRO t-shirt. But then I think the guilt wore off a bit, because all I got the next year was a CSIRO peaked cap, which, you know, I've got a million of. Not CSIRO ones, but peaked caps. Yeah.

There's an instrument here from a Japanese professor that measures the ozone layer, too. He pays $1000 to the police service every year but unlike the CSIRO's ozone-measuring equipment mentioned above, all I do is post off little data cards to him about every three months when they fill up.

Theo used to read the town electricity meters but when he left in 2008, he gave that job to me, which is quite good as it means a bit of extra income and isn't too difficult. I read all the electricity meters in town. There're no water meters. And I look after the ABC transmission hut, that downloads all the ABC and free-to-air commercial channels from a satellite and rebroadcasts them to the town. I go around and again, I know how to push buttons. The road signs are electronically controlled from Adelaide now, but as with anything electronic out here, you've got dust, you've got geckos, you've got insects. They play up from time to time so I go down and reset them. Before the electronic signs went in I used to have to change them by hand.

When the river floods I measure and check it three times a day, again for the Bureau of Meteorology. I check it more often if it looks like coming up a fair bit. It's important the weather bureau has an accurate idea of river heights because with computer modelling they can work out what it's going to do further downstream.

In February 2007 there was a break-in at the Birdsville Roadhouse. That was a huge crime for Birdsville. The town was still surrounded by floodwater, so the offender had to be in town. I could rule out 90 per cent of the town straightaway because they were over fifty and had been law-abiding citizens all their lives. They weren't likely to start doing break-ins that week. In a town with a summer population of about sixty people, that narrows the suspects down to a handful.

That, and people told me, 'It'll be so-and-so.'

And they were right.

The problem was, I didn't have any proof. Unfortunately, the roadhouse manager, Theo Nel, was away, so I couldn't get access to the security-camera vision, which was in the safe. So I made enquiries and got different versions until Theo came back.

The security vision revealed a young male wearing really big clothes. Like, five sizes too big. He had climbed in through the toilet window, which someone had left open. So I assumed it was an inside job. There was a young apprentice working at the roadhouse and, even though he wasn't the person in the security vision, he was in the frame. There was only him and a middle-aged woman working the counter and she was the one who had reported the break-in.

The whole contents of the till had been stolen: $1200. In the security vision, this young guy went up to the machine that weighs the fruit and started pushing the bottom right-hand button. But nothing happened because it was a weighing machine, there was no tray on it. So I assumed the offender had been told which button to push on the till, but he was pushing the button on the wrong machine. After about five minutes of pushing this button, he worked it out, went to the cash register, and pushed the bottom right button and the till opened. He grabbed the contents and left. That was the vision.

Under closer examination, I could see the offender was

wearing distinctive Adidas sandals. You could see one of them had a big red blotch on the strap that goes over your foot. When I went to one of the houses in town to make enquiries, there were two Adidas sandals at the front door, one with a red blotch. So I knew he was involved. I seized the sandals as an exhibit. Then he didn't say anything, which is his right.

I took out a search warrant, searched the house, but didn't locate anything. Then I went to the house where the apprentice was staying and conducted a search there. I located some of the money in the ceiling and the apprentice confessed. He put in his mate, who then confessed as well. It turned out he had the rest of the money hidden in a video recorder. It was inside the flap but I didn't look there at first. Almost all the money was recovered.

The main offender was charged. He got probation, I think. The brains of the outfit, the apprentice, got the sack from Theo's and was given an official police caution because he was a juvenile.

What was a bit worrying was they also had a sugar bag full of those little things you put in soda bottles, little gas canisters. Back in 2007 I didn't know what they were going to do with them, but inhaling nitrous oxide is now a form of drug abuse mostly associated with the inner-city drug scene but rarely encountered outback, mainly due to the lack of availability of the canisters. They had a sugar bag full of those poppers, where you pull the string to make them explode. I don't know how they got them all. They also had instructions on how to commit crime and disguise yourself by wearing big clothing, and covering up any tattoos and all your fingers and your head. Unfortunately for them, there was nothing in the instructions about wearing Adidas sandals with distinctive blotches.

Any money that wasn't recovered when the boys confessed

was paid for by the parents of the apprentice, who were very upset with him. They were very respected members of the community. They'd got him the job with Theo and he threw away a good trade. His mother was crying. They were especially disappointed in him because they worked for the Brooks and the Brooks owned the roadhouse. Even though it was leased to Theo, but still.

Years later, at my farewell, there was a positive outcome. The father said that even though his children had run off the tracks (the apprentice's brother was the one who knocked off the bar mats), neither of them ended up with a criminal conviction and I think they learned from that. Unfortunately it took this young fella a while to come clean but when the money was found he had to. He's moved on. I think he's got a baby, a child now, is in a relationship and running a station. At the farewell, he and his associate presented me with a bottle of black hair colouring, to make up for all the grey hairs they caused me.

There was another incident just a couple of days later. I believed the getaway driver for the roadhouse robbery was this middle-aged bloke in town. I couldn't prove it and nobody would say it, as in, make a statement that wouldn't be dismissed as hearsay in court. However, information from the juvenile offender led us to him. Well, he told the woman who worked at the roadhouse, and she told me.

Then I received information that this bloke had been showing X-rated videos to minors. I went around to his house and seized the videos. He got charged with that and with running over signposts as he left town. I could match the tyreprints at the scene with a car he was driving.

On 5 April 2007 I got a report that a council road grader had been broken into 67 kilometres north of town, at a location called Mooneys Grave. Tools and equipment had been stolen. I drove up and examined the crime scene. I could see tyre marks from a two-wheel drive vehicle.

I got back to Birdsville around 11.30 a.m. and continued my investigations. Once again, when there's a crime in a town where you've got all good people who don't usually offend, you look at who's new. I did a quick run through the caravan park. It was grey nomad, grey nomad, grey nomad. I could cut them out, basically. Then I looked at the security-camera vision at the roadhouse and saw this red two-wheel drive ute and three young people: two males and a female.

They'd already left town, so it was a matter of working out which way they went. They couldn't go west, through the desert, because their vehicle was a two-wheel drive. So they'd either gone north, east or south. I got onto police at Bedourie (188 kilometres north), Windorah (386 kilometres east) and Marree (521 kilometres south). Around 4 p.m. I found out they were heading south because they'd paid for chocolates and drinks at the Mungerannie Hotel (315 kilometres south) with a large amount of coins.

Down at Marree, the police officer had been waiting for them all afternoon. At around 6.30 p.m., when they still hadn't appeared, he drove up the Birdsville Track, looking for them. They'd run out of fuel and were stuck on the side of the road. The only thing they hadn't stolen was fuel. That's probably what they should have got first. The stolen property was located in their vehicle and an offender was charged at Marree with unlawful possession. The property was returned to its rightful owners.

The crime was committed 67 kilometres north of Birdsville and the offenders were picked up that day, 500 kilometres south. Fortunately, in Birdsville we're in a fairly unique geographical position and there's only three ways out of town – four if you're equipped to cross the desert. And not many people use the roads. You know, when you're policing somewhere like New South Wales, down on the coast, offenders could go anywhere. So it's a lot easier here. And there's not that much traffic. I mean, we've been sitting here for ages and I don't think there's been a car go by. One? Yeah. (Laughter)

By this stage, after my first three or four months here, I thought, What have I got myself into? I've had a break and enter, someone rockin' a roof, someone runnin' over guide posts, someone showing porn to minors, and someone stealing from up the road. In city policing you get a job every day at least but for here, that's a fair bit going on. I thought, Gee, I'm in the middle of a crime wave. Fortunately for the community I solved those ones so it was good for me. It means you're doing something about it, which is what they want you to do. It's not just what you're paid to do.

In June 2007 I had another case to investigate. Don Rowlands went to the tip and saw all these fish frames, the heads and spines of a large number of filleted fish, and suspected someone had been netting across the river, which is illegal because it can severely deplete fish stocks. He had a pretty good idea who it was so he called Fisheries and they executed a warrant on that person's place. Unfortunately, they didn't find anything. Rumour has it that the net and more fish were in an esky on the front verandah, covered by something, but by the time we found that out, the evidence was long gone.

No-one was charged over that. Rumours continued to back up Don's suspicion about the person who did it. Unfortunately, that's still one of my cold cases.

Later that month two dingoes started coming into town. They ripped a pet dog to pieces outside the police station at one stage. People were getting worried because there were young kids in town and these dingoes were hanging around. You see dingoes around the district all the time but these ones were causing trouble, getting more comfortable with being close to people.

The council wanted them destroyed. They were eventually caught in cages but the town foreman at the time didn't have a firearms licence so he called on me to destroy them. It was a difficult thing to do because they were looking at me and I don't like shooting things at the best of times. You have to do that sort of thing though, to save a problem down the track.

The following month, in July 2007, I attended my first car accident. An optometrist from Victoria rolled his car. He had a whole lot of stuff – like jerry cans – in the back and he was really lucky that nothing hit him or his partner. Nevertheless, he and his passenger were injured. A passing motorist brought his passenger into town because he had a big cut on his head and I brought the optometrist in.

My son Robbie came out to that accident, too. He was out here on holidays, working for Theo. He was only sixteen or seventeen. He put the car on the trailer and all that sort of stuff.

That accident happened out near Durrie, as in Durrie Station. However, the nurse from Birdsville thought it happened at Bedourie. It sounds similar. So he headed north to Bedourie instead of east to Durrie. Back in those days, everyone who was needed at the scene of an accident (police, nurse, recovery specialist) left separately in their own vehicles as soon as they were ready to go. By the time I got there, and there was no sign of the nurse, I thought, I'd better just bring them back in.

After that, I arranged it so we'd all leave together (or at least the police car and ambulance). I made sure that where we were going was the place we were supposed to be going. Around here, you've got Bedourie, Betoota, Durrie. They all sound the same, except they can be 100 or 200 kilometres apart. If you go the wrong way, it can mean hours and hours of driving for nothing. After that incident, I always made sure to find out from the vehicle where they left from, what landmarks were around them (if any), which way they travelled, to make sure everyone had the right address, or location.

On my way back to town with this optometrist, I got talking to him about reading glasses.

I said, 'What about those glasses you buy for five bucks?'

He said, 'There's nothing wrong with them. Optometrists tell you there is so you buy expensive glasses.'

After that I just bought the $5 ones. So that rescue saved me money.

After his accident, the optometrist came and visited me a couple of times. He thanked me for looking after him.

My job certainly changes when winter comes and more tourists are in town. The phones are going a lot more. If there's rain, it never really stops. People ring up looking for information on the roads. In summer the phone never rings and no-one comes in. It goes from that to people coming in on a regular basis. And back in the days when there were no mobile phones in town I'd pick up a lot of jobs that involved going to the caravan park or around the town trying to find tourists to pass on a message from family members in an emergency. Sometimes I'd have to pass on the news that someone back home had died or someone was very sick.

CHAPTER 3

MOVE ALONG, NOTHING TO SEE HERE

Everything was ready to go for my first iconic Birdsville Races, the highlight of the year, in early September. I had all the police down from Mount Isa and the operation order all done. I'd had numerous meetings with David Brook, the president of the Birdsville Race Club, because I wanted to make sure my first races ran well and were properly policed. I'd covered all the bases.

Then, out of left field, equine flu hit Australia. No-one could move horses across state borders. So that put an end to the 2007 Birdsville Races.

Remarkably, 4000 people still turned up.

The organisers still tried to hold the event but they just didn't have the horses. They went from horse races to running wheelie bin races. And the bookies had betting on interstate races and so on.

The organisers' line was 'Who needs horses?'

They definitely needed horses.

It didn't have the same atmosphere. People come here for the horses. There are a few things you can do without at a horse race, but horses isn't one of them. Know what I mean?

Aside from the wheelie bin races, they had races with little toy ponies pulled along on strings. The toy pony races stayed on in following years. That was probably because it gave people the opportunity to cheer for a horse called My Face, as in 'Come on My Face'. They actually had an auction of the toy ponies one year, to raise money for the RFDS, and while most horses got bids of less than $100, My Face went for about $1600. It was then donated to the pub. They also had racing mops and shit like that. All pretty lame sort of stuff.

From the point of view of policing, the event still ran as it would have.

Getting ready involves cleaning the courthouse here. The inspector stays in the barracks, so you have to make sure they're in good shape. You've got to get firewood, you've got to get a barbeque, clean the place up, do a roster, brief everyone on what jobs they need to do, which places to patrol. I got good advice from David Brook that first year. He told me to make sure to have a visible police presence around the hotel, Brophy's boxing tent, the race track and caravan park. And he was right: that works.

The Birdsville police population during the races goes from one officer to about thirty. Two South Australian police come up. Various police come down from Mount Isa: cops from the Traffic Branch, the CIB, the inspector, Stock Squad and TAC Crime. Most of them just roll out their swags wherever there's a spare bit of dirt. Some sleep in the courthouse.

Every year just before the races I send an email saying, 'If you're gonna come, the accommodation is an 1880s courthouse with basic conditions. You've got a shower, roof, toilet and a bit of a kitchen. There's no air conditioning. Birdsville can be hot and windy, with the occasional dust storm. If you think it's not for you, let me know and we'll get someone else.'

And they've gotta share rooms with other police. But they all love coming down. If they think they're coming to Birdsville, they're really rapt. It's one of the iconic events that people want to come to. Police get paid to come down so no-one ever replies to the email saying, 'I'm not comin'.' No-one's ever said no.

What's it like going from one officer to thirty? It's good. Got someone to talk to. (Laughter) Some people reckon, 'Oh, you're busy.' But you're not. Imagine, now, single officer, there's a murder, or overdue aircraft, or a search. You've got to do it all yourself. During races you've got twenty-nine other people on hand to help.

At night, I hand the phone over to them. So if there's a job, I don't have to worry about it. It's all done by them. So you have a good time. You work during the day but that's more about liaising with race club officials, the pub, Brophy's, the caravan park, sorting things out. Road closures and so on. And you leave the policing to the Traffic Branch, the Generals and CIB.

They used to come Thursday and start work Friday, the first of the two race days.

I said to the Inspector, 'Can I get someone down earlier?'

He said, 'You'll be right.'

The problem was, as the years have gone on, more and more people have been coming to the races earlier, and leaving later. So it got to the point where, on the Wednesday before race weekend, there are 2000 people at the pub. And just me to police them. So now they come down Tuesday and start work Wednesday.

And I get the copper from Bedourie (Tim Farran in the early days) to come down after the Betoota Races, which are the week before. The Betoota Races used to be held after the Birdsville ones, but now they're before which is the best thing they ever did.

You've got people coming to Birdsville for weeks before the races and it gives them something to do. So Tim would work the Betoota Races with me and then come down here from Sunday onwards.

Given there are 4000 or more people in the desert, drinking alcohol virtually from the moment they arrive, the event is noted for being remarkably trouble-free. There're a few reasons for that. One is, policing the Birdsville Races is like policing your parents and grandparents. I dubbed it schoolies for over-fifties. I should have patented that because it's been used a lot of times. The people who come would rather talk to police and get their photo with them than bash 'em. People are generally in a good mood. They're here on holidays, a long way from home.

I think, too, visible police presence is a factor. We practise low-impact policing. If someone's drunk, police will say to their mates, 'Take him home, he's had too much.'

And if they don't, option B is back to the cop shop. There's a lot of that. If you police to the letter of the law, you'd probably have a few arrests a night. A few people intoxicated or pushing each other or something but if it can be quelled quickly by police saying, 'Take him home' then it's left at that.

Brophy's boxing tent helps because the people who probably would have a fight have a fight in Brophy's. Normally they get towelled up and we don't hear another peep from them. I've told Brophy he's worth at least ten coppers when it comes to people playing up.

Saturday and Sunday, there's also court, the only time it's held in Birdsville. Being an ex-prosecutor, I do it. I think the prosecutors in Mount Isa were looking forward to me retiring because now they can come down for the races. The magistrate from Mount Isa or Brisbane attends or does a phone hook-up with the court in Birdsville so people who've come to the races don't have to return to Queensland to attend court from wherever they've come from in Australia

Then, Monday morning, it's like the races never happened. Tumbleweeds blowing up the street. Everyone's gone and it's back to being a one-officer station. It's a big shock to the system. You look out the window and there's no-one there. You're used to going up the street because you get to know all the stall holders who come out for the races over the years and they're like friends and they're all gone. You go out to the river. No-one there. All the police are leaving. Or have already gone. And you know you've got a long hot summer ahead of you. A long, hot, lonely summer. (Laughter)

That's just part of the shift from major police operations to officer-in-charge of a one-officer station. You've just got to deal with what your duties are, whether you're working in a one-horse town where you're the only person there or you work in the city where you've got other police to help.

With a single-officer station, when there's an incident, you've got to be aware of what a lot of other people are doing, because you're effectively in charge. You've got to make sure the ambulance is coming. If you need to cut someone out of a vehicle, you've got to get SES. You've got to contact the Flying Doctor. You've got to do all that sort of stuff and activate whatever resources you need. That often involves asking for help from the rest of the community, which is why their support is so important. They're right there when you need them. And let's face it, out here, if you call for backup, you've got to wait at least two hours.

In September 2007, after the races, I got sent on a Search and Rescue course in Rockhampton. The course is based on experience from search and rescues the world over. It's best practice. Like aircraft accident investigations, where they find out what caused the accident and take steps to ensure it doesn't happen again, they find out what went wrong with a search and use that knowledge to help subsequent searches succeed. The course covered map reading, GPS, the tried and tested practices in relation to all kinds of search and rescues. For example, for a lost kid, the first thing you do is search the house thoroughly, because he may be hiding in the house. Then you do a quick search. You go out everywhere, just driving around, hoping to track him down. If that fails, you then go to a planned search.

It also teaches you how far people can get in any period of time and you'd be surprised; it's a lot further than what you think. A toddler can be kilometres and kilometres from where they went missing. You'd think they wouldn't get more than 3 or 4 kilometres. Then there's talk on how long people can last in certain conditions. That determines how long to keep searching for a survivor, although these days, the decision to call a search off comes from a lot higher than me. It has to come from an assistant commissioner. We will always search for days after the average survival times, until there isn't any hope. We need to keep families and loved ones in mind.

No sooner had I returned to Birdsville than I got two search and rescue jobs in two months. Both were initiated by Search and Rescue in Canberra. They called me directly. The first distress call, in October, was quickly sorted out. The second one, in November 2007, was 300 kilometres east, on the Cordillo Downs Road.

At that time of year, the heat can kill you in a matter of hours.

I contacted Cordillo and asked them to start looking, if they were able, while I headed out there with Theo. We got to the area three hours later and soon found a motorbike rider broken down by the side of the road. He'd set off the EPIRB after his brother, who was travelling with him, rode past and didn't see him. He hadn't come back. So either he was still waiting for his brother somewhere down the track or something had happened to him as well.

So we started looking for the missing brother. Canberra sourced a plane in Cairns that was flying down with night vision. After some difficulty, searching everywhere he might have set up camp, we managed to find the other brother. We also managed to cancel the plane before they got there, which saved a fair bit of money. Fortunately, everyone was safe and well.

Around the same time, the *Police Bulletin* ran an article noting that Theo had been awarded a certificate of appreciation 'for his invaluable assistance to police over a ten-year period in the township'. I submitted the application because his knowledge and specialised skills in outback vehicle recovery had made him indispensable to a number of police who had staffed the Birdsville Police Station.

Theo is a larger-than-life sort of character. He'd come out from South Africa after the apartheid era ended. He used to drive a truck over there, and he says that at night, he'd to have to take the tarp off and drive the truck onto the tarp so it wasn't stolen.

He came out to Australia with virtually nothing. He built himself up working for Nell and David Brook then took the lease out on running the roadhouse. He was a real entrepreneur and he worked really hard.

Theo took me under his wing, taking me out on rescues, out driving, and he taught me about all sorts of things to do when you're out in the desert.

He'd go like a cut cat. He'd go out, get a car, bring it back, go out and get another one, come back. Anything you needed, he'd give you a hand with. One rescue, he was coming back towing this big camper trailer. The car it belonged to had broken down and was limping back. Anyway this woman came up on the radio and said, 'Oh you won't get it up Big Red.'

Big Red is reputed to be the highest dune in the desert. And Theo goes, 'Just watch me darlin'.'

And up he went. He didn't get all the way to the top so he went sideways across Big Red and up again. And he didn't get up again, so he went sideways along and then up and over with a big jump. Landed.

As I said in the *Police Bulletin*, he could drive a truck up Mount Everest. He was that good.

By December, my second summer in Birdsville, things had quietened down a lot. Then I got a call to the hotel. One of the barmen had got his door smashed in. According to him, the cook had smashed it, so he reported it to the manager, who reported it to me. While that fairly short chain of communication was running its course, the cook left town.

I went around and investigated and found that the barman had cannabis in his room. Then I found cannabis in the other bloke's room. He wasn't there but he was flying back in. So I waited for him to fly in. When he arrrived he had more cannabis on his person. I knew both these fellas, obviously, but you're sworn to do your job so that's what you've gotta do.

They both got put on Drug Diversion. That's a program for drug offenders where you go and watch a video and they do a talk on the dangers of drugs. The victim with the broken door ended up flying up to Mount Isa for Drug Diversion. And the other guy, I think he failed to turn up to his. He ended up going to court and getting a fine.

It was only cannabis, not a large amount, personal use type stuff, but between that and the broken door, I had to act.

In January 2008 I got a call that a community member had threatened someone else with a knife.

I think this bloke was staying with someone and he'd worn out his welcome. He was eating their food and staying there and they asked him to put in some money for food and accommodation. He got angry and, according to the victim, he produced a knife.

He ended up getting charged with a couple of offences and on another occasion he did have a knife. He and his partner had ongoing problems and they kept me entertained for the best part of twelve or eighteen months. There was domestic violence. A bit both ways, too. Wilful damage.

Once the fella got locked out of the house by his partner so he put a besser block through the air conditioner on an extremely hot Birdsville night. So that got him in the house because she had to open a door or window to get some ventilation. Otherwise she'd have died from heat exhaustion. He came up to the police station once at about three in the morning and pushed the buzzer. I went out and he was lying on the ground holding his stomach. It's alleged she pegged a stubby at him. In the guts.

They both got charged with various offences that year: assault, domestic violence, wilful damage, those types of offences. On one occasion, he left town. He actually walked out of Birdsville and passing cars offered him a lift for two or three days but he kept walking. I think it took until he was 100 kilometres from Birdsville before he eventually accepted a lift.

In some of these violent situations, people are actually armed. It's not normally a situation that a police officer would handle on their own but most times you can get someone to give you a hand. Like an elder to talk to them, or someone else to talk to them. A relative. Calm them down.

The main thing is to calm the person down so he doesn't hurt someone or hurt himself. That's what you do. You go around, talk to him. By knowing all the locals, you call someone by his first name if he starts causing trouble. Obviously, if he's in a house and it's a hostage situation, then you have to get other police but if you can just talk to him face-to-face, normally you can resolve it. It's when you can't talk to someone, that's when you can't resolve issues.

In April 2008, I got a call that there'd been a fatal heart attack at Big Red. Bev and Ross, the clinic nurses, and I got there and found a man there who was well and truly dead. He was an older person, but not overly old. I think he was in his sixties. He was still working.

He was travelling with his son, his son's wife and his grand-children. He'd wanted to drive up Big Red and he got about 3 metres from the top. He stopped and got out of the car, walked around the back and his hat fell off. He bent down to pick it up and dropped dead of a heart attack. His son and daughter-in-law worked on him, but to no avail. We got there probably half an hour later.

Between us, we had to carry the body up the hill to the ambulance. We were sinking down to our knees in sand and it was really exhausting. And Bev, who was in her fifties, she worked as hard as Ross and me. We got him up the top and we all collapsed, just exhausted. You know where you can't move. Utterly spent.

Then we put him in the back of the ambulance and brought him back to Birdsville. This was in the days prior to mobile phones in Birdsville, so the family made all their phone calls from the police station. I let them make their calls, made them cups of coffee, because it was very sad for them. You know, their father and grandfather had died in front of them, right before their eyes.

Then we tried to get a death certificate because it makes it easier for the family, as well as for us. So we got onto the fella's specialist in Victoria and he was going to think about whether or not he could issue one. Then, unfortunately, someone from the family rang him up and abused him for not doing it and that was the end of that. We didn't get the death certificate.

In the end he had to get flown to Mount Isa, then flown to Rockhampton, then flown to Brisbane. He had a longer trip when he was dead than when he was alive. Then at the John Tonge Centre, which is the mortuary in Brisbane, they burnt all his clothes, which the family was very annoyed about. It was just a pair of shorts and a work shirt. They also found $100 in his top pocket, which we had missed. They were upset about that.

Then the son rang and asked if I'd write a letter so that his father could go from Brisbane to Victoria by ambulance.

I said, 'No, I can't write that. They'll think I'm an idiot.

Ambulances are for sick people.'

He said, 'Well, if you do write it, we'll get it for free.'

I said, 'Well you probably won't because they'll just say I'm an idiot.'

I refused to write the letter, which he wasn't happy about. Then they made a complaint to the police service about the clothes getting burnt (which had nothing to do with me and why they wanted them back I don't know), the money being found and the fact that I didn't write that letter. You can only do what you do. Imagine, though, for an ambulance it would be a three-day trip to Victoria, than a three-day trip back. It would take an ambulance out of action for that long.

That whole incident was a bit disappointing because I tried to do everything I could to help them out. I suppose people grieve in different ways and, like I've said before, you've gotta have someone to blame. I think I was that someone to blame.

One of the great Birdsville controversies erupted on 13 April 2008, when the town foreman made a formal complaint about a helicopter landing on the oval opposite the pub.

I said, 'Well what do you want me to do about it?'

He said, 'I want 'em charged.'

He had concerns that the chopper had damaged the oval's underground irrigation system. Something like that.

What happened was, some tourists had hovered above the pub. I think he was whingeing about that, too. They'd taken some photos, then they'd landed on the oval to take a photo with the pub in the background.

So I took a statement from the foreman, I submitted it to the aviation authority, CASA, and CASA said, 'The offence they've committed is illegally parking a vehicle on the oval. Get the council to issue 'em with a parking ticket.' (Laughter)

So I told the foreman that and he said, 'Forget it, I don't want to go ahead with it.'

So that was the end of that.

It might look like you're sweating the small stuff when you follow up on things like that, but the thing is, if you don't take it further, it looks bad for you in the eyes of the person who lodged the complaint. So you're better off going through the motions, taking it as far as you can. Let 'em get it off their chest. Half the time you know what the result is going to be. This wasn't the most earth-shattering of offences. We could prove that the helicopter did land on the oval, but CASA didn't seem to think much of it.

The threat of a parking fine does seem to have prevented any further landings. Although the average price of a helicopter is a million bucks and I don't know what a parking fine is, but it's probably not going to worry 'em anyway. That said, later in the year, during the floods, the emergency helicopter bringing vital supplies to Birdsville landed on the road right outside the pub – to deliver beer.

May 2008 was the first time I went all the way to Poeppels Corner (the junction of the Queensland, Northern Territory and South Australia borders, 171 kilometres west of Birdsville) to do a rescue. I'd been out there before on patrols. I'd also gone out there with Theo, but not in the police car. I just tagged along with him, a work experience type of thing. (Laughter)

We had a vehicle broken down west of Poeppels, with a

burnt-out clutch. I thought it would be a good chance for a writer who was new in town, that's you Evan, to come along and see what happens out in the desert on a rescue. By this time Theo had left so Padraic O'Neill, an Irish backpacker, was doing the mechanical work at the roadhouse. He came out to either fix the vehicle or tow it back to Birdsville. And his then girlfriend, now his wife, Olivia, came with us.

By the time we got the group together and loaded up the vehicles, it was late afternoon. We headed off west, negotiated Little Red (a section of the Big Red dune that's not so high), then you and me in the police car got over the next sand hill. We struggled but we did it. But then Padraic towing this big car trailer couldn't make it so we came back over and tried to give some moral support or advice on how to get to the top.

Padraic tried half a dozen times maybe. It was obvious that he wasn't going to succeed because even with a long run-up the best he could do was half or three-quarters of the way up the dune. There was still a long way to go, a big dog leg to the right at the top, and then over.

It wasn't going to happen so we decided to go the long way round. I knew we could go down the Birdsville Track 200 kilometres, then up the Warburton Track to Poeppels. There're almost no sand dunes along that route. The Warburton Track travels north-south, the way the dunes run. So most of the time you're travelling between the sand dunes. You still go over half a dozen to a dozen sand dunes but this is over 200 kilometres. Unlike the direct desert route, the QAA Line and French Line, where you're up and over, up and over, all the time.

We had to help Padraic back over Little Red, then we headed back into town, refuelled there, and by this time it was dark, about seven or eight o'clock.

When we got to the Warburton Track turn-off, it was probably eleven o'clock. We travelled along until we crossed over Warburton Creek, which was dry. Then we camped there the night. Probably only 10 kilometres in. Early in the morning, we headed north. We left the trailer on the big saltpan near Poeppels Corner because the sand dunes are pretty hard going from there on.

We went to Poeppels and I said to Padraic and Olivia, 'While you're here, we should have a quick look.'

We knew none of the people we were rescuing were injured. They were in a four-wheel drive and they had plenty of water and food. So, an extra fifteen minutes was neither here nor there when you're travelling for the best part of a day and a half.

While we were at Poeppels we saw Dave from Mount Dare (on the other side of the desert) and it was your idea to get him to tow the vehicle back to the trailer because he had a flash little car. And he agreed.

We went on and it was about 30 kilometres in that we found the vehicle and a retired professor and his wife. They were playing golf while they waited for us, practicing getting out of sand traps. Lovely people. They gave us some fruit cake.

Padraic worked out the clutch wasn't going to be fixed so he had to tow the vehicle back. Dave towed the broken vehicle with Padraic in it steering and braking. We took everyone else back in the police car to where the trailer was. Then we loaded the car onto the trailer.

By this time it was late afternoon. Then we headed off south with Padraic and Olivia towing the trailer, and you and me and the retired couple in the police car.

As it got dark, we had trouble. The police car could negotiate the sand dunes alright but it was very hard for Padraic because now instead of getting up a sand dune with just a trailer, he had a trailer plus a three-ton car on the back. So sometimes we had to dig away the top of a sand dune, then snatch him over. We did that over several dunes. Some were easy. Others took a lot of effort.

By the time we got back to the Birdsville Track we all breathed a sigh of relief because it meant no more sand dunes. It was probably midnight by then. Then we travelled up the track. Everyone was exhausted. We stopped every now and then to let Padraic catch up and see how he was going. Olivia was with him, so we knew that she'd keep him awake. We were all keen to get home, which we did around 3 a.m.

That was a good rescue. Everyone did their part. We got the people back. They spent the night in the police barracks and then a few extra nights, too. They had to get the new clutch and they ended up spending a week in Birdsville. We did a deal: they did the garden for me, and they'd get accommodation in return. And they did a real good job, too. It's slid a bit since then.

By that time I was a lot more confident about knowing my patch. I'd been out with Theo and Don, and I knew that at the turn-off on the saltpan it's 163 kilometres going east back to Birdsville. Poeppels is eight kilometres further on. And it's 183 kilometres south down to the junction with the Birdsville Track. And 200 odd north up the track to Birdsville. So going south then north more than doubles the distance you travel, but it's a much better way if you've got injured people or vehicles.

I say to people having trouble at Poeppels, 'If you've got plenty of fuel, go south. Go down there. And make sure you see me or ring me when you get to Birdsville. So I know you're back here.'

Padraic was only relieving at the roadhouse at that time. He'd been working at Cordillo Downs on a temporary work visa and let slip that he was a mechanic, and the Brooks, who own the roadhouse, needed a mechanic there. Padraic probably preferred working at Cordillo but he and Olivia also really loved Birdsville.

I said to him, 'Why don't you take over the garage? David and Nell are really keen for someone to take over. I'm sure you could come to some agreement with them.'

Olivia said, 'Oh, but my sister's having a baby.'

I said, 'You Irish, someone's always havin' a baby.'

They ended up going home to Ireland but I think their hearts were in Birdsville and they were hoping to be able to come back. The Irish economy was going through tough times after the global financial crisis. They got married in Ireland and we were actually invited to the wedding but unfortunately Sandra's passport had expired. By the time we got it renewed it was too late. I would have loved to have gone.

They came back to Birdsville a few years ago now. And now they're part of Birdsville. Padraic has a chopper licence and he flies out to the Brook properties to do whatever mechanical work is needed. Olivia is secretary of the race club committee, they're in the social club, on the school P&C. They've got three kids. They told me the other day that they'll probably stay here until their eldest child, Patrick, goes to high school. I think he starts school next year or maybe the year after. That means at least six more years. They just love Birdsville.

If you look at Padraic, you'd think he was an Aussie ringer. He wears the cowboy shirt, the jeans, the boots, the Akubra. Until you hear him talk, you think, 'He's the real deal, I'll get a photo with him.' Born and bred in Ireland. Very handy. A good mechanic and a lovely bloke, too.

Not long after we did that Poeppels rescue, we did a rescue where a vehicle had snapped in half, a few dunes into the desert, west of Birdsville. They'd hit something hard while accelerating to get up a steep sand hill. The vehicle was hanging on by just the bottom of the railing of the chassis. And Padraic welded it back up so that the car could be driven. Not bad for welding in the middle of the desert, working round the fuel tank, things like that. But some guys can just do things. Padraic's one of those guys. He gets the job done.

Later that month, I was made a special constable for the Northern Territory, with a ceremony in Alice Springs.

I drove across the desert with Don the Ranger to be sworn in. We spent three nights in the desert, then went to Alice Springs and stayed at the casino. That was good after three nights in the desert. I got sworn in and was given a card saying I was effectively a police officer in the Northern Territory, with the same power as any other police officer: power of arrest, power of search, seizure and all those things that police the world over have.

Then we had to come back to Birdsville. We started working out whether to go north and go along the Plenty and Donohue highways to Boulia, then down. Then Don said he saw a sign in the mall that said 'Coober Pedy 380 kilometres'.

I said, 'Don, that's not far. That's only four hours' driving.'

So we headed off south about two o'clock and we're driving and driving and we got to this place out of Alice Springs called Jim's Place, and we stopped there. There's a dingo at Jim's that gets up and sings along with the piano. So we watched that and thought that was pretty funny. A backpacker was playing the piano and the dingo was singing. Then we went down to Kulgera and met the police officer there. We talked to him and then we kept going.

It was getting darker and darker and then we worked out that the sign Don saw was in miles. It was one of those old milestones that you sometimes see in country towns, that are kept there for a bit of historical interest. So it wasn't 380 kilometres, it was 688. By now it was dark, there were cattle on the roads and all the other dangers of outback Australia to think about. We decided to pull up at Marla. We got to Marla and went to the police station there, looking for a bed for the night.

They were really good and let us stay.

So we stayed in the barracks there the night. Had a few drinks.

We headed off the next day and went to Coober Pedy. We didn't get there until about lunchtime. From there we went to Marree (370 kilometres). Stayed the night there. By the time we got down there it was dark again. And from Marree we went back to Birdsville (521 kilometres). It was a total of 1579 kilometres, instead of 1000 travelling back across the Simpson or 1200 through Boulia. I was away for a week.

I called police communications in Mount Isa and said I'd been away for a few days.

I said, 'Any messages?'

They said, 'Oh no, is there anything you want? Do you want to speak to the inspector?'

I said, 'Oh no, it's okay.' (Laughter)

I think there was also a medal ceremony in Mount Isa I had to get back for. That was a police long service and good conduct medal. Ten years of not being away from your station for long periods. (Laughter) Actually, I shouldn't laugh. It's particularly important to be at your post when you're in a one-officer station, because when you're not, it leaves your area without any law enforcement. As it was, I'd planned to be away for six days and it ended up being seven. The Bedourie cop also relieved while I was away. Anyway, not long after I got back to Birdsville I went up to Mount Isa and got presented with that.

Everything was terribly dry in the middle of 2008. Despite the occasional floods, most of Western Queensland had been in drought for the previous eight years.

Back then, in June every year, we would have the Birdsville Gift on the Queen's Birthday weekend. The idea was to have a running race to rival the Stawell Gift. We used to get runners here; they all came in on a bus. In 2008, they had a concert, too, on the night of the race. They called it the Lift the Spirit, Defy the Drought concert, with Graham Connors, who sings 'The Road Less Travelled' and 'A Little Further North'.

As soon as Graeme started singing, it started pouring rain. And it never stopped. All that night. And the next day. The runners who were in town for the race were stuck here because the bus couldn't get out. They were here for almost a week. Eventually most of them flew out, and that was the end of the Birdsville Gift. It was never held again. So the rain killed the Birdsville Gift but it broke the drought as well.

There had been rain around Birdsville before, during my time, but this was the start of an extended wet period that changed everything. The desert plants thrived and soon burst into an abundance of flowers that transformed bare red sand and gibber country into swathes of yellow, white, red, purple and green. The rivers started flowing and were brimming with fish. Flocks of budgerigars flashed red, yellow and green across the sky. Good rains transform the desert. When they do, you realise that all through the dry spell it's just in survival mode, waiting for a whiff of moisture to give it the green light to make the most of it.

Not long after it started to rain, we got an EPIRB activation. Two motorbike riders were stuck about 50 kilometres east of Birdsville. Fifty k isn't that far but the roads weren't good. A couple of centimetres of rain and the dirt roads become too soft to travel safely, especially with a heavy vehicle towing a trailer. Often, roads may be passable but they're closed to protect them from damage, which will eventually make them impassable anyway.

These riders had been travelling on two bikes, then one bike broke down. So they both got on the other one and in the end that one ran out of fuel trying to get through all the mud. So they set off an EPIRB, and we (relieving officer Dave McCarthy and I, because I was about to go on holidays) went and got them. While we were getting ready to go, we learned there was another traveller stranded as well. He hadn't made it as far as the motorbike riders.

Dave came out with me, as did a backpacker who was work-ing at the garage. Padraic had gone back to Ireland by that stage. We got to these riders and put the bike that was out of fuel on the trailer. Then we headed further out to locate the other person.

We were going through floodwater and the car was travelling well. It probably wasn't that deep, about half a metre. We were using the guideposts, which are 900 millimetres high, and keep-ing in the middle of the track, which is where the road surface is hard. But then it just got deeper and deeper and we couldn't see the guideposts. I didn't realise it at the time but one of the motorbike riders in the back of the car had a video camera and captured all of what happened next.

I said to Dave, 'What do you reckon?'

Dave said, 'I dunno.'

Then he said, 'Oh, trouble. I think the road would be a bit higher that way. Wouldn't it? It might be a bit harder and a bit . . .'

I said, 'Further over?'

'I'd say go the high side. Don't you reckon?'

'Yeah.'

And all of a sudden it got really deep.

We had a bow wave, where the front of car is pushing the water up so high that you can see it from inside the car, which is often the last thing you see before your vehicle drowns. Dave starts going, 'Oh fuck.'

Then the water came over the bonnet. He's going, 'Uh oh.'

Then it came up to the windscreen.

Now I was going, 'Fuck!'

He's going, 'Oh fuck.'

I said, 'Back?'

'Yeah, let's get the fuck out of here.'

That's when we decided to reverse out.

Now I was driving backwards through floodwater. No idea where the road was. I was asking Dave, 'How we goin', mate? Straight back?'

He's guiding me, 'No go a little that way. Yeah that way. Keep goin'.'

Fortunately, we were able to get out, after which we decided to get the person to walk through the water to us.

(The video of this incident is on YouTube as 'Police car in Birdsville floods', courtesy of motorbikin.com.au)

We came back to Birdsville and I think the bike riders stayed there a few days themselves, until they were able to go out and retrieve the other bike. It took quite a while for the water to go down.

One of the fellas we rescued was a professional bike rider, Phil was his name. He takes people on bike tours all over Australia. They actually sent me a DVD of their adventures and of them getting rescued. It was too hard going through the mud. It just got deeper and deeper, too much mud, too much water. It just stopped the bike in its tracks but we got them back, which was good.

During these floods, there were some other people who got stuck, too. At one point they were on the only bit of high ground they could find, a cattle grid, where the road goes up and over the grid (out here the grids are installed above ground with banks built up to them so they don't fill with sand). They were completely surrounded by water. We had to get them to walk through water to get to us. They were in the distance and they had to walk out. We told them not to go on if it got too deep, and to watch the guide posts. If you can see them, you know it's alright. If you can't see them and it gets too deep, go back. The water wasn't flowing fast. It was just floodwater. They made it out, too.

More travellers got into difficulties in July 2008. At the end of the month I had a two-wheel drive vehicle that had a series of flat tyres and no money to pay for new ones.

First of all, this bloke had got a flat tyre at Mount Leonard, 170 kilometres east of Birdsville. Chook Kath, manager of Mount Leonard Station, had given him a tyre to get going. Then he got to Birdsville, but now he had two flat tyres. So I rang the mechanic, Mark, to give him two tyres and some fuel to get him going.

The car had come from Moree in New South Wales. I noticed the rego label was five years out of date. I didn't ask the driver for a licence because I knew he wouldn't have one. That may not be correct procedure but sometimes you don't want people to stay in town. If they tell you they haven't got a licence or you ask for it and they haven't got one, then you have to take action. If you don't ask, they just go and sometimes it's better if they do. Otherwise, places might get broken into or things might get stolen.

The people in the car were going to a funeral in Mount Isa, so they headed off north. Then they got another flat tyre. This is halfway between Birdsville and Bedourie, so we took out another tyre to them. Then off they went again. I don't think they made it to the funeral because they had more mechanical problems after leaving my patch. It was about a week later. But we got them going to where they wanted to go. If they'd stayed in town, they'd have had nowhere to live. They didn't have any money, but people have to eat. Sometimes people in desperate times do desperate things. I knew these people had family in Mount Isa. And there're all the support services up there, like Centrelink, blah, blah, blah.

Was there any suspicion about a two-wheel drive from Moree going to Mount Isa by a less-than-direct route and on dirt roads? I don't know why they came through Birdsville. A drug run? No, they just seemed like people that I didn't want in town.

Another incident I had to deal with was a German backpacker working in the roadhouse who decided to add her own message to a postcard a tourist had asked her to post. She wrote, 'Having a great time in Birdsville. Birdsville rocks.' And signed her name. Then she posted the card . . . to the guy's wife.

When the wife got it, she put two and two together and came up with about eighteen. She rang him up and he rang me.

The backpacker didn't mean anything bad. She was just writing as a friendly girl. Which the wife didn't appreciate. Anyway, I rang his wife and said, 'Look, she was given the postcard to post and she just wrote on it. Nothing more.'

If you ask me this husband and wife might have been having troubles anyway but this sort of didn't help things. The suspicions were there.

Was a crime commited with that incident? There probably was but it wasn't like this girl opened someone's mail to see what was inside. She just wrote on a postcard. I think I've still got a copy of the postcard that he sent me because I kept this file. And what would a magistrate do with that? She wrote on a postcard. It wasn't in the custody of the post office at the time. It had been given to her to post. That's what happens when you take short cuts. It backfires on you.

We had a big car rally come through Birdsville the following month, organised by Dubbo Rotary from New South Wales. The Betoota Race Club organised a breakfast for them on Nappabillie Creek, just east of town. That's on Geoff Morton's property. He gave a talk to them.

I was there supporting the charity. I was in full police uniform, but serving breakfast for the rally. You have that at community events. Lauren, my daughter, used to pitch in all the time. We'd help at the school, too. The school would cater for events or Bev the nurse (and Geoff's wife) would do that on behalf of the Betoota Race Club. And we just helped. There's not many people in town. Birdsville's a place where you can afford to give that time and it's good for the community to see the police officer helping out and supporting events. You also get a free feed out of it.

At the rally breakfast, a lot of people came up and gave me back stolen property they'd souvenired from the pub. You know, salt and pepper shakers, bits and pieces. Again, they gave it back to you, and, by the letter of the law, they've stolen it. But what are you going to do? They gave it back, so well and good. I took it and gave it all back to the pub.

Doing events in police uniform is a very deliberate choice. People see that you're helping and you're part of the community. You're doing your bit as the local police officer to support the community in town. It's another way of recognising that you rely on them to help you when you need a hand as well.

It's a good impression for others as well. People from city areas usually only see police when they pull them up for a breath test or to give them a ticket. In a small town it's good because they can come and talk to you and you can talk to them about driving in the area and just talk one on one. They get to know you as a person, not as a police officer.

Later that day I had to attend a car accident. Another rollover. It was 20 kilometres west of town, between Birdsville and Big Red. The driver was part of the Dubbo event. He'd rolled his car coming back from Big Red. He wasn't hurt but we took him up to the clinic to get him checked out anyway.

All the accidents you attend out here are rollovers. When people are driving on dirt roads, if they get into a skid, they panic, hit the brakes, and roll over. Fortunately, most times they get out of it okay. A few bumps and scratches. That's why it's so important people wear seatbelts when they're driving in the bush.

If you roll without a seatbelt, you're going to die or be seriously injured. With him, the worst thing dented was his pride, because he wrecked the car, which meant one less person on the run.

Around that time, whenever a vehicle and/or caravan rolled over or was involved in an accident, the new mechanic, Peter Barnes (who'd worked for the Brooks off and on for years), would put the vehicle on the back of his recovery truck, bring it back to Birdsville and park the truck at the side of his garage in full view. Sometimes the wrecked vehicle would be there for weeks.

Every time that happened, an endless stream of people would come to the police station to ask about it. Where did the accident happen? Was anyone injured? How fast was the vehicle going, how did it happen, what speed, were they wearing seatbelts? Were they flown out by the Flying Doctor, is there a design fault with the caravan or camper, any alcohol involved, was it driver error? And a million other questions. Invariably, I would then be told a story about some other traveller they knew of doing something silly. Never them, mind you.

I would always spend time answering some of the questions, obviously without disclosing anything confidential, and always provided some road safety messages. The main one was driving to the conditions, which may mean driving at 5 kilometres per hour or even less when you're going through water or muddy conditions. Don't drive like they do in TV ads, where they're always going flat out, risking damage to the vehicle and injury to the occupants. After a few months of answering thousands of questions I said to Barnesy, 'Any chance of moving the truck out of sight?'

He said, 'I was thinking exactly the same thing. They come and ask me exactly the same questions.'

Barnesy moved the truck to his holding yard and it saved both our voices.

Towards the end of August I had a person in town reported as a suicide risk. People who knew him were concerned for his welfare because he said he was going to the Dingo Caves, 20 kilometres north of town, on his own.

If you get a call that someone is concerned, then you've got to take it seriously. It might be true. So I investigated it and got the person to see the nurse.

It turned out he just wanted time alone, a bit of time out. There was no risk to himself. He didn't have any thoughts of doing self harm.

I didn't think the person who reported it had overreacted though, because the person they were worried about had said he wanted to go off by himself. There was concern for him. Genuine concern. I checked it out. He was spoken to by the nurse. And it was left at that.

You can't ignore the fact that mental health issues and suicides occur more frequently in rural areas. One of the reasons is that it's very hard in a small town to go and see the local nurse. The nurse knows you. It's different in the city, where if you go and talk to a nurse, a health professional or a police officer, you're probably never going to see them again. You're anonymous.

When it comes to going to the clinic or the police station here, I'm not saying that everyone knows but bad news travels fast in small communities. Well-intentioned as everyone may be, sometimes it gets out. Or people think it will get out, so they're more reluctant to seek help, whether it's for domestic violence, mental health issues or whatever. You know the person, you've probably had them around for dinner and you've been around to their place for dinner. Or you play tennis with them. Have a drink with them at the hotel.

For a police officer, this is another area where you have to be like Switzerland. You've got to be completely neutral and completely confidential. People expect it.

If you suspect someone is having a problem, you really have to try to get to the bottom of it. You might say to them that people are concerned. You don't tell them who you've been speaking to, but you say, 'Look, you just need to get checked out. So, if you see the nurse and the nurse is happy, well and good.'

Most people are happy to do that. If the person is paranoid, that might be a bit harder.

September 2008 was the first year I policed the races with actual horses.

Once again, the event ran smoothly, helped by the fact that most of the over-fifties schoolies were in a holiday mood. Most were camped on the common, scattered widely so they were separated from each other. They also saw police when they came to town, conducting breath-tests, riding motorbikes around the common, and foot-patrolling outside the pub. There was a visible presence at the racecourse, hotel and stall precinct. That helped a lot.

At the 2008 races, the retiring chief magistrate, Marshall Irwin, came out with his wife and held court for the minor offences that had to be dealt with. We had a few cases on. One involved a person who had fired a parachute flare that landed in the airport, then denied responsibility despite the fact that he was standing at the boot of his car surrounded by orange smoke. And the fact that there were more unlit flares in his car. I think the magistrate saw that for what it was. It was more a prank than anything else, so he fined him about $150. No conviction recorded. You don't want people setting off flares but the offence was down the lower end of the scale, really.

Later that year, in November, Penny Wensley, the then-Governor of Queensland, visited Birdsville. She came out and I met her in the Birdsville Hotel. She was a very nice lady. She had a talk to all the locals and got involved with everyone here. She was easy to talk to. Very personable.

I think she was here for the Outback Tourism Awards. They were held out at the race track and they had stock in the middle of the track and big drums full of fire to create an outback atmosphere but it was blowing an absolute gale so everyone was huddled in the marquee. It was a windy night out there. It had been perfect weather in the days leading up to the event and then that night it was so windy and dusty.

Later in November 2008, more floods. There was quite a bit of rain around the town, then we started getting reports that a lot of water was coming from the Diamantina's upper catchment. I was told that when it arrived, in early January 2009, the town would be cut off for an extended period.

When it comes to floods, you can rely on local knowledge about what to expect. These are people who've been here all their lives. And they don't exaggerate. They say the country around town's going to be flooded but you look up in the sky and there's not a cloud to be seen. Then you go down to the river and it's getting higher and higher. The water level's rising every day. Then one day it breaks its banks and spreads out and there's still not a cloud in the sky but there's water everywhere that has come down from a thousand kilometres away.

Birdsville's in a good location when the floods arrive. The airstrip is in the middle of town and it never floods, it remains dry. It never closes because of flood water. Unlike somewhere like Rockhampton, which closes for weeks when a cyclone passes. The rest of the town remains dry, too. When you take off in a helicopter, it's like you're looking at an inland sea and Birdsville's an island in the middle of it.

The locals just take it in their stride. They've got their food. They know that if they run out, the council will organise a resupply. Everyone goes down for a talk at the grid or wherever the flood level is. They watch the level to see if it's still rising or going down. When there's a flood, or a flood is expected, one of my duties is reading the flood levels three times a day for the Bureau of Meteorology. I put the levels in on the weather terminal that's housed in the police station.

So in November 2008, people were saying, 'It'll come down, it'll be this high and flood this area.' They can tell you almost to the day when the floods will arrive. Fortunately, the flood wasn't going to arrive before Christmas, but it wasn't far away.

In the days before Christmas, I started monitoring the progress of a German woman who'd been sighted on a bicycle on the Windorah to Birdsville road. A stockman had seen her getting dirty water from an almost dry dam near Durrie Station. This was at the hottest time of the year. Obviously, there was concern for her welfare. You don't want her to die in the Australian outback.

I drove out to check on her, and she said, 'I'm fine. I don't need any help.'

She didn't say no, though, when I offered her clean water and oranges and stuff. Then she came through Birdsville. She was in town on New Year's Eve. I remember talking to her there. She was probably in her fifties. She headed down the Birdsville Track when she left town and we monitored her progress. I got into contact with the South Australian Police so they'd keep an eye on her, too.

Then I lost track of her for a couple of days. No-one had seen her. So Sandra and I went down to find her. We followed the bike track and when we found her, she was off the road under a tree. Turns out she had been travelling at night, in the moonlight, and camping up during the 40-degree heat during the day.

I talked to her about the risks she was taking, travelling through this country at the hottest time of the year. She was pretty stubborn. She'd ridden here (to Birdsville) and she was riding down there (to Marree). She wanted to do it and I couldn't stop her. She wasn't breaking the law. Sometimes you're better letting people go, but monitoring them every day. You get other people to keep an eye on them as well so if they do get into trouble, you know exactly where they are.

This woman had the right gear: long clothes, to keep the sun off, and this old bike loaded with lots of cordial bottles full of water. A lot of it was brown. So I gave her food, clean water and monitored her the whole way down to Mungerannie (315 kilometres south), just to make sure she got down alright. When Mungerannie reported that she'd made it, South Australian Police monitored her from there on.

———

New Year's Eve at the end of 2008 also brought with it one of my first 'dumb tourist' rescues, as opposed to people just not knowing what to do, like letting their tyres down a bit to drive on sand. It was a man with two kids in their pre-teens, a boy and girl. They were driving up from Innamincka, towing a camper trailer. This bloke decided not to get fuel in Innamincka because it was $1.97 a litre and he found out it was only $1.70 in Birdsville.

He was about 100 kilometres from Birdsville when the fuel light came on. So he unhooked the camper trailer he was towing, thinking he'd get further not towing anything. In the camper trailer was 100 litres of water, food, beds, shelter, blah blah blah, and cooking facilities.

Off they go again. Then they picked up these people who had two flat tyres. Then they're coming along and between them these five people had two 600 ml bottles of water. Then they get a flat tyre.

They got out and changed the tyre. It's 47 degrees. When they've done that, they drink the water, as you would. It's hot work. Then off they go and about 40 kilometres out of Birdsville, they ran out of fuel. It was always going to happen.

So it's 47 degrees, three adults, two children, no water. So then the man and his son, just a kid, try and walk in.

They got 4 kilometres and the son said, 'This is foolhardy, I'm going back.'

Thankfully, the young fella made it back to the car. They still had no water though. It was all in the camper trailer. They'd drunk what they had.

Fortunately for them, a car came along, picked the father up, and brought him into Birdsville. I think he had to really convince them to bring him in, because they were going the other way.

He said, 'Look, it's a matter of life and death.'

The vehicle dropped him off at the police station, then left. He told me what was happening and I got fuel from Barry Gaffney and out we went. I put fuel in the car and gave the kids water. The two people they picked up, I gave them water, too.

The funny thing was the woman said, 'Oh, have you got a satphone?'

And I said, 'Yeah.'

And she said, 'Can you ring this number? It's roadside assistance and they'll bring out two tyres for us.'

And I said, 'Darlin', you're in the middle of nowhere. They won't be comin' out here. It's New Year's Eve. Come back to Birdsville. You can sort it out there.'

So I took them into Birdsville and old mate put fuel in the car and headed back for his camper trailer. Then I drove up the road to where these people had two flat tyres. It was maybe 100 kilometres out. I picked up their two flat tyres and brought them in. I dropped them off and the bloke said to Barry, 'Oh, you've gotta fix these tyres.'

Barry said, 'Well, you've gotta pay for them.'

They said, 'Roadside assistance will pay for them.'

Barry said, 'Until someone pays for 'em, you're not gettin' 'em.'

So she was in the phone box to roadside assistance for about an hour.

Then someone rang me up and said, 'We've got this woman in a phone box wanting us to pay for two tyres.'

So I went up and saw her and said, 'Look, why don't you just pay for them and sort it out later?'

Then they wanted me to drive out and put these two tyres back on the car.

I said, 'Nah. You have to pay for the garage fella to take you out.'
It was like $400.

It was New Year's Eve. I've already driven hundreds of kilo-metres out to get the tyres for them. I shouldn't have even done that for them but I did. So they cracked the shits about that, because I wouldn't drive out and put their tyres on.

Then they went around asking the property owners who were in town and they all said, 'No, we're here for New Year's Eve.'

In the end they ended up paying John Hanna, a barman at the pub, $400 to drive out to put the tyres on the car. He got a flat as well, wrecked his own tyre, and that was any profit he might have made gone.

I said to them, 'You've just gotta pay. We've gotta pay for these things.'

And consider, they only had a 600-ml bottle of water. They could have paid a much, much higher price. You'd usually drink two litres just changing the tyre on a hot day.

The moral of that story still is: tell people your travel plans. No matter what the price of fuel is, fuel up. There's nothing more use-less than a brand-new car if it's got no fuel. It doesn't matter how good your car is, if you haven't got fuel, you ain't going anywhere. And the other moral is: if you think you can call roadside assis-tance when you're in the middle of outback Queensland on New Year's Eve, think again. Because they didn't come out. A helicopter didn't appear and drop off two brand-new tyres for these people.

You need to think smart. A caravan with 100 litres of water in it? Hang onto it. The history of this region shows what has happened to people who left the water behind: they've died.

The expected flood arrived just after New Year's Eve. The town was cut off and the roads were closed.

I went on holidays and while I was away we had a highly suspicious car accident. These two young fellas in a four-wheel drive ute managed to get to town. They had a couple of beers at the pub. Then they quickly left. At night. Not long after, they crashed their car where floodwater had cut the road away.

The road they were driving on was closed. So there was a strong suspicion they were up to no good.

I don't know what they were up to. Drugs were mentioned. Well, I might have mentioned that. Unfortunately, we couldn't get to the car because of the flooding. It was weeks before the floodwater went down. If I could have got out there, I would have looked to see footprints going somewhere and then looked for something buried.

It was just strange. They came to town, had a couple of drinks at the pub, and quickly left. Down a closed road. At night. Mmm.

That will probably be a mystery I'll never solve, but there was definitely something wrong there. Of course, I looked at the details of the driver and the car to see if he had any history. He didn't. If he'd done anything wrong in the past, he'd never been caught.

From early in 2009 until March, the town was cut off by floodwater. It's a bit different policing the town when it becomes an island. First of all, you don't have any people coming through. You don't have the tourist traffic on the roads, so it's relatively quiet. You've only got the town. You get a bit, not stir crazy, but a bit of cabin fever, I suppose. You can't drive anywhere, but even if you normally wouldn't leave town, it's different when you can't. You end up going past the clinic to the edge of the flood-water and you can spend an hour just talking to people about the river. About the height. Then you might go for a run in the flood-boat for something different to do.

For police work, it's pretty quiet. You've got the river heights to do, the weather to do, and making sure the town is supplied with food, which is mainly done by the council anyway. You've got the odd phone hook-up with senior police to let them know how the town's travelling. The locals have been going through this for donkey's years so it's not something that worries them.

We also have to keep an eye on the stations, which can also be isolated. That year we ended up doing runs to Roseberth in the flood boat, to drop off medication. Then we went down to Pandie Pandie, just to visit them as well. We'd go down and give them a bit of company, have a cup of tea, take out a cake, have a bit of a talk to them. The other stations around have airstrips. We do phone hook-ups with them to find out if there're any issues. They've all been there before. They make their own fun.

If there is an emergency, we have contingencies in place. Say someone needs to be evacuated, we have a helicopter for that. If the airstrip at a cattle station is unusable (the dirt strip may be boggy or under water), then we get the helicopter.

By February 2009 there was an escalating cycle of violence between the couple who'd been keeping me busy since I'd arrived in town. There had been ongoing domestic violence incidents but they worsened until I arrested the bloke. In the end he was given bail on the condition that he didn't reside in Birdsville. I was sick of him and he needed to be kept away from what was a toxic relationship. He and his partner fought constantly and the violence was increasing. So we put in a circuit breaker. He went and lived with his family up at Bedourie. Then he moved to Boulia. Then he disappeared. Which suited me. (Laughter)

The floods of early 2009 turned out to be among the biggest ever in Western Queensland. It was the third biggest on the Georgina River–Eyre Creek system and there were big floods on the Diamantina River and Cooper Creek systems as well. With masses of water coming down all three waterways, it became clear that the water would reach Lake Eyre. It wouldn't just reach the Lake, it would fill it, a spectacular once-in-a-lifetime event. It would create an inland sea and an explosion of wildlife rarely seen anywhere on the planet.

In late March 2009, the Georgina was still in flood north of Birdsville. That led to a rescue 30 kilometres west of Cluny Station. The car involved had got to the intersection of the Birdsville–Bedourie Road and the Bedourie–Windorah Road. There was a big ROAD CLOSED barrier on the road heading south. But the driver had been told at Bedourie that the road between Bedourie and Birdsville was open. It *was* open but via a sign-posted detour going around Lake Machattie, which was along the road to Windorah. So they get to this big 'road closed' barrier and they just decide to drive around it.

They said later, 'Oh, we got told that it was open.'

They got to the Cuttaburra Crossing, where the water was still flowing. It's a sea of water, it's as wide as the Amazon, and they drove into the water and immediately got stuck. It was always going to happen. There was a husband and wife up front and in the back were two old people. One was the bloke's father. I think he was in his eighties.

For me to get to these guys meant a drive right around the Cuttaburra, around Lake Machattie. About 200 kilometres. But that's what's good about Birdsville: you can rely on property people to help you. So I asked Steve Cramer, manager from Glengyle, to pull them out for me.

The old bloke said to Steve, 'I knew we were in trouble when he went around the "road closed" sign.'

His son came down and saw me when they got to Birdsville and he said, 'I'm really angry. They told me the road was open.'

I said, 'Well the road *is* open but you went past a "road closed" sign.'

The road that was open was around Lake Machattie. So if he'd looked at the way to go, he wouldn't have had any trouble. Instead he went around a 'road closed' sign and kept going. When someone is telling you which way to go in the outback, you need to listen.

In April 2009 one of Jimmy Crombie's foals got attacked by a wild dog or dingo. So we called down Ross, the nurse. He had quite a big job because as well as being one of the clinic nurses, he was the local vet as well. Unfortunately, the foal's lung had been punctured in the attack and it was in a bad way, so I had to put the animal down.

Then Jimmy said, 'I'm going to borrow Brookie's gun and I'm going to shoot every dingo in Birdsville.'

Poor old Jimmy has only got one eye. I rang up David Brook and said, 'Whatever you do, don't give Jimmy your gun.'

Not that David would have anyway.

Jimmy is an Aboriginal elder. He was born in the desert. He doesn't have a birth certificate and can't read or write but he's very well respected in town. He's a very good person who's well-liked by everyone. He used to be a stockman around outback Queensland on the properties around here.

At one stage I did try to get him a birth certificate, or at least work out roughly when he was born. I've got a big folder on that. He said he was born on Pandie Pandie Station, which is in South Australia, so that makes it harder, because you're a Queensland police officer dealing with another state's bureaucracy. I sent off form after form, so much paperwork. I took statements from people who have known Jimmy for a long time, like Barry Gaffney, David Brook and Don Rowlands. I was trying to ascertain how long they'd known him, when he'd been a kid, that sort of thing.

In the end we gave up. It just got too hard. He didn't really need a birth certificate because he won't travel overseas. I think he's never left Birdsville. He's got a licence. He's got Medicare. He gets a pension.

Jim's got a date that's on his licence but he thinks the actual date may have been a year earlier. He came in once to ask Sandra (after she came out permanently in 2010) for another year's back pay on his pension because of the incorrect birth date. He didn't get that.

I think his age is pretty close to what's on his licence. I think the police years ago worked it out just by talking to people. The actual date, they'd have made that up. Maybe they worked out that he was born in summer or spring. But Jim wouldn't know. Jim's mother was actually alive when I came to Birdsville but she was in no position to give us any information. She was very elderly. Jim's probably in his late sixties or early seventies now.

CHAPTER 4

ON A WHEEL AND A PRAYER

In mid-May 2009 I got a call from Geoff Morton on the radio. I've got a radio in the house so people can contact me directly if they can't get to a phone. There was nothing unusual about Geoff calling me because it had just rained and he often wanted to know how much rain Birdsville (which is surrounded by his station, from which the town precinct and common was excised back in the nineteenth century) had got.

So I said, 'Oh, we got 12 mls, Geoff.'

He said, 'Oh, that's good, but I've lost a wheel off my aircraft.'

So I go, 'Oh, that's not good.'

Obviously, it was battle stations then. Geoff wasn't just radioing from down the road, he was up in the air. I asked him if it was okay for him to fly around while I got things happening.

He said, 'Fine. Apart from the wheel, the aircraft's intact.'

I started contacting all the necessary people: the inspector, the nurse, the fire brigade. You came up, and Barnesy, people that are handy. So we all get to the airstrip and we worked out a plan of attack. The plan was for Geoff to fly around for an hour to burn off as much fuel as he could. If something bad happened, it was best if there wasn't much fuel in the tank ready to ignite. He agreed to that, which was his decision. As he's the pilot, with sole responsibility for his safety and that of his aircraft, no-one can presume to tell him what to do. You don't want to be telling him to do something when he's up in the sky.

I remember, when the plane flew over the airstrip you could only see one wheel. You know, gee, it sunk in at that point what was really happening. He's only got one wing wheel plus the nose wheel. You definitely need two wing wheels to land safely.

While Geoff was using up fuel, we were working out the best way for him to land. Birdsville has got a bitumen landing strip going north–south and a dirt landing strip going east–west. I thought it would be better for him to land on the dirt. There'd be less chance of sparks and stuff like that. Fortunately, David Brook was there, and he's a pilot. He called in some expert advice from pilots at a flying school in Adelaide.

They said, 'No, the best way to land is on the bitumen airstrip so the strut doesn't dig into the ground.'

Obviously, we'd closed the airstrip to all other planes. Paul Veal, the council foreman at that time, was there. He did a good job. The whole town came out to watch what was going on. Bad news travels fast. There's people crying, because a lot of them loved Geoff. The whole community was there.

We went up to the end of the runway, the northern end, and as Geoff came in we followed him down in the fire engine, the police car, council vehicles with fire-fighting equipment, and the ambulance. Geoff's wife, Bev, was one of the clinic nurses, but she was away at the time. So Ross was there with the ambulance.

When Geoff touched down, it was a good landing. A perfect

landing. He came down on the good wheel and the nose wheel, kept the wing with the missing wheel up for as long as he could. Then he put it down and it just skidded ever so slightly and came to a stop.

He got out. He was checked by the nurse which is part of the procedure. I told the inspector he'd landed.

He had said, 'If he crashes and burns, contain, isolate, get it underway and we'll call the investigators. You can only do what you can do.'

The inspector was happy that he'd made a proper landing. No-one was hurt. Everyone was happy. The whole town was happy. And I'm sure Geoff was happy, too.

We got a photo of us all around the aircraft and that was that.

I asked Geoff what had happened and he told me he lost the wheel when he hit a pelican. They can do a lot of damage. Very strong beaks.

We don't have anything to indicate it was anything else.

There were a lot of pelicans around at that time. The floods that had come through earlier in the year had continued down to Lake Eyre, bringing a flood of wildlife in their wake. And a flood of tourists wanting to see Lake Eyre.

Birdsville became a major hub for the tourist influx. A few things happened to promote that. The late Paul Lockyer put out a doco on Lake Eyre that was very well received. Paul made part of that documentary in Birdsville. I think 800 000 people saw it the first time it screened. Then Don Rowlands got his photo on the front page of *The Australian* newspaper with all the pelicans up at Lake Machattie. After that, tourism boomed. People have it on their bucket list to fly over Lake Eyre when it's full of water.

Planes were picking up people from capital cities, flying them to Birdsville for lunch, then down to Lake Eyre. They'd come back for an afternoon drink or snack, then head back home. So people were leaving home and then returning in one day. They didn't have to overnight. There were toilets on the plane and someone doing a commentary on Lake Eyre as they flew over. They'd travel down over Lake Eyre one way then everyone would swap seats for the return leg, so if you had an aisle seat, you'd then get a window seat. Those planes came all the time.

There were also charter operators based out of Birdsville. They were flying Cessnas that would fly down with five passengers. They'd do a flight over Lake Eyre and come back. They were going out full all the time. A lot of the pilots ran out of hours they were allowed to fly per day and they had to cancel flights. There were just too many people wanting to go and not enough pilots to take them.

And Lake Eyre was filled for two or three years and it transformed Birdsville. There were pilots in town, plus the planes flying in for lunch then going out. I think they were still going down there in the third year, but the lake was starting to recede a lot by then.

I met Paul Lockyer when he was here making his documentary. Nell Brook introduced me. He was a lovely bloke. He was a great friend of the outback and really promoted it. That's what Nell said. Tragically he died in 2011, with pilot Gary Ticehurst and cameraman John Bean, in a chopper crash while making another documentary on Lake Eyre. I've got a copy of the doco he made. The colours and presentation really show the outback for what it is.

By 2009 I'd been living in Birdsville for nearly three years and had become part of the community. Sandra still wasn't with me but our daughter Lauren had been here for the first year-and-a-bit and the town had really looked after her. Sandra used to come out on holidays and so did Robbie.

It was around that time that Geoff Morton said, 'Oh, Sandra won't come and live here.'

She eventually proved him wrong.

When Lauren wasn't here, or Sandra, there was still plenty of social life. When you were here, Evan, we'd play golf and tennis, and that continued after you left in mid-2009. We played tennis on Wednesday, year round, with the Brooks. Then we'd normally go have a drink at the pub, sometimes we'd have a meal. I'd go to the pub on Friday, too, when all the community got together, and normally have a meal there.

I got invited to the caravan park for dinner, to Dusty's, to Don and Lyn's. I had a bit to do with Don. He's been a good friend of mine since I got here. And you and Michelle. So I was never really bored.

I had work as well. I was going up to Mount Isa for training, conferences or whatever.

Sandra came out on a semi-regular basis for a week or two at a time. In school holidays she'd try and come out for most of the time. It was better when she was here but I survived when she wasn't, too.

I was on the social club and ended up getting elected vice-president. I didn't really do much work when there was an event on. I'd be there all day as a police officer, because there would be a bar serving alcohol and it's not good for me to be behind the bar selling alcohol.

I certainly worked on the working bees and if the club needed something picked up in Mount Isa, I'd get it for them. I'd attend all the meetings. At events, I'd be there to stop trouble. Mind you, in Birdsville, if there was a dispute, other people would usually come in and separate them. So it was easy to police in that regard but it was good to have a uniformed police officer there and people knew that.

Then we started having barbeques on the courthouse verandah. We started those not long after you got here. I think you guys were going down to Pelican Point (on the billabong) and I said, 'Nah, I'm not goin' down to Pelican Point. Best place for a barbeque is the courthouse. You've got power, you've got toilets, you've got shade, a fridge, a fire if you want one, and it's handy.'

Next thing, you turned up, said, 'Alright, we're havin' a barbeque here.'

And we kept having barbies here. We had many good barbeques here. We ended up having your send-off here.

I've had hundreds of barbeques at Birdsville and probably only one at the house. The other nine-hundred and ninety-nine were at the courthouse. It's just a magical place. It's got that feeling about it; 1880s building. Built the same year as the hotel. Old courthouse, police station, customs house, a lot of history there and it faces the right way, so you're protected from the westerly wind. You haven't got the afternoon sun beating down on you. Yet you can step around the corner and see the sunset, which is magical. And there's plenty of room to sit under the shade and have a nice cool drink in the cool part of a hot day.

Now when police come out for the races, we always put on a barbeque there. Always. Dusty gave a barbeque to the courthouse, sort of a permanent loan.

He said, 'If I ever get booked, it goes.' I *think* he's only joking.

After the races are over, you sit around a fire. A lot of people don't do that very often these days, with modern society. The council brings in two truckloads of wood. Dusty supplies the barbeque. The gas is supplied. Everyone bunks in there. It's pretty basic but you've got the essentials of life: roof, shower, toilet, cooking facilities. What else do you need?

We also open the courthouse up for other events, mainly for charities or for people coming through on rallies. A lot of folk who come through are a bit soft. They don't like sleeping on a swag on the ground. It's one of those things where people stay, then tell friends and tell friends of friends, and it's as if it's on TripAdvisor: where to stay in Birdsville. We've had thirty or forty people staying here.

When someone is coming, I give the place a sweep. You've helped me clean. The place has lino floors, big rooms, you can fit lots of people in there. You don't tell people about the snakes. Some things are best just left. You warn them about snakes. You just don't tell 'em there're snakes in there.

I think it's good for buildings to be used. They soon deteriorate if they don't get used. So I've let people stay here on a pretty regular basis. It might be four or five times a year. People know it's here. They ring up.

Visiting police from interstate sometimes ring up, too. Asking, 'Can we stay at the courthouse?' I always think, What would happen if I rang up Parramatta Police, or Geelong Police, and said, 'Oh, look, I'm comin' through. Can I roll a swag out at the Parramatta Courthouse?' I don't think I'd get the same treatment or the same response that I give to them. (Laughter) I think I know what the answer would be: 'Nah mate, you find a motel.'

One of the more memorable barbeques was when Tom Kruse, the legendary Birdsville mailman, came to a barbeque on his last trip to Birdsville before he died. Tom became famous after the international success of the 1954 film *Back of Beyond* that showed him battling up the Birdsville Track, when it really was a track, in his Leyland Badger truck, delivering mail and supplies to the stations along the way. It showed him traversing the flooded Cooper Creek and using sheets of corrugated iron to get over the sand hills. The family of his offsider, William Butler, still live in Birdsville, and the film also shows David Brook when he was a very small child.

Now it was June 2009 and we'd organised a barbeque for your send-off. I knew Tom was in town. I'd invited Nell to your do and she said, 'We've got Tom Kruse coming. We're having a meal at the pub.'

I said, 'Nah, come down to the courthouse. Come down to Evan's barbecue. Tom'd probably love to come down instead of sittin' at the hotel.'

We've all sat at the pub plenty of times. You eat a steak and chips, or schnitzel and chips, and a salad or something.

He came down, and he was a frail old man, very tall, but he was still as bright as a button. It was like having a celebrity. Well, he was a celebrity. And he told me later that he hadn't sat around a fire for twenty years. He was in his nineties then. Still bright. He told a few stories. And it was a really good night. He was there with his wife. I think both of them have passed away now.

I think his daughter was there. Nell and David were there, too. He signed that book of yours, *Land of Mirage,* that had his picture in it. That was a good night and I think he enjoyed it, too. It was fitting that his last time around a campfire was in Birdsville, on the Birdsville Track.

CHAPTER 5

THE MIDDLE OF AFGHANISTAN

On 23 May 2009 I received information that a 63-year-old American tourist had crashed his motorbike on a sand hill at Poeppels Corner. He had serious head injuries. In a situation like that, the ambulance wasn't an option. Throwing a patient in his condition around on rough roads for a couple of hundred kilometres (or more if you go the longer and smoother way around), isn't recommended.

As luck would have it, a helicopter happened to be landing on the airport apron out the front of the Birdsville Hotel at the same time I got the call for help. The owner of the chopper was staying at the hotel so I asked the publican, Brian Hanna, to approach him about helping with an emergency rescue.

He'd only been in town a couple of minutes but he said 'no worries' straightaway.

I travelled out to the crash scene along with the nurse to rescue the rider. He was treated at the scene before being brought back to Birdsville for transfer to Brisbane with the Flying Doctor.

It was another of those situations where you have to be

resourceful and adaptable, and be able to rely on the community, or members of the public. There's usually no argument, even when it comes to requesting use of a multi-million-dollar aircraft. In this case, though, not only was the owner of the helicopter happy to make it available, he refused to take any payment to cover costs. I think it worked out being $2340 for fuel alone.

On 10 June 2009, there was another, very similar, emergency. Another motorbike rider had gone over the handlebars on a sand dune in the desert 30 kilometres west of Poeppels Corner.

I got an EPIRB activation from Canberra. The support crew for the bike rider also had a satphone and had contacted the Flying Doctor. They described his condition. He couldn't move. He had neck and back injuries, spinal injuries. He had limited movement in his fingers but he couldn't feel his toes.

As with the rescue three weeks earlier, we didn't want to put him in an ambulance and bounce him over several hundred sand hills. You could make his injuries worse, or permanent, or even kill him. Also, it was going to take a long time to get there.

I said, 'We need to find a helicopter.'

You don't need a mustering helicopter, which we have in spades around Birdsville. You need a helicopter that can take the nurse, a stretcher for the patient and a police officer, so you can do an investigation. And you need to find it fast. Not just that day but well before nightfall. When we got the call, I think it was lunchtime. You quickly lose the light at that time of year and the helicopter can't land in the dark because they don't know what's below, even though it's the desert out there. The helicopter had to be able to get to Birdsville, load up with medical supplies and the nurse, and then get out to the accident before it got dark.

I rang Inspector Trevor Kidd to notify him about what was going on and he said, 'Look, there's no police helicopter in Mount Isa. It's up at the Gulf of Carpentaria doing something.'

Mornington Island, in the Gulf, is the northernmost part of the Mount Isa police district. It's over 1200 kilometres from Birdsville. Even if the police helicopter had been available in Mount Isa, it still would have been difficult because they'd have to fly 700 kilometres to get down here.

We keep looking, starting local and then going out, getting wider and wider until eventually, it's pointless. If you find one in Alice Springs or something, it's just too far. There's also a matter of cost, too. At that point, you don't give up but we weren't coming up with much. Blank. Blank. Blank.

So I'm on the phone to the inspector, saying, 'Gee, I don't know where we're going to find a helicopter. I've tried this, this and this.'

Then, as I'm talking to him, I started finding it hard to hear him. There's this incredibly loud noise outside. Just BOOM-BOOM-BOOM-BOOM! Big motor noise. Really loud, then EXTREMELY LOUD. And I looked out the window, thinking, WHAT IS THAT? And over at the airport, an army Chinook helicopter is landing.

I go, 'INSPECTOR, I THINK OUR PROBLEMS ARE SOLVED! WE FOUND A HELICOPTER! AN ARMY CHINOOK'S JUST LANDED!'

And he says, 'Wow, that'll do.'

So I said, 'I'LL GO OVER AND SEE THEM AND RING YOU BACK!'

So I went over and saw them, introduced myself to Captain Pat

Schadel, from Townsville's Fifth Aviation Regiment, C Squadron, and said, 'Look, this is the situation. We need a helicopter that can take someone who's got spinal injuries on a stretcher, plus a nurse and a police officer.'

He said, 'Yeah, we'd be happy to do it.'

Helicopters don't come much bigger than an army Chinook. They're one of the biggest helicopters in the world, currently worth about $80 million. It turned out to be a good job for them. They were on a training exercise and had landed to refuel. They were really keen to help.

Obviously, the request had to go through channels. You can't just say, 'Come on boys. Let's go.' It has to go through police command; it has to go through army command; and that took probably forty minutes. It was remarkably quick, when you think about it. I rang the inspector, and the inspector had to get onto the assistant commissioner. You can't just jump onto a military helicopter as a civilian, even though you're a police officer, and go somewhere. There's an approval process and it's got to be done and done properly. Otherwise, if you go out, get him and come back, you're in a world of hurt.

In the army, I don't know the rank they had to go to for permission but it was pretty high, because they were deviating from their training. And they were planning to take me, a nurse and an injured person onboard. We also thought we might need a couple of extra civilians because we wouldn't be able to carry the injured fella ourselves. As soon as everyone in town saw a Chinook was going to do the rescue, they were sure they had to go, too. A long queue formed. Plenty of volunteers.

Bev came down and she had all the medical gear, the spinal stretcher (the one they wrap around you and pump up so you can't move a millimetre), all the medical equipment. We were there waiting, talking and going through what we would need to do on the helicopter: wearing the helmet, the pre-flight safety stuff, all that.

While we were talking, a doctor who was there on holidays put two and two together that we were doing a rescue, and came over and offered us her assistance. The closest doctor to Birdsville is 700 kilometres away, so she was a really important person to have onboard.

We included her in the briefing prior to going out and as a name to go on the helicopter.

When approval was given, the Chinook crew were happy. There were five in the aircrew, enough to help with the stretcher, so it ended up being only me, Bev and the doctor who went.

It was midafternoon when the rescue mission got underway. The chopper had been fuelled and off we went, into the desert. We flew at a couple of thousand feet.

It was really noisy inside. Like, deafening noise. Even with earplugs and earphones and a helmet on. Everyone was shouting. There were little windows in the sides of the chopper but they also had the back door down, a big cargo door. You could look out and see the ground below and the airman was just standing on the back of it, just hanging onto a handle. He had a safety harness on, though.

It was quite an adventure. I mean, how often do you get to go on an army Chinook? And you think you're in the middle of Afghanistan, looking out at the desert there. I was lookin' around and the rotors are going and it's windy, it's noisy, but it was good. It probably took us thirty or forty minutes to fly the 200 kilometres out to the accident.

It was a lot easier than driving. It probably saved us nine hours getting out there. And by the time you get ready and get the ambulance out there, the whole rescue would have been two days: a day there, dark when we got there, then we'd have to take a break, because you just get too tired. Then it would have been a long, long, long trip back.

We arrived at the scene and the pilots did a lap around the site. You could see probably ten or fifteen bikes there and four or five support vehicles. There were quite a few. And you could see all these big wide eyes looking up at you. (Laughter) They knew a helicopter was coming, because Search and Rescue had told them.

You can imagine what they thought when they saw this great big helicopter, a big army Chinook, doing a lap of them. We could have brought the whole crew in it – the riders, the support team – we could have brought them all back. Not all the cars, but all the bikes as well.

We landed on a low sand dune about 500 metres from the accident because the dust and the noise were just incredible. You're talking two big propellers flicking up sand. People were coming down on bikes to meet us. Then we walked up, the whole crew, except the pilot and airman who stayed on the chopper, as the rotors were still running.

They'd done a good job on the fella. They'd made a neck brace out of tyre tubes, to keep his neck still. They had him lying on his back. He was surprised to see us, to say the least. He couldn't believe his eyes.

I said to him, 'Wait until you get the fuel bill.'

The guy could talk, but I didn't take details at that stage. I let the medical people do their bit. I could always find out his name and do accident details later. He did say he came over a sand hill, hit a bump and went over and hit his head. Face planted. Then hurt his neck.

He was in quite a bit of pain but the doctor gave him some pain relief. The medical crew, the doctor and Bev, were looking after him for half an hour before we moved him. I took a couple of photos of his bike and the medical crew treating him.

It was funny, too, because all the people had cameras on. They were taking photos of the Chinook, they couldn't believe it.

The patient was loaded on the stretcher. Then we had to carry him back. All the air crew took turns carrying him. We were walking through sand and it was a fair hike. As we carried him, the aircrew covered his face to stop him being smothered with sand and crap. When we were getting close to the helicopter, dust was going absolutely everywhere. When we got to the back of the helicopter, the heat from the exhaust of the chopper just idling was really hot. And it was incredibly noisy.

The American pilot just said, 'Boys, you've just got to suck it in. Just carry him onto the back of the chopper.'

They put him on the ground, covered him with a silver foil blanket, and six people carried him on. Then all the extras got off and we took off back to Birdsville.

He was pretty comfortable in the Chinook. We could talk to him and he was able to respond, he just had trouble moving his legs and his hands. The doctor had him in a spinal stretcher so he couldn't move anyway. There was a lot of vibration, and it was very noisy. Extremely noisy. If you didn't have earplugs, earphones and a helmet, you'd go deaf. So despite his spinal injury he was also given hearing protection, to avoid adding to his injuries. The doctor supervised that. Every so often, the crewman who was hanging out the back would put his thumb up and nod, checking that everything was alright.

When we got back to Birdsville it was still daylight. We were out and back in a bit over two hours. It was the best way to get him back.

When we landed at Birdsville, the Flying Doctor was already there. The plane had started from Charleville when the rescue got underway. It's only two hours flying from there. He was transported from the Chinook straight onto the Flying Doctor, then taken to Brisbane.

By that time it was too late for the army guys to continue their training exercise. So they spent the night in the police barracks. The whole crew. I had a beer with them in the pub. They were interesting blokes. The pilot had only just returned to work after an accident. He'd been flying a Blackhawk and crashed, breaking his back and his legs. The American airman had seen duty in Afghanistan and Iraq. He was interesting to talk to.

The motorbike rider was very lucky that the Chinook landed when it did. I've asked the locals, and there hadn't been one land at Birdsville before and there hasn't been one since. Except on that one day that it was really needed. We felt incredibly lucky.

And the outcome? I think he had a jarred spine. He spent about three days in hospital and was then released. He made a full recovery.

He was on *Sunrise* about five days later. Sitting there, back home. I was on it, too. There was a lot of media attention. The army wanted it out as a good-news story, which it was. This was around the same time former Labor leader Mark Latham called Australian military personnel meatheads.

It was a good story for Search and Rescue, too. And the police, because we were able to respond to it. For the nurse and the doctor, it all worked well. So the superintendent was keen to let the media know about it. It was on *Sunrise*, in the *Herald Sun*, the *Army News*, on the front page of the *Townsville Bulletin*, then the *Courier-Mail* and all the rest picked it up. Seven News did a story on it. It's something that just doesn't happen every day. A motorbike rider gets injured and an army Chinook turns up at a little speck on the map in outback Queensland.

Not long after, there's a knock at the door and I go to open it. Dick Smith. He wanted to know all about it. So I showed him all the photos and told him the tale of the rescue.

One evening at the end of June 2009, there was a 000 emergency call made from a phone box in Adelaide Street, the main street of Birdsville. The caller said shots had been fired. Someone had been shot.

You think, Oh, that's pretty serious.

Having been one of the first responders at Hoddle Street, I'd been through that kind of drama for real. This time, experience told me it wasn't like that. I live probably 150 metres from the location of these reported shots but I hadn't heard anything. There'd been no firearms go off. When a shot is fired, you hear it. Especially if there's multiple shots. I've heard shots being fired. I know what they are.

I looked up the main street. It was dead quiet. There were a couple of people outside the pub, talking. There were no bodies lying around. There's no-one on the street, no people ducking for cover or cars taking off really quickly. It would be a different story if there were. The phone would be ringing hot. So I knew this was a hoax. The caller had said there were multiple shots fired or people had been shot or something.

I didn't even put a gun on. I wasn't required to carry a fire-arm at that time, but you are now, ever since the latest terrorist attacks. I just went up there. It was quiet. I talked to a few people. They said there were a couple of kids hanging around. One was a ten-year-old, so I went and saw him. He admitted to making the phone call. I took him home to his mum.

His mum said, 'You're always pickin' on 'im.'

I said, 'I'm not. I've hardly spoken to him. I've brought him home because he's making calls that people have been shot. It's a serious offence. You need to talk to him.'

I didn't want to charge him with anything or even give him a caution. She just needed to talk to him. It's a stupid thing to do. People can get hurt, responding to that, or people can jump to the wrong conclusions and something bad could happen; to him or to someone else.

He was sorry he'd done it but I was hoping his mother would be more grateful to me and be dirty on him for doing the wrong thing, a stupid prank like that. He was only ten but still, it was a pretty stupid thing to do. Instead, she stuck up for him.

The young fella was scared. He thought he was going to get into trouble. I told him what a stupid thing it was. I could have come up there armed to the teeth, with my firearm drawn, not knowing what was going on. In today's climate, imagine if some-one did that now. What would happen? Police would start closing down roads and suburbs.

The young fella was reasonably contrite. His mum wasn't.

There's an old oil rig out on Durrie Station that has been there for years but in 2009 a dispute arose over the ownership. I think what happened was, this guy had got money off some rich dentists in California to drill for oil but he bought this shitty old oil rig that couldn't do anything and took it out to Durrie. I think he got a permit to drill there. Then he went broke or he disappeared and the dentists tried to sell the oil rig to someone, or someone else bought it. It got really convoluted. It was a game of passing the hot potato, the hot, mouldy potato.

Eventually this Australian guy who'd been living in America turned up in July 2009. He had some claim to it. So I took him out, and he took some photos, and he identified it. I took a lengthy statement from him because he had to go back to America the next day. Then I just attached it to the file. Some detective in Mackay had carriage of it and that was about the end of it. It was written off as a civil complaint. Someone had just scammed some rich dentists – $250 000 each. About six of them. And people were still throwing good money after bad trying to get their money back. It was never going to happen. Meanwhile, there's this oil rig on Durrie that's never turned a sod of dirt and was about ninety years old. Not that old, but it's old. It's still there today, rusting away, a monument to a con that extended from California to outback Australia.

In mid-August, a convoy of vehicles was travelling west along the Birdsville–Windorah Road near Betoota when a vehicle travelling east drove onto the wrong side of the road, forcing first one vehicle, then a second and finally a third off the road. After passing the third vehicle, the offending vehicle did a U-turn and pursued the west-bound vehicles, cut in front of one of them and forced it to stop.

The offending vehicle was a four-wheel drive utility with two males in their twenties. Their ute was set up for pig catching and there were a couple of pig dogs in cages on the back. There was dried blood all down the side of the ute (hopefully from pigs). The driver got out and approached the vehicle he'd forced off the road and verbally abused its driver, telling him he had to pay $360 for flicking up a rock and breaking his windscreen. He then dragged the victim from the car, threatening him and demanding money.

Fortunately for the victim he was travelling in convoy with several vehicles, all separated by distance so they weren't sucking on each other's dust. Three of the cars coming up the rear caught up to the victim and the weight of numbers meant the offender had to back off and decamp. The victim looked at the offender's windscreen as he drove off and saw numerous cracks and star-shaped chips on it; it was obviously quite old.

This matter was reported to Bedourie Police and OIC Darren Mills conducted an investigation. I assisted and interviewed some witnesses.

The offender was located and charged with demanding money with menaces, assault and dangerous driving. He later pleaded guilty after a plea bargain, which saved the victim and witnesses having to travel to outback Queensland to give evidence. Who knows what would have happened to the victim if he was by himself?

Later, at the races, the offender was charged with drink-driving and also got towelled up in Brophy's Boxing Tent. Not a good races for the offender. Karma I think is the word. Justice was not only done but there was a bit of natural justice thrown in for good measure.

———

The races in 2009 ran smoothly, except for one stupid drunk. I got called to the pub because someone was abusive and wouldn't leave when asked. I got there and there was a bloke so intoxicated he'd pissed himself. I suggested to him that he go home and have a camp. His response, 'Get fucked'. (Laughter) He was the last person I locked up at the Birdsville Races. Wrong answer.

He spent eighteen hours in custody because he refused to give his name. Then he got bailed with the condition that he was not to return to licensed premises. So that cut out the pub and the race track, and on Sunday he got fined $500 for drunkeness and not leaving licenced premises when asked. So hopefully he learned a lesson out of that: next time he goes to the races, he behaves himself. And he doesn't tell me to get fucked. (Laughter) Maybe go home and have a camp.

After the races there was an accident involving one of the vendors who came out each year to sell collectable hat badges.

Roger was a larger-than-life guy aged eighty. He'd been a sailor, as was his brother. His brother died in the Voyager accident in the 1960s. Whenever he came out for the races to sell his badges, I would ask him, 'How's it going?'

He'd always say, 'Who gives a shit? I'll be dead soon anyway.'

Roger was driving home after the races, heading east along the Windorah Road. He'd got about 100 kilometres from town when he rolled his van about three times. He was injured, mainly head injuries.

Nadine and Darren Lorenz from Durrie Station attended the scene, along with their staff and some of the Mount Leonard staff. The ambulance and I arrived about an hour later. The way Nadine tended to Roger I was sure she was a nurse in a previous life. She wasn't a qualified nurse, but she had heaps of experience as a remote station manager's wife, providing first aid to ringers, stockmen, staff, her husband, her kids, as well as any motorists that rolled over on the dirt roads near her property. She always assisted.

Roger was worried about his badges so we all walked along the road – police, travellers, station hands, ringers – picking up heaps of Roger's badges that were scattered all over the ground.

Roger had old security doors that he used as tables. They'd been on the roof of his van. He said, 'Make sure you get my tables.'

I said, 'Yeah Roger. I will.'

They were all wrecked. I told Chook Kath from Mount Leonard to take them to his tip. Out of Roger's ear shot, of course.

Roger was conveyed by ambulance back to the Birdsville Clinic, where he waited for the Flying Doctor to arrive. He kept saying, 'I need to know if my vehicle is insured.'

I said, 'We'll sort it out later. You have some bad injuries the nurse needs to attend to.'

Roger was getting very agitated about his vehicle so I rang up his insurance company. I was on hold for twenty minutes, repeatedly being told my call was important. Finally, I got onto a pleasant young woman and explained the situation to her: Roger rolled his vehicle, the vehicle was wrecked, Roger was at the clinic about to be evacuated by the Flying Doctor to Toowoomba, he needs to know if his wrecked vehicle is insured.

I gave the phone to Roger. Roger immediately says, 'ARE YOU A PERSON OR A MACHINE? 'CAUSE I'M NOT TALKING TO A MACHINE!'

The young woman must have said she was a person. Roger said, 'ARE YOU SURE? 'CAUSE I'M NOT TALKING TO A MACHINE.'

She told him his wrecked vehicle was fully insured and he was happy.

I had a lot of time for Roger. I really liked him and enjoyed his company. He hasn't been out for the last two races. I heard someone stole all his badges from his car in Ipswich a while ago. I hope he's going well. He's a tough old fella.

Not long after, there was another rollover that didn't go so well. It involved a car and caravan that both rolled in very wet conditions on the dirt road between Birdsville and Bedourie. The car, caravan and contents were wrecked but the old couple in the vehicle weren't injured.

I conveyed both of them back to Birdsville, to the police station, to make some phone calls. I gave them a cup of coffee while this old fella rang his insurance company. He spoke to a young woman who advised him they would get the princely sum of $150 for meals, accommodation, airfares, incidentals and so on. That's $150 all up, not per day. Old mate started abusing the person on the phone.

During a break in the conversation, I said, 'Mate, you can't get up her. It's not her fault; it's what you signed up for.'

If you're coming to Birdsville, you need to know what benefits you'll get from your motoring association and insurer if you have a breakdown, accident or other emergency thousands of kilometres from home and find yourself without transport and accommodation. You need at least a week's accommodation, airfares, meals, vehicle hire and incidentals. If you're stranded on a Friday, the next plane to Brisbane is the following Tuesday. Spare parts can take up to ten days to arrive. Accommodation, if it's available, is expensive. The hotel is $175 a room. Buying cheap insurance could end up costing you heaps more if you get stuck in a remote area. And after almost ten years at Birdsville, I can tell you that getting stuck happens to dozens of people every year.

Basic motoring association or insurance cover also only pays for about 50 kilometres of towing, or nothing in remote areas. It's 520 kilometres from Birdsville to Marree, 400 kilometres to Windorah. It costs approximately five grand to do a vehicle recovery from Poeppels Corner to Birdsville. That's before accommodation, meals, airfares and everything else. Things can go from bad to worse really quickly. It can happen in a blink of an eye.

One couple with young children were stuck in Birdsville for over a week waiting for a radiator. The lady said, 'Barnesy should have a spare radiator for every type of vehicle at his garage.'

Barnesy said, 'I'd need a shed bigger than Birdsville to store them.'

Sunday, 22 September 2009 should have been my day off. Instead I got a call from one of the support vehicles for two women walking across the Simpson Desert and the Munga-Thirri National Park. They contacted me on a satphone saying they'd lost the track near Annandale Station, an abandoned homestead on Adria Downs Station, overlooking Eyre Creek.

I rang Don the ranger for advice, then relayed his information about which way they should go back to them. They were on the western side of Eyre Creek. The two women who were walking were raising money for the Heart Foundation. And they were lost. Don said they needed to go back to a particular point but they didn't understand. I don't think they were near the track Don was talking about, but it was the only way they could cross Eyre Creek. They needed to use the flood crossing that's used when the normal crossing, 45 kilometres south, is impassable.

We had a few conversations back and forth and they didn't appear to recognise any of the landmarks Don was pointing out to them. We later discovered that the position they were giving Don wasn't actually where they were. And where they thought they were wasn't where they were either.

Don and I decided it was better to go out, get to roughly where we thought they were and find them, rather than let them get completely and utterly bushed and then have a major search on our hands.

Don came with me in the police vehicle. It was Sunday afternoon by then. I think we left around lunchtime. Out we went. I drove. Never got bogged once. There was water everywhere.

Don, with all his bush skills, was giving me directions: 'Go over this sand hill. Go right. Go left. Go right.'

I thought, Why don't we just drive in a straight line?

Then we got a call from the people on their UHF radio, so we knew they were within 20 kilometres of us. We could hear them. Eventually, we went over a sand hill and there they were. Don found them.

They were going the wrong way. They were heading south. The crossing was north, back the other way, then east. It's the only point they could have got across.

We pulled up and one of the women who was meant to be walking was in a vehicle by that stage. She got out and gave me a big hug and said, 'Oh, you're a sight for sore eyes. Thanks for comin' out.'

We talked to them and Don said, 'Nah, you're goin' the wrong way. You've gotta come back and cross at the crossing. Then you keep heading east, then you get onto the track out to Adria Downs homestead, which you can't miss, and go to Birdsville.'

They said, 'Oh, thanks for that.'

I went to drive off, still talking to them and I got bogged. Just the back wheels. Dug in. I didn't want to keep going because you just dig in further.

I said, 'Mate, can you give us a snatch off?'

He says, 'Yeah, no worries.'

So he snatches us off, all proud about doing that. It took about two minutes. He pulled us back a metre. Then off I went again.

So they followed us for a while until they got onto the track. Don showed them where it was. Across the plain. You can see it. Well-defined. They couldn't get lost. We told them that if they did, they could give us a ring again.

We headed back to Birdsville and I didn't think much more about it. We'd gone out there and put them on the right track. That's the right thing to do because we didn't want them to get completely bushed. Then, if the radio or satphone goes flat, or they start making poor decisions about what to do, or they split up and one goes one way and one goes the other way, or whatever . . .

We didn't get back until 7 o'clock at night. So that was Sunday, our day off. And Don and I don't get paid overtime. If you work, you work. That's part of your duties. If you work three days without a break, too bad, so sad. If you get called out on Friday night and spend thirty or forty hours rescuing someone from the desert, you don't get a day in lieu on Monday. You're expected to be at your desk. Obviously, if you're tired, you can have an easy day but you've still got to do the weather and you've got to be there if the inspector rings up. You've still got a police station to run: licences, registrations, people making enquiries about roads.

You've just got to suck it in. You know that when you sign up for the job. There're times, too, when you might go a couple of weeks where nothing happens. Then you just clean the station, sweep out the dust, whipper-snip and take out the rubbish. But when you work, you work. That's just what you do.

Anyway, Don and I were happy that we went. Then it was just a watching brief until they got to town. You don't just say, 'We went out and found 'em. Put 'em on the right track.' Then it's a month and, 'Oh, haven't they turned up yet?'

So I put it on the whiteboard and it was only after they turned up that I closed the job off. You've got to be really strict on that. What happens if they get lost again, or whatever?

Two days later, they made it to Birdsville. I knew that because I said, 'Make sure you let me know.'

These two old dears walked from Annandale to Big Red and it took them two days. I thought, Gee, that's a quick walk when you're in your sixties or your fifties. About 70 kilometres.

Then, a few months later, this bloke wrote a lengthy letter detailing his trip in *Network News,* the newsletter for High Frequency radio users, which includes a lot of outback drivers. I found the letter really offensive because when it got to Don and I, it was like: they didn't need rescuing; we had nothing else to do so we came out for a pleasant little drive in the bush; he called Don 'the Aboriginal ranger', like he was Jackie Jackie, the tracker; and he wrote that I'd got hopelessly bogged.

They were really flippant about it, as though we only did it for an enjoyable drive in the bush. We're always out in the bush and you don't enjoy the drive when you're going to a job. You're not driving along looking around, stopping, having a cup of tea and, 'Oh isn't that nice over there, we'll go over and have a look at that.' You're driving to get there as quickly as possible, so you don't lose the light or have them get more bushed.

Time is really important. Get there. Nip it in the bud. Get it done, while you've still got daylight. And what happens if something happens in Birdsville while you're in the desert? Something could happen that you've got to get back to in a hurry. So the last thing you're doing when you're out there is enjoying a drive in the desert.

I was really offended, so I wrote a reply. It's the first time I've written a reply to a letter:

> There are a few issues I would like to bring to yours and the readers' attention in the letter by [name withheld].
>
> Did [name withheld] need to describe the Queensland National Parks and Wildlife Ranger as the Aboriginal ranger. Both Don and I find this demeaning and condescending. Would [name withheld] have referred to a ranger of Italian descent as the Italian ranger? I think not.
>
> As for it being a pleasant break for the policeman and ranger to get out in the bush this is so far from the truth it is not funny. That is how we earn a living. We are always out in the desert or down the track rescuing persons disorientated (read lost), broken down, injured or needing assistance of some type.
>
> Both Don and I don't mind going out into the desert and assisting persons. We don't expect any thanks for doing so,

as it's part of our duties, but both of us took offence to the
tone and flippant nature of the letter describing us and the
duties we performed when all we were doing was helping this
fella and his party.

So after my letter, he wrote another letter, bagging me. He said *they* found *us*. And he's talking about Don, who knows the desert better than any person living on planet earth. GPS on two legs. I didn't know where they were, but he did. He tracked 'em down, using all the skills and 40 000 years of DNA in him. And if he says they're going the wrong way, they *are* going the wrong way.

After that I just gave up. I wasn't going to reply because then you get into keyboard warrior territory. So I said, 'Oh well.' I was happy because I'd said my piece. Then people came in and said, 'So glad you replied. We thought he was an idiot, too.' People actually wrote to me. One person came up to me and they were almost crying, saying, 'I'm so glad you wrote that reply and I was so annoyed about what they said about Don.'

It was good to get that positive feedback. Some time later, a *Network News* reader, Barry Slattery, wrote to me and had the final say:

When his group got to the area of camp 20 and started their
'shooting from the hip' navigation, I could very easily see
why you and the ranger opted to head out there straight
away, rather than wait until you're having to search for three
vehicles and two women on foot, all separated from one
another.

The only thing I will mention about [name withheld's]
quip about you getting momentarily stuck, is that he was

*always quick to point out shortcomings of others but failed
to recognise his own fallibilities.*

*I will very soon be travelling in your region and rest
assured I won't be making any presumptions about you
having nothing better to do than come looking for me
(although I have no doubt at your preparedness should a
genuine emergency arise).*

Only a few days after that rescue, on 24 September 2009, I woke
up to a howling dust storm. It was so bad you could hardly see to
the police station from the house. It was massive. It went through
Sydney and much of the east coast of Australia. I thought, Crikey,
I'm just gonna have a quiet day in the office today. You'd be
stupid to drive around or do anything.

No sooner had I thought that than the phone rang. So I pick
it up. And the person on the other end said, 'Search and Rescue
Canberra here.'

My heart just sank.

They don't just ring up for a chat, you know. They're not
gonna say, 'Oh, how you goin'?' What are you doin' today? Got
much on?'

They ring up to give you a job.

They said, 'We've got an EPIRB activation, 15 kilometres west
of Poeppels Corner.'

That's right in the middle of the Simpson Desert.

So I began planning for a trip into the desert. The trouble
with an EPIRB is you don't know what's happened: they might be
injured, or their car has rolled over and they're trapped inside, or
they're bogged. They've got a flat tyre. Or, you know, they've run
out of chardonnay. You don't know, but you've got to prepare for

the worst: that someone's injured or they need urgent assistance. People don't just set 'em off for no reason.

So the plan was for Don to go up with a Birdsville-based pilot, Lou, to fly over and try and glean what was happening on the ground. Barnesy had gone out and I was to drive out, too. So Don and Lou waited a while, hoping for the weather to improve, which it didn't. Meanwhile, I went looking for someone to come with me.

Don said, 'There's this new fella in town, Hugh Brown, go around to his place.'

So I went around and he wasn't there. I said, 'Don, I can't find 'im. I'll just get goin'.'

He said, 'No, I think he's at the information centre.'

At this stage, I didn't know Hugh was a photographer. Don had just said, 'He'd be handy to have around, handy on the end of a shovel.' (Laughter, because when I went on rescues with Neale, I spent most of the time digging.)

So I went to the information centre and found him, introduced myself and said, 'I need someone to come out to the desert. Do you want to come for a run?'

He said, 'Yeah, I'd love to but can I go home and get my camera gear?'

I said, 'Sure, grab some tucker, too.'

If I'm going out into a tricky situation, it's always better to have someone with me. If anything goes wrong, hopefully it won't go wrong for both of us. It's safety in numbers. You've got help changing tyres. You've got help if the vehicle falls on you while you're changing a tyre, help if you get bogged.

We left and you could hardly see. Not long after, the plane took off, even though the conditions were no better.

We went over Little Red and I couldn't see the track and I

hit this big rock and I thought, Oh no. We drove along about 50 metres and boom-boom-boom-boom-boom. We've got a flat tyre. Flat tyre number one. So we're under the car changing it and it's like a blast furnace, with the heat and all the sand. Painful, terrible, and as we're changing the tyre we hear the plane fly back over. Heading back to Birdsville. The visibility was just too bad.

My heart sank again.

We weren't going to know what was happening on the ground. Lou said the conditions were atrocious, so in a way I was glad she turned back. We didn't want a downed aircraft to add to our problems. We changed the tyre and headed off again. We were going over sand hills where you couldn't see over the other side. A couple of times we lost the track and we had to go back and find it.

When we were on the French Line, we lost the track again. I got out of the vehicle, and I'm looking for it, and it was just sand flying everywhere. The French Line is a defined track, and normally you can easily see it, but that day you couldn't. While I was looking, Hugh managed to take photos, one of which ended up on the front page of newspapers around the world. You could really see how bad the conditions were. Luckily, I found the track and we got going.

We got another flat tyre just before we got to Poeppels, going over a rock again. So then we were on wood, down to no spares.

We got to the scene late in the afternoon. Five o'clock. Still very dusty. There we found John White, the driver. He was fairly old, sixty-five. He'd rolled down this big sand-hole. The vehicle had landed on its side. He said that, at one stage, when he set off the EPIRB, he had trouble seeing the ute. He'd walked a short distance away from the ute and even though it was a matter of

10 or 15 metres, he had trouble seeing it. So when he got back to it he just climbed into the back and huddled up in there. The vehicle had a canopy for storage. He got in there to get out of the dust.

He was lucky. If he'd wandered off, we'd never have found him. He'd have become bleached bones in the middle of the desert. He did the right thing by staying with the vehicle. His only injury was from a blow to the head.

Barnesy was already there and other tourists had also turned up and were waiting there, because of the weather conditions. There's a photo of me talking to Mount Isa on Barnesy's satphone because mine was broken, the aerial on the vehicle had bent because of the wind. I told them we'd found our guy and cancelled the EPIRB.

We had to leave the rolled ute there, because it was on its side. John White went with Barnsey and we followed them back to Birdsville. Barnesy's car has the same type of tyres as the police vehice, so we knew we could always swap them if we got another flat. That's why we followed him back. We didn't get a flat on the way back, but the dust storm had eased a bit at night.

We probably got back about eleven o'clock and got John checked out by the nurse. John stayed at the barracks until Barnesy went out a couple of days later and got the car.

There was a lot of media attention on that rescue, too. It was the same storm that blanketed Sydney, with that famous picture of the Harbour Bridge shrouded in dust. That was all dust from the Simpson Desert. The BBC contacted us, as did a lot of newspapers. John and I were interviewed by Neil Mitchell on 3AW in Melbourne. John told *The Australian* newspaper how his canopy didn't stop the sand getting in so he'd folded his beard up to make a dust mask and pulled his Akubra down over his eyes.

While he was wondering if he was going to come through his

ordeal, he'd thought about his late wife. He told her she'd looked after him for forty years and asked her to look after him for one more day.

John stayed in the police barracks for about a week until his car was fixed, then he headed off. He still comes back to Birdsville today. We've become really good friends, actually. He was very grateful that we came and got him. He was so happy. He's been travelling around by himself since his wife had died and now Birdsville is like a second home to him. He knows Don, Barnesy and me. In some ways the accident was a good thing because he made a lot of friends. He was probably pretty lonely before. Everyone knows him in town now so he comes back and is treated like a local.

He actually came on a rescue with us. A guy was hurt down the Warburton Track and his mates left him high and dry. We got John to drive the ambulance. Another time, a bike rider came off and had a badly broken leg. Down at the clinic the nurse didn't have anything to cut the boot off with and we couldn't pull it off because he would have really suffered. John's one of these guys who's very handy. He came in with tin snips and cut the rider's boot off.

When John comes out, he stays a week or two. He helps out around the place, doing odd jobs, things like that. He was also crew on the sailing of the HMAS *Birdsville*. That was a tin boat we made up with HMAS *Birdsville* painted on the side, when we had yet another big flood that left a huge lake in front of Big Red. Normally, it's just dust and sand. Instead, you could go boating in the desert, which we did. We put a container with a chimney on it and lit a fire, just leaves and stuff, so smoke was coming out, and I was playing a guitar, an eel-ectric guitar, and we were floating in floodwater at the foot of Big Red. That's a photo by Hugh Brown, too. And John's in the background. That was about a year after his accident. You can see it was all flooded. No dust then.

That's not the first time that's happened. After a mishap, if people are waiting to fly out or get their vehicle fixed, they end up becoming attached to the place. I remember there was one couple with their kids who had travelled around Australia, got here and damaged their radiator and it took about ten days to fix. They stayed at the barracks as well. With a taipan.

The fella said to me later, 'I drove all around Australia, saw all the sights like Uluru and Monkey Mia and the Kimberleys and all that stuff. And all the kids talked about was their time in Birdsville: how much they loved staying at the police station, going to the school, going to community barbeques, having coffee at the cop shop in the mornings, smoko, kicking the footy with the local kids on the oval.'

He said, 'We wasted our money. We should have just come to Birdsville, put a rock through the radiator, and stayed for a couple of weeks.'

His kids loved it and they all got to know the real Birdsville, instead of coming in, staying at the caravan park, going to the pub, and leaving the next day. They embraced Birdsville, learned what made it tick, got to know the locals and had a great time.

As for the taipan, the world's most venomous snake, someone spotted it in the breezeway of the police station early in the day, which was a worry because there was this family and kids about. Then when we were having morning smoko, it tried to come in through the front door. It poked its head through the gap under the screen door. Immediately, about six people tried to go out the back door, all at the same time. Fortunately, all the commotion scared the taipan away. Then you and I spent the next hour mowing the grass all around the station down to about a millimetre, so the taipan wouldn't have anywhere to hide and would relocate.

A week after the rescue with John, there was a distress call involving a family in the desert 300 kilometres west of Birdsville. They'd abandoned their camper trailer and only had two litres of water left when two of their three children became really sick. They could still drive the vehicle.

Eventually we worked out that the children were actually carsick, which is understandable with the constant bouncing, slowing and accelerating, twisting and turning as you negotiate sandhill after sandhill. We got them to get water from passing travellers. Then we monitored them all the way into Birdsville while Barnesy went out and got the trailer.

A lot of people say trailers should be banned in the desert but I reckon if you want to take a trailer, it's up to you. I reckon there's a lot of laws; it's just another one. A lot of people like to go across the desert and take their trailer so they can keep going to Alice Springs, instead of doubling back to get it, then going the 1200 kilometres or more the long way round. And a lot of trailers are built for four-wheel driving.

You've just got to understand that you can have all sorts of problems with the trailer breaking down. Then you've got to pay to get it out. I wouldn't take one over myself. It puts too much strain on the vehicle and you've got an extra two wheels or four wheels, you've got an extra axle, an extra frame. A lot more can go wrong. A lot of people regret it.

In the desert you don't really want to be burdened with a

trailer because if it starts raining, you want to hightail it out of there anyway. You don't want to hang around if it's raining. You want to get out. Also, if you can't get over a sandhill, and you reverse it down and jack-knife, you can't go forward to straighten it up.

You can also get hooked over the top of the dune. If you're just in a car or a ute on its own, you can usually get off by rocking backwards or forwards, but if the trailer is hanging on one side and the vehicle is on the other, the only way out is to dig.

A lot of trailers bite the dust out there and have to be carted back. I'm only guessing, but I'd say four or five a season don't make it across for one reason or another. I've pulled a couple back myself. Don and I have gone out and brought them back.

Around October 2009, I was outside the Birdsville bakery after having a morning coffee. An elderly male approached me and we had a conversation regarding Birdsville: weather, road conditions, etc. It was a pleasant conversation but at the end of it he asked, 'How long have you been been stationed at Birdsville?'

I replied, 'About three years.'

He patted me on the shoulder and said, 'Never mind, son. Hopefully your next posting is better.'

He then walked off, obviously feeling very sorry for me. If only he knew, I applied for the posting and enjoyed Birdsville so much that I (and eventually Sandra) stayed another six years.

Where else are you fifteen steps from work, you go home for lunch, and when the children are visiting you see them all the time and not just after a long day at work? There are no traffic snarls, you never have to worry about finding a park, there are no tolls, and you can walk anywhere in town within a few minutes. Everybody knows everyone in town and on the surrounding properties on a first-name basis. You don't need to worry walking around at night, from a crime perspective. Admittedly, deadly snakes are an issue, but there's always something.

True, it is very hot in summer and it can be very isolated, but aren't London, New York and Paris freezing in winter? I can assure you London is, having lived in England as a child when my father was posted to Australia House. Even though they're beautiful cities, if you live and work there, you struggle to work on crowded public transport, work and then struggle home. And you do it day after day. I know where I'd rather be.

The scenery at Birdsville is stunning and the sunsets take your breath away. You get out in the desert, off the tracks, and you know there's not another human being for hundreds of kilometres. The sandhills look like no person has ever walked on them and some of them probably haven't been walked on for a few hundred or a thousand years.

The changing colours stop even experienced desert travellers in their tracks. At night the stars are so close you feel you can reach up and touch them. You also see satellites dart across the sky, but while the ingenuity of modern man is just above you, this timeless untouched land is all around you.

On 3 November 2009, the minister for police, corrective services and emergency services, Mr Neil Roberts, the police commissioner, Mr Bob Atkinson, assistant commissioners Clem O'Regan and Alan Davey, the ambulance commissioner, David Melville, and their entourages all visited Birdsville.

They got off the plane and said, 'Hi Neale, how you going?'

They knew all about me, having obviously been briefed before they got here. They were very congenial, friendly people.

When visitors come to Birdsville, you put on a nice smoko for them, and you drive them around the sights: the pub, the spot that water comes out of the bore, the race track, the South Australian border, the Burke and Wills tree and the Royal Hotel Ruins.

The day they came out was Melbourne Cup Day. I said to them, 'Why don't you come up the pub and meet the locals?'

So they did. Obviously they just had water, you know. And the locals met them. They were friendly to them. And I think they had a good time up there: talking to people, talking to ringers, talking to stockmen and retired stockmen like Jimmy Crombie. You could just tell that they enjoyed interacting with the locals, instead of sitting around, having a cup of tea at the police station and nibbling on a biscuit.

The commissioner and minister don't often visit such remote stations. I think they were doing a run through a number of out-back stations and I was on the list. I'd had a big year with some quite high-profile rescues. They knew all about that.

Someone just rang and said, 'The minister and commissioner are comin'.'

And I said, 'Yeah, no worries.'

Then you clean the station, make sure your shoes are polished and all that. You put on the best outlook for the station that you can. You have the place spick and span. It's an important visit and they've got to be treated like that. Make sure the grass is mowed, watered, everything is tidy, and take all your files over to the house and hide them over there. (Laughter)

You make sure they enjoy their stay and it's a positive visit, because it reflects on you if it's not.

In the middle of November 2009, we closed the Munga-Thirri (Simpson Desert) National Park for summer. That was the first year that was done. (At the time of publication the park closure was from 30 November to 14 March.)

The reason is that it's just too dangerous. With the radiant heat, even if you breakdown in the car and you're well supplied and equipped, it's just too hot. It's dangerous for us to go out there, too. The police car can roll on a sandhill or get stuck like any other car.

You've still got nine months of the year to cross and that's the time to do it: the cooler months. And it's a very hard trip at the best of times without adding 47-degree days and radiant heat from the sand. If something goes wrong, it's going to go much more wrong in the summer months.

So 2009 was the first year the desert was closed. Not long after, Dave from Mount Dare put out an email to various members of the outback community (businesses, police stations and information centres) detailing the nearly fatal consequences for someone who not only defied the closure, but did so on his own, in a vehicle not suited to the terrain, and not properly equipped and supplied. At one point he got bogged, couldn't get the vehicle out because he didn't have a shovel, ran out of water and couldn't call for help because he had no radio or satphone. I think he might have dug the vehicle out with his bare hands. He had to do that a few times.

He crossed the desert and got away with it but it wasn't a very smart thing to do because if anything went wrong he was in a world of hurt. After what he went through, I don't think he was going to do it again. It underlined why the desert was closed. But he made it out so he can tell his grandkids he crossed the desert in defiance of the laws. But the laws are there for a reason, like seat-belt laws and drink-driving laws: to save people's lives.

The closure has been in force ever since and it works well. It's well respected. People realise it's too hot at that time of year. Then you can get summer rains that'll make the desert impassable. You know what it's like, Evan, when those salt lakes are full of water. You get in one of those, you'll never get out.

The best time to cross the desert is in June, July and August. That's when I tell people to go. It's easy on you, easy on the vehicle. You can enjoy the beauty and driving over the dunes, but do it in comfort.

As happens every summer, by December 2009, Birdsville had become a very quiet, sun-baked outback town. There wasn't much going on and I was a week from taking an extended holiday. Then, on 9 December 2009, this idiot from Pandie Pandie drove up to the police station. I watched this car drive down the main street of Birdsville, turn at the corner where the police station is, and pull up out the front.

This ringer got out of the vehicle, came in and said, 'I'm here to get a driver's licence.'

I said, 'Well have you got one?'

He said, 'Nuh.'

I said, 'Well why did you drive the car up here?'

He said, 'Ah well, too far to walk from Pandie.'

I said, 'Couldn't you get someone to drive you? It's a bit cheeky driving up to a police station without a licence. Plus it's illegal.'

I checked him on the computer and he'd actually been disqualified from driving down in New South Wales and he still had eleven months to go on his disqualification. So he drove up to get a licence and ended up getting charged with driving while disqualified. The matter went to court and he lost his licence for a further two years.

Some people just aren't that bright. What can you do? He'd broken the law right in front of me. He was twenty-five or something. He knew he wasn't supposed to be driving. The magistrate who disqualified him would have told him that.

What he was trying to do was get a licence in Queensland, hoping the computer system wouldn't follow him across the border from New South Wales, where he got disqualified. Unfortunately for him, it did.

The interstate disqualification policy came into being after a major accident in 1989. The person involved had licences in at least three states, and the licences had already been suspended in two of them. He was driving on another licence when he was involved in an accident with multiple fatalities. Things changed after that. If you're disqualified in one state, you can't drive in other states.

This ringer thought he might be able to sneak through in a one-cop station, that maybe I was still in the age of quill pens and papyrus. Birdsville is equipped with a lot of computer systems, like all other stations. That's the case whether it's Thursday Island, Birdsville, Bribie Island, wherever. So that idea didn't work. Miserable failure, in fact.

———

Not long after, I went on leave. As I wrote in my monthly column in *Desert Yarns*, the Diamantina Shire's community newsletter:

> I am taking holidays from 19 December 2009 and will not be back until 5 March 2010. I am off with Sandra to Hong Kong and then on a cruise to China where we are going to the Great Wall of China. I want to see for myself if it really does keep the rabbits out.

I was still in Sydney when I got news that there'd been an accident involving the Birdsville station's brand-new police car. I'd gone to Townsville to pick it up. So by the time I got back to Birdsville it was almost due for the first service.

A young officer, Jess, had come down to relieve and was heading up to Bedourie to get the car serviced. It was very slippery because it was wet and the car went over an embankment and rolled onto its side.

The inspector rang and said, 'Oh, Jess has rolled the car.'

I go, 'Oh no, that's terrible. How is she?'

He says, 'We don't know, just found out about it.'

So I was worried the whole day about Jess; she was a young thing, really likeable. It was hard to get through to get any information but finally we found out that she wasn't injured. The car had just rolled on its side so she got a fright more than anything else.

The car got towed away to get fixed. Then it rained and the place was flooded, so I couldn't go and pick it up. The car went into the vehicle pool in Mount Isa. By the time I got it back, it had gone from a new car with less than 9000 kilometres on it to a car that had been driven by twenty different police officers. It was an old car.

When you're the only cop driving the police car, you treat it like it's your own or better. When you go on holidays, you stress to the relieving police officer to look after it, keep it clean, because it's really important your car is in good condition. That's what's going to get you out in the desert and get you back. And this new car was better equipped than the previous one. It was a Land Cruiser Troopie (troop carrier). It had an actual recovery box in it, with recovery gear. It had a fridge, an extra spare tyre bay, a place for those Max Trax, durable plastic ramps that help give you traction if you're bogged. Anyway, alas. Although little did I know that, while it had a hard life before I really got to use it, it was about to get a whole lot harder around Birdsville.

CHAPTER 6

BAPTISM OF WATER

My fourth year in Birdsville, 2010, was a huge year for floods. Right through. Birdsville was isolated for a while in March. I was doing river heights, the flood boat was being used on a regular basis. It was used on and off all through 2010, in what's supposed to be a desert.

Despite all the rain, early in April, the school went out to the Dingo Caves, 20 kilometres north of town, for a camping trip. The teacher went out there with Don and Lyn Rowlands and me. At the time, the school consisted of ten primary-school kids across a number of years and one teacher, plus teacher's aides (one of whom had been my daughter Lauren). The school caters for children who live in town, while School of the Air, or Distance Education, is available for children on stations who live too far away to go to school every day. The station kids and the town kids get together regularly for social events and sporting carnivals, which are sometimes their only chance to play team sports because it's the only time they've got enough children for a team.

Don and Lyn talked to them about animal tracks, showed

them examples of different tracks, showed them bush tucker and so on. I talked to them about police work, why laws are enacted, and how they're not made by police, they're made by the people. I explained that politicians make the laws, so the people make the laws and police enforce them. Then there were general conversations relating to child safety, stranger danger and things like that.

It's a different policing role, going out for a couple of days and camping out. A lot of the time was just interacting with the kids, making dinner with them, talking with them. The kids in town know you as a person anyway. They know you as the local officer but they also know you and call you by your first name. On a camping trip they get to see you when you're off-duty, cooking, sitting around a campfire talking, telling jokes and stuff like that. A few of the parents were there. They came and went at different times as well.

No sooner had I returned to town when I got a call. It was 4 April 2010 and locals John Hanna, a barman at the pub and brother of publican Brian Hanna, and Wolfgang John, an artist, were missing along with some of their friends. They were both knowledgeable outback drivers and had gone out to Big Red.

About five o'clock in the evening, Gus from the pub rang and said, 'They should have been back at three. It's now five, should we give 'em another couple of hours?'

I said, 'No, we'll go now.'

I went and picked up Gus. My son Robbie was in town so he came along too. To get out there we had to take a long detour because the usual road to Big Red was flooded. So we went round on the golf course track. It was nearly dark but there were Wolfie, John, Dia and friends of Gus.

I said, 'Where's the cars?'

They said, 'Oh, out there.'

I'm looking and then I see little specks in the middle of this wide expanse of water. There were the cars. Miles away.

John said, 'Can you pull us out?'

The cars were on the track but the whole track was under water.

I said, 'No way, John. I'm not getting your car back.'

I loaded them all into the police car. There wasn't enough room to put them all on the seats, so some had to jump in the back with Wolfie's dog. We got them back to town and the next day Barnesy spent all day pulling the two vehicles out.

They should have known better, especially John Hanna. His car was so far out, ay. We're talking a kilometre along this stretch of water. Just . . . miles. I thought, What was he doing out there? He was never going to get through. He tried, I suppose.

Two days later, on 6 April 2010, a station plane spotted a motorist bogged 75 kilometres south of town. It turned out he'd been there three days. To get there, though, he passed through two ROAD CLOSED signs and a barrier across the road, with ROAD CLOSED on it, to go down the Birdsville Track. There was no way he was going to get through. The road was closed for a reason.

At the place he got bogged, he was in South Australia. The fine for driving on a closed road in South Australia can be over $1000. This fella didn't tell anyone where he was going either. He was stuck for three days and no-one was going to come after him. You couldn't get two people that stupid. So he was in a world of hurt.

Fortunately, a mustering plane flew over, saw him and raised the alarm. Peter Barnes and I went down and got him.

He'd been bitten by a zillion sandflies. He was just covered in bites. The sandflies were about in huge numbers because of the mud. He was out of food and he was drinking water out of puddles. He wasn't about to run out of water. He was surrounded by it.

He was well and truly bogged but Barnesy pulled him out. Then we got him back to Birdsville.

He told me he was going to see his sick mother. He told Barry Gaffney he had to go pick up a caravan. Anyway, he got a ticket from me for disobeying a road sign: $120. That sign he'd ignored was in Queensland. Lucky for him.

The funny thing with that rescue is, the golden rule of the bush is: never leave your vehicle. However, if you look at his situation, he'd had a meal at the pub so he had a full stomach. He had water and food in the car but not much. And if he was thinking, he'd have said, 'Right, I'm here. No-one is coming down the track. It's closed. It's been closed for ages. No-one is going to come up the track.'

So it might have been better to walk back along the track to Pandie Pandie. It was 56 kilometres away. He could have travelled at night. He was fit and healthy. You don't like to tell people that but that's probably one of the few times when it might have been better to leave the vehicle. As it was, he was getting weaker and weaker, getting bitten by all these insects, and the bites were getting infected. He was out of food, so he was going to get weaker still if he stayed where he was. There was plenty of water on the way back so he wasn't going to die if he'd started walking. How far can you walk in a day? At 4 kilometres an hour, you'll make 30 kilometres or 40 kilometres in 8 to 10 hours. So in two days that bloke would have been at Pandie Pandie. He was stuck three days. Something I thought about.

Barry Gaffney said it was a bit harsh giving him a ticket but I said, 'Mate, we spent a fortune in fuel and time and effort getting him out of trouble. Me and Barnesy had to go down and get him, and we were at risk because we can get bogged just as easily as him.'

The fine was only $120. In South Australia, it's about $1250. I could have rung South Australia and they could have mailed a ticket up.

If you do stupid things, there has to be consequences. He passed two 'road closed' signs, then a barrier across the road. Surely it should sink in that someone doesn't want you to go down that road. Maybe because you won't get through. Whether he had a sick mum or he had to pick up a caravan, or both, he shouldn't have gone down there.

Late in April 2010 I got called down to the school to deal with a brown snake that had been spotted in the school grounds.

Dealing with snakes can be tricky, and not just because they're venomous. The copper at Bedourie was interviewed about snakes, which were very common up there because of the flood and he was asked, 'What do you do with them?'

Tim Farran said, 'I relocate them.'

Next thing, he got into trouble because people who love snakes said he might be taking them away from their family or their nest or whatever.

Catching snakes is an interesting function for a police officer to perform. Do you know how much training you get at the police academy in capturing dangerous reptiles? None.

That's one of those moments you feel like saying, 'Why are

you calling me? Don Rowlands is a park ranger. Try him.'

The funny thing was, I spoke to the kids and said, 'What do you do if you're bitten by a snake?'

And they said, 'Oh, we'd run home and tell mum.'

Running is about the worst thing you can do. The poisons will go straight through your system.

If there's a snake in the school, that's a public health risk. You don't ever want kids to be bitten by a snake, but in Birdsville the risk is even greater because there's no anti-venom in town. Small body. They run home. If it goes through their system, it's going to be serious.

So, the option is to catch and relocate. I went out to the school with John Hanna, who caught it and we took it out on the road to Pandie Pandie and released it there.

Usually, the best way to deal with snakes is to leave them alone. Snakes generally avoid people because we're too big to eat. Most people get bitten when they're trying to kill them or shoo them away. If you have to relocate a snake, call on the experts who know how to approach them. Your local National Parks office should be able to help there.

For outback people, one of the most popular events in Birdsville is the annual bronco branding competition. In 2010 they were held in early May, on a weekend when the town wasn't flooded. Bronco branding competitions involve a rider roping a calf and pulling it up to a panel where three other team members secure it, tip it on its side and two hold it down while the third brands it using a paint brush (instead of a hot iron). The team that brands three calves quickest wins but the calves often have a fair bit of say in proceedings as some resent being pulled, tipped and branded more than others.

One of the competitors was an elderly male from Camooweal who had heart problems. His doctor warned him not to go to Birdsville and he said, 'If I die on a horse in Birdsville, I'll die happy.'

That's exactly what happened. Unfortunately, it happened while he was competing in the bronco branding, in front of the entire crowd, including young kids, tourists, everybody.

As it happened, there were health professionals from Longreach running programs, handing out pamphlets, and the clinic nurses were there with the ambulance, so it was all hands on deck doing CPR. They had a defibrillator there. They went back twice to the clinic to get more adrenalin. I assisted with CPR, as did other police and station hands with first-aid experience.

Eventually, the batteries to the defibrillator went flat. He passed away. He was taken to the clinic. His family were really sad but at the same time they were grateful for the emergency services, the nursing staff and police who were there to help. But he had just had a massive heart attack. I don't think anything would have saved him.

I noticed that Bev, one of the nurses, she was so compassionate to the family. She was looking after them, holding their hands. She really cared for them.

Back at the clinic, we let the family spend as much time as possible with him. Then I had to take a report for the coroner, unless I could get a medical certificate explaining that the cause of death was the result of a medical condition, which I think was what happened. He was conveyed up to Mount Isa and I think he was buried at Camooweal.

I wrote about what happened in *Desert Yarns*:

> A magnificent effort to revive [name withheld] was conducted
> by Birdsville nurses (Beverley and Ross), visiting medical staff
> and other persons present including Bedourie police officer Tim
> Farran. They were all committed, professional, dedicated and
> acted in a caring way to ensure that everything that could be
> done was done to revive [him]. Unfortunately, despite the very
> best of efforts [he] passed away. . . He died doing what he loved.
> Rest in peace.

Not long after, my daughter Lauren, who'd been the Birdsville
QGAP officer for three-and-a-half years resigned, to concentrate
on her studies at Toowoomba University. She wrote a farewell
message in the May 2010 edition of *Desert Yarns*:

> The time has come for me to bid farewell to Birdsville and
> the fantastic Diamantina community. When I first moved to
> Birdsville I didn't think I would last long, as I arrived in one of
> the hottest months of the year (January), with every road closed
> due to floods and I was missing home greatly. However, after
> meeting all the friendly locals from Birdsville and Bedourie, I
> became very fond of this place and began to call it my home.
> I have had many great times here, met great people and have
> experienced the incredible outback life. I have thoroughly
> enjoyed my time here and this place will always hold a special
> place in my heart and I will always treasure the memories of my
> experiences. I'm in my third year of uni now, studying a Bachelor
> of Education, which is becoming more demanding but I will still
> visit Birdsville in the uni holidays to catch up with the locals and

spend time with Dad. I would just like to thank everyone in the Diamantina Shire for the amazing opportunities and memories that I have encountered living here. You're a great bunch of people who have made my time here a good one!

Around that time, there was a report of a single vehicle rollover near Glengyle Station, 120 kilometres north of Birdsville. Tim Farran, the officer-in-charge at Bedourie was closest, so he attended the scene. A small Suzuki vehicle (like a rollerskate with seats) was on its roof in the middle of the road with no occupant in sight.

Tim worked out that the vehicle belonged to a woman who had recently moved to Bedourie to work for the council. Fearing she'd hit her head and wandered off, Tim enlisted the help of the manager of Glengyle Station, Steve Cramer, with the search. Steve immediately dropped everything and got his plane up and all his staff on horseback, motor bikes and in vehicles looking for the driver. Once again, you never had to ask outback people twice. They were always ready to help.

Tim contacted me and I began making enquiries to see if this woman had made it to Birdsville. I also got ready to join the search. By now it was late afternoon and time was of the essence. I was in conversation with the Birdsville nurse when a truck pulled up and a woman got out. She said, 'This nice man [indicating the truck driver] drove me down to Birdsville after my accident. You owe him a beer.'

I said, 'We've had aircraft, police and a whole cattle station out for more than three hours looking for you. You could have left a note in your car or waited until someone from the emergency services turned up. You've caused many people a lot of worry and stress, and wasted everybody's time when it could have easily been avoided. I don't owe him a beer, you do.'

She then opened her purse and gave the truck driver $5.

I said, 'Beers at the Birdsville Hotel are $6.'

She said, 'That's all I can afford.'

I also told her to contact Glengyle Station and thank them. She never did.

She was going down the Birdsville Track to pick up her brother. He'd also recently moved to Bedourie but was driving a little white Honda Jazz that got four flat tyres. Four, one after the other, but as each one went, he just kept driving. He ended up wrecking the vehicle.

Barnesy bought the wreck, repaired it, and left it at Windorah. Then, a couple of years later, our vehicle's radiator failed at Windorah when we were going to our daughter Lauren's graduation at Toowoomba. Barnesy lent us the Honda Jazz. It was a very slow trip dodging all the kangaroos but we made it to Lauren's graduation.

By the middle of June, there were still roads affected by floodwaters all around the town. This led to a joint patrol with myself, Don Rowlands and South Australian police officer Nicholas Hempel. Joint patrols are an opportunity to liaise with colleagues we usually only talk to on the phone, to familiarise ourselves with areas we may not have visited for some time and to develop joint operations capabilities, which the general public can see in action.

We went down to his station at Marree, a 550-kilometre trip each way.

We met Nick at the point where the Birdsville Track crosses Cooper Creek. For decades, if the Cooper is in flood, a drive-on, drive-off punt has been provided by the South Australian Department of Transport to ferry vehicles across. This can involve a distance of a couple of kilometres, too far for a bridge, which could be washed away anyway. So our joint patrol included what could be a once-in-a-lifetime experience. There are photos of the three of us taking the punt across the swollen waters.

I wrote later in *Desert Yarns*: 'I'm not used to putting on a lifejacket to patrol the Birdsville Track. Usually it's just flies, desert tracks and sand storms.'

At 3 a.m. on 28 June 2010, I got a call from Trevor Kidd, the inspector in Mount Isa. He said, 'Tim [Farran, the Bedourie cop] went out to check on a couple of truckies that were bogged or something and he hasn't returned. His wife is worried about him.'

So I got in the car, kitted up and went up to try and track Tim down. Three in the morning. I was about 100 kilometres up the road (avoiding cattle, and the occasional roo) when I heard that Tim had returned home. So I went back to Birdsville. It was hardly worth going to bed because it was about five when I got back, and you've got the weather to do at six.

With a job like that, you've got to go. A police car can hit a beast or roll over or something can happen like it can to any other car. You've always got it in the back of your mind, that maybe something has happened. A lot of times with rescues you go early rather than late so you're on top of it. What are you going to do? If you're lying in bed worrying about someone, you might as well get up and get going.

Another aspect is that he's in a vehicle with fairly sophisti-cated communications equipment, and so am I, and yet he wasn't reachable. Sometimes you have trouble with satellites. So he may not have been able to use or be reached by satphone. Or the job was taking longer than he thought and he didn't want to wake his wife. I don't know why they couldn't contact him. He might have been out of the vehicle when they rang. In any event, there was a fairly immediate response, until we knew all was well. Maybe that's why police are referred to as 'first responders'. If someone is worried, you don't say 'let's wait and see'.

There was a different kind of job on 5 July 2010, involving one of the worst tragedies in the history of the Birdsville Track. I was asked to escort a woman to the place, 100 kilometres south of Birdsville, where five members of the Page family had perished at Christmas 1963. This woman, Avril, and her brother, who came with her, were descendants of the family. Avril's mother might have died as well but she hated the outback so she stayed home while her parents and two youngest brothers headed for Clifton Hills where her eldest brother was a ringer. It worked out a smart move. Her mother and father and three brothers lost the track on their way from Clifton Hills Station to Birdsville and then they ran out of fuel. They left their vehicle carrying 20 litres of water, but got tired of carrying the water and abandoned it. The bodies of the parents and two youngest boys were found at a dry water-hole not far from where they left the car. They wre buried there. The eldest son's body was found on the next sandhill, where it was buried.

The daughter who stayed at home never really got over it. She died at a relatively young age. She was in her sixties, I think. Her daughter, Avril, had a headstone specially made to erect at the place the four family members had perished and I went down to give her a hand, as did Sully, an old World War II veteran who comes out to Birdsville every year. Avril was with her partner, and her brother and another partner, and their kids.

When we arrived, the billabong just behind the grave site was full of water from all the rain we'd had. I was thinking, Gee if they'd had that water there, they wouldn't have perished. But that's the outback for you. We spent all day putting the headstone up. We concreted it in and made a surrounding of stones for the grave. It came up really good.

I'm not sure if that was the first time any of the family members had been to the site. One of the reasons I went with them was to help them locate it. It took us a while to find it, too. Eventually we tracked it down with the help of a GPS.

It was quite moving for the daughter and son. The kids were pretty young but they probably appreciated it, too. They'd have known the family history. The daughter, though, she was very keen. She was the one who instigated it all. I think her brother came along to show his support.

On 1 August 2010 I got called to a disturbance at the caravan park. There was a bloke from Sydney staying there with his wife and two kids. At a neighbouring camp site there was a woman who had a dog that had been running around loose. He told the dog off. Then the woman yelled at him and one thing led to another. He ended up headbutting her, opening up her forehead. She had to go to the clinic.

I found him at the hotel. He came down to the police station where he was interviewed and charged. He was convicted of common assault at Birdsville Court later that year. He pleaded guilty.

He was a typical family man but there was no excuse for

Senior Constable Neale McShane, Officer In Charge at Birdsville Police Station, western Queensland, looking for a desert track in the dust storm that raged during the rescue effort for John White in 2009. This image made the front page of newspapers around the world. *Photo: Hugh Brown*

ABOVE: John White's stricken vehicle after it rolled into a sand hole obscured by one of the worst dust storms in Neale's time at Birdsville. *Photo: Hugh Brown*

RIGHT: Left to right, mechanic Peter Barnes (Barnesy), John White and Neale McShane in Birdsville after John's rescue.

TOP: Neale on a desert patrol, Simpson Desert, 2015. *Photo: Mick Molloy*

BOTTOM: Typical desert conditions during a joint patrol in 2015.
Photo: Sandra McShane

Every year at the beginning of September the famous Birdsville Races see the population increase by up to a hundred-fold for two days. *Photo: Evan McHugh*

Neale, Mel Hovenden and Trent Jansen with boxing tent impresario Fred Brophy, a regular at the Birdsville Races. *Photo: Sandra McShane*

Some of the thirty-plus police working at the 2008 Birdsville Races. Many were accommodated in the 1880s courthouse building in the background.

Patrolling the Birdsville Races includes police on trailbikes who ensure campers on the town common aren't put at risk by off-road driving antics.

Clearing weather over the Birdsville Hotel, 2013. *Photo: Neale McShane*

Neale with the vehicle he relies on during desert rescues, outside the Birdsville Police Station, 2015. *Photo: Mick Molloy*

LEFT: A long way from anywhere. Neale at the distance advisory sign on the outskirts of Birdsville, 2015. Note the official spelling of Mungeranie, spelled locally as Mungerannie. *Photo: Mick Molloy*

RIGHT: Neale with future prime minister Malcolm Turnbull during his visit to Birdsville in April 2015. *Photo: Sandra McShane*

During the 2010 races, rain and floods cut the town off after the population had swelled to over four thousand. *Photo: Neale McShane*

An unexpected desert adventure, in 2010, wearing lifejackets to cross the flooded Cooper Creek by punt during a joint patrol with Ranger Don Rowlands and South Australia Police officer Nicholas Hempel.

Aboard the good ship *Birdsville*, playing an eel-ectric guitar in floodwaters at the foot of Big Red in 2010. John White, rescued during a dust storm in 2009, is in the background. *Photo: Hugh Brown*

Neale with wife Sandra and daughter Lauren in 2011, on Big Red, with floodwaters in the background. *Photo: Damian Wrench*

Bogged on a desert patrol in 2009, Neale (right) was assisted by Jimmy Crombie (left) and Evan (centre) in deploying snatch straps so Ranger Don Rowlands (out of picture) could pull him out. *Photo: Michelle Havenstein*

It was all hands on deck in 2009 when station owner Geoff Morton radioed that he'd lost a wheel after a mid-air collision with a pelican. Fortunately, he managed a perfect two-point landing. *Photos: John Hanna*

ABOVE: One of Neale's 'luckiest' rescues was in 2009 when a helicopter capable of carrying a patient on a stretcher was needed and an Army Chinook materialised in answer to his prayers. *Photo: Neale McShane*

LEFT: Late night transfer to the flying doctor for an injured motorcycle rider, in this instance a Queensland Police inspector, near Betoota in 2013. *Photo: Neale McShane*

ABOVE: The Diamantina crocodile, probably released into the river at Birdsville by a practical joker. It took some months in 2013 to capture and relocate the creature to a wildlife sanctuary. *Photo: Sandra McShane*

BELOW: Noodles the camel outside the Birdsville Bakery during the 2012 Races. He was popular with tourists but that didn't stop someone shooting and beheading him a few weeks later. *Photo: Blythe Moore*

This shoe tree was a point of
interest for travellers on the
road from Birdsville to Bedourie,
until it was set on fire in 2014.
*Photos: Michelle Havenstein,
Neale McShane*

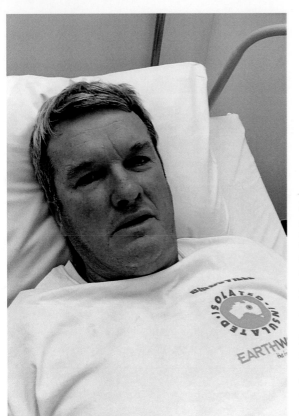

LEFT: Neale in the casualty ward of Princess Alexandra Hospital, Brisbane, in May 2015, after suffering a stroke that left him unable to walk or speak and facing months of rehabilitation. *Photo: Lauren McShane*

BELOW: With fellow officers Shane Long (right) and Paul Jackson (left) on his final Simpson Desert patrol, 2015. *Photo: Sandra McShane*

Friends, police and most of the Birdsville community celebrated Neale's retirement after ten years as OIC Birdsville at a special event in November 2015. *Photo: Michelle Havenstein*

Neale and son Robbie enjoying one of the many stories told during Neale's retirement event. *Photo: Michelle Havenstein*

Neale and wife Sandra relaxing during Neale's last trip through the Simpson Desert before his retirement, 2015. *Photo: Shane Long/Paul Jackson*

what he did. His wife was very angry with him, and rightly so. He just lost his temper and did a stupid thing. His wife was very apologetic.

I said, 'You've got to listen to what your wife tells you, mate.'

It was just a brain snap or whatever.

It was fairly dramatic for Birdsville but just because you're in a remote area doesn't mean there's not going to be any crime. Usually it's minor crime out here but it can become serious, like that incident.

Later in August, it was still raining and people were still getting into difficulties. On the Arrabury Road, 220 kilometres east of town, there were reports of motorbikes being pushed along the muddy track. Then a car and caravan travelling the same road became overdue.

As luck would have it, on 24 August 2010, the minister for public works and ICT, Robert Schwarten, was flying out for a visit to Birdsville, so we asked if his aircraft could divert to search for the missing travellers. He was the minister in charge of QGAP at the time and was bringing out the head of the program on a tour of Western Queensland QGAP sites. He was at Thargomindah when the call came in so I got approval, got onto him and asked him to do a run up the Arrabury Road. He was keen to do it.

It was really good that he gave up his time and the use of the government jet to do the search. The people on the plane, his minders, were really excited. It's a big job for them, looking for people, instead of their usual jobs pushing paper around.

They found the people, too, which was good. They were

waving. And they were stuck. Well and truly stuck. They were surrounded by floodwater. So we got a helicopter from the Moomba oil fields to go and rescue them. There were three bikes, and a car and caravan, in two separate groups. They were separated by 5 or 10 kilometres but didn't know about each other.

The chopper did the rescue as a 'community assist'. That means it doesn't cost the taxpayers money. They dropped off supplies to them first, because there were too many to take in one trip and making sure they had food was a priority, then they picked them all up later.

After the plane found the bikes and the car and caravan, it continued on to Birdsville. Unfortunately for Sandra, who had finally moved to Birdsville and had just taken up her job as the QGAP officer, the plane arrived too late for the minister to appreciate all the effort she'd made. The police station was spick and span and she'd organised smoko but by the time they'd done all the trips around, it was too late for smoko.

Later, Minister Schwarten wrote to thank us for hosting him during his visit and for the chance to help with the search and rescue. There had been some media coverage of it and he said, 'Thanks for making me look good.'

The following day, 25 August 2010, we had three people stuck on the Birdsville Track at Clifton Hills, 140 kilometres south of town. Water was coming down everywhere.

In my notes from that time, I described the Birdsville Track as slippery and wet. I was slipping all over the place when I went to pick them up. The problem was, I knew heavy rain was coming so I had to go then, before it got much wetter.

Normally, I'm used to driving over sand dunes and in dusty conditions. Every now and then you have the same road but it's totally different because it's soaking wet. It's a real effort to keep the car on the road. You can slide and be going sideways down the road for hundreds of metres. Then you go sliding down the road for hundreds of metres the other way.

The trick is to stay on the road. That's where the hard road surface is. And you've just got to keep the vehicle going because once you stop, you'll sink. If there's water over the road, you use the guidemarkers because they're 900mm high. If you can see three-quarters of them, you know you're right. If the water is up round the top, don't go through it.

I went down to get them. It turned out they'd gone through a creek and the car just stopped. They were down near Clifton Hills Station for about three days. I got some guys from Clifton Hills to pick them up and drive up the track to meet me coming down. The travellers were actually police from Victoria, including an assistant commissioner. I brought them to Birdsville, they stayed at the courthouse, then Tom the mailman flew them down to Adelaide the next day. We got them to do another search on the way down, too.

A family had been reported missing on 26 August so I got Tom to fly down the Birdsville Track on his way to Adelaide to see if he could spot them. He did, and they weren't there. They were missing for a while and we ended up starting a major search. Turns out they were bogged out past Windorah, down near Cooper Creek. They'd been there for a week or so. Windorah is hundreds of kilometres away from Birdsville. This family had changed their itinerary without telling anyone. Instead of being down the Birdsville Track, where they were expected to be, they went in a completely different direction. When they were reported missing and hadn't called in, they weren't anywhere near where they said they'd be. They were actually in the Windorah police officer's patch so he took care of that one. Eventually someone came along and got them out, which was lucky.

In the midst of all that, in August 2010, a special bike ride was organised by a fellow named Jim Cairns for three paraplegics, including himself, and one quadriplegic. All four injured guys were revisiting the places they had suffered their injuries and making a documentary about it.

Jim's motorbike accident was in Birdsville when he was on a Redex ride in the 1980s. He was riding along doing 160 kilometres an hour and he slowed down to 150 to overtake a car on the inside on a sweeping bend, because the dust was blowing towards the outside of the bend. He lost control, came off and was badly injured.

He ended up in Perth and is now a very successful man. He was the general manager of operations for Caterpillar in Western Australia.

He rang me, told me he was coming out and it so happened that we had a large amount of rain that delayed his trip through the desert. They came to Birdsville late one night. We heard them first, from the sound of their specially modified buggies.

Sandra said, 'Oh my God, there's bikies in town.'

They were like bikies but they were just riding around, finding out where things were. They ended up staying at the pub for only one night because they'd been delayed three days and as it was coming up to the races, after that the pub was booked out. You're talking four disabled people, support people, film crew, so there were at least a dozen of them. By time time the Birdsville Track had closed because of all the rain, so they couldn't leave town.

So I put them up at the courthouse.

I struck up a friendship with them. They were great people. Jim was a great guy. I went out to Big Red with him and he took me up on his buggy. You could see that he used to be a motorbike rider in his younger days because it was all flat out. I was glad to get out of the buggy in the end.

We had barbeques with them. Jim had a really good attitude about life. You don't come across many like Jim in your lifetime, but you're really glad to meet them. He got on well with Sandra, too.

They got an opportunity to leave a couple of days before the races and they took it. We had police coming down to stay at the courthouse and the forecast suggested that leaving was a good option. They headed off down the Birdsville Track, which had reopened, and fortunately they made it.

Afterwards, Jim sent me emails about how the doco, *The Ride,* was going and then he sent Sandra and me an invitation to the premiere screening in Perth twelve months later.

I said, 'Oh, I'd love to go to Perth.'

So we drove from Birdsville to Mount Isa, stayed in the barracks at Mount Isa overnight, then flew from Mount Isa to Brisbane, and Brisbane to Perth. We stayed in the middle of Perth, which is a beautiful city. We had a great time there. We went to Fremantle and looked around. Then we had dinner with Jim and his wife and a few of the other people on the ride. They took us up to Kings Park and showed us the sights. Then we went to the documentary screening. It was very well received by the people there.

Then we returned to Birdsville by the same route. Perth to Brisbane, Brisbane to Mount Isa, Mount Isa to Birdsville.

I still keep in contact with Jim from time to time. I really enjoyed him coming to Birdsville and helping him was another of those experiences most police might have once in a lifetime but which happens all the time here.

By 27 August 2010 there was a lot of rain coming down. People were being reported missing or overdue and the missing persons running log was just getting longer and longer. We were going through them, tracking them down. You've got no mobile coverage out here, except in town, so when people change routes without telling anyone, it's a case of doing good old police leg work, ringing Mungerannie, all the outlying stations, all the police in Marree, Bedourie, Windorah, trying to track people down. Out here, though, people are really helpful. They'll always keep a lookout for you.

As I mentioned, Sandra moved out here permanently just prior to the 2010 races. When I'd come out, it was stinking hot, a baptism of fire. When Sandra came out, it was the exact opposite: a baptism of water.

CHAPTER 7

THE DUST HAS SETTLED

A week before the 2010 races, we could see a lot more rain coming. On Monday, 30 August 2010, the weather bureau said we were going to get between 30 and 40 millimetres on the following Friday and Saturday. That was bang over the race period. The rule of thumb is that 17 millimetres of rain will shut the roads around Birdsville. We were going to get twice that.

I started explaining that to people who were ringing the police station: 'We're expecting this amount of rain. Decide if you want to come. The roads are going to close. We'll definitely close the roads.'

Some people in Birdsville didn't like that because they don't want people to avoid coming to the races. Yet it's important that police give accurate and correct information out to people. I ended up putting the weather forecast on the front door of the police station, the five-day forecast: '30 to 40 millimetres on Saturday'.

As it was, we got 34 millimetres, so it was pretty right. (Laughter)

My colleagues and I also started looking at contingency plans for rain at the races. That involved all sorts of things. I knew some police were coming down on their days off, so I asked them to bring down their uniforms, in case they had to be recalled to work. I was planning for people to be stuck in town, planning for the worst. The old story: plan for the worst, hope for the best.

I had regular meetings with the Diamantina Council and the race club. I was keeping senior police, the clinic and the senior sergeant in charge of disaster management in Mount Isa informed.

So I was on the front foot. I was planning for the roads to be closed, so when they were, everything would be in line. I was all ready to go, ready to deal with it.

What I didn't foresee was a police employee, on 31 August 2010, starting to show symptoms of having a stroke.

He was a radio technician. He comes down every year to keep all the portable radios police have going. He came down and on the Monday he couldn't move his arm. So we called the nurse down. At that stage the nurse was really busy because a local girl had just had a miscarriage. Eventually the nurse got to see him and said, 'Just have a rest. See how you go.'

Then Sandra, who had first-aid training from her years as a flight attendant, went and saw him and he had more symptoms of a stroke: his face had dropped a bit, he was cold and clammy. So the nurse called him back to the clinic and saw him there.

What came of that was, he didn't want to get flown out by the Flying Doctor. Stubborn old prick. So the deal was his wife would drive him up to Mount Isa the next day.

The funny thing was, after he got out of the clinic, he came back, and he was angry. He said, 'Who dobbed me in?'

He'd found out people had said, 'You've got this, you've got that.'

And his wife said, 'I did.' (Laughter)

Sandra was there and she was really worried because he was so angry. So next day he and his wife drove back to Mount Isa. Police saw him at Boulia having a durrie and a bit of fried chicken before he continued on to Mount Isa.

Months later, he sent an email to Sandra that had a subject line that read: 'Look what you've done!'

It turned out he had big problems with his heart. And because Sandra had said he might have had a stroke, he had to see a specialist in Mount Isa. That's the deal. They had to operate on him. It turned out to be a minor intervention but it nipped in the bud something that could have been really serious and could have killed him.

He was man enough to say, 'Look what you've done!' That was the heading on the email. And the text said, 'You saved my life.' Then there was a big spiel about what was wrong with him and how it was diagnosed.

Friday, 3 September 2010, was the first day of the race meeting. As predicted, there was heavy rain and wind.

The race organisers moved each race forward so one race would finish and they'd start another one soon after it. They should have just cancelled the races because it was just too dangerous. The race course was a mud pan; soaking wet mud.

After about three races, they just had to stop. It didn't stop raining. There were big wash-outs forming where the water was running through the public areas. In town there were big pools of water because the drains were being overwhelmed by the volume of rain. That night, it kept raining hard, with strong winds, into the early hours of Saturday morning. Everyone who was camped on the town common, between the town and the track, about 1500 people, had to be evacuated. The place had become a sea of water. Their camp sites turned into absolute quagmires. The common looked more like a refugee camp than an outback racing carnival.

We said, 'Come into town, you're going to get flooded. Just grab a spot, anywhere in town. Pull up a bit of mud.'

The next day there were caravans and tents everywhere. There wasn't a spare bit of dry ground. The town was full.

Every fence, *every* fence was draped with wet clothes. Right along. Every fence in Birdsville was a clothesline: doonas and clothes.

The t-shirt people sold out of every t-shirt. Even 5XL was going because people had nothing dry to wear.

They said, 'Just give me a t-shirt.'

They bought anything that was dry.

By then the track was a lake. At one stage, they were trying to pump water off the course but they never had a hope. It was like a swimming pool. All flooded.

By Saturday we'd got 34 millimetres of rain, as predicted. There was a howling wind that made the conditions even worse. We opened up the sports centre. Heaps of people camped in there, and around there. Just everywhere. Welcome to Birdsville. The motto of the races is: the dust never settles. Well, the dust had settled.

At the police station, we had all the dramas: phones going, organising resupply of staple foods and essential medicines, people coming to the counter crying because they had to get home for work. All the roads were closed. We had 4000 people stranded in town. We had the contingency plan in place but you looked out from the police station and all you could see was people.

And my kids were here. We had friends here. If you ever run out of friends, move to Birdsville, because you get heaps during the races. So while I was trying to provide for 4000 people in town, Sandra and I were hosting quite a few of our own while our larder was shrinking rapidly.

Everyone wanted to know what was going on and all that, so we had police at every roadblock. They had to stop some people from leaving town. You're better to have people in town where you've got all the services than stuck on roads way out in South Australia, Queensland, all over the place.

The airstrip remained open so we had supplies coming in. All the caterers sold out of everything. Even Dusty sold out of everything. All the milk went, all the bread. Dusty baked more bread and there was a mass panic as people tried to get some. He sold all his pies. He sold everything.

The thing was, people usually go to the races on Friday and Saturday, then head off after breakfast on Sunday. Everything is geared to them leaving Sunday morning. Now you've got 4000 for lunch on Sunday, then dinner, and so on. At one sitting they'd eat as much as everyone in Birdsville would eat in a month. So no wonder everything started selling out. As always, there were winners and losers. Caterers did really well that weekend.

This was also when the federal election was on, and there was a hung parliament. We took the election off the front page of newspapers around the country. The Birdsville Races were on the front page. All these people stuck in town. There was a lot of media interest.

Then the charter planes came in. It was $1200 for a one-way flight from Birdsville to Adelaide or Birdsville to Brisbane.

People paid that. Those planes were going out full. People have got lives to lead. They might have weddings to go to, important business meetings or they've got a holiday booked to go overseas. Heaps of cars got left in town and these planes were flying out all the time.

The pub rationed beer. They sold out of cigarettes. They auctioned the last packet of cigarettes on Sunday afternoon, for $130, and the money went to the Flying Doctor. Although the Flying Doctor probably isn't the biggest fan of cigarettes.

In the midst of all that we were flying food in. The food was distributed through the local businesses: the roadhouse, the bakery, the pub and Gaffneys. They sold it. Also, a lot of people bring a lot of food when they come so they were using that up as well.

We didn't have a real problem with food. It took the caterers a while to run out. It was probably the Monday before they did. Meanwhile, we were bringing in bread, we were bringing in flour to make bread, fresh fruit, all that sort of stuff. Staples. Not cigarettes or beer.

I also had thirty or forty police stranded in town with me. They took it in their stride. We kept moving them around so they weren't stuck on a roadblock all day. They worked tirelessly, even when conditions were pretty terrible. Officers who had come for a holiday and got called back to duty did so without complaining.

I kept everyone informed about what was happening. I said, 'As soon as the roads are open, we'll get you out.'

Instead of policing, I was getting them to go around to talk to people and explain what was going on. People were seeking out police at roadblocks, or they'd come down and look at the water. We hardly had any problems. Most people just took it in

THE DUST HAS SETTLED

their stride. It was a bit of an adventure, if anything.

There were still plenty of things for people to do. Lots went to the pub. Fred Brophy had boxing shows on Sunday night, when in other years he wouldn't have. So he was another winner. And he kept people entertained. Fred is one of the legendary figures of the outback. His boxing tent gives members of the public the opportunity to step into a ring with one of Fred's professional boxers. Some do it for a bit of fun, others train for months to prove themselves in three short rounds. The crowd pays to see how they go.

The race club organised different events. When the skies cleared, Sandra did one of her first star shows, using her knowledge from working as a guide at the Cosmos Centre in Charleville, on the oval. She used a high-powered laser pointer to identify stars, constellations and the Milky Way, then she had a telescope that let her audience take turns to see the rings of Saturn, Jupiter's moons, the Jewel-Box Cluster and other astronomical features.

There were different things happening to keep people informed. I spoke at a public meeting outside the pub on Monday. There were about 2000 people there.

I said to them, 'You guys have been stuck here for four days. I don't know what you're complaining about. I've been stuck here for four years.'

That got a laugh. Then I told them, 'You're better off to be here where you've got medical facilities, you've got food, you've got heaps of planes flying in with more supplies. There'll be bread, there'll be milk, staple foods, you'll be able to buy. There'll be no price gouging. It'll be the same price as what you'd pay in Birdsville any other time.'

Which is bloody expensive anyway. (Laughter)

I said, 'If you've got any problems, come down and see us. The roads aren't ready to be opened yet but as soon as they are, we'll get you out of here.'

There were all sorts of rumours going around that we were keeping people in town so the pub could make more money. That certainly wasn't the case.

We spoke to the bus people because they were keen to get out first. It looked like the only way we could get them out was north. So if you were going to Brisbane, you'd have to go north to Bedourie and Boulia, then east to Winton and Longreach. Instead of going direct east. An extra 1000 kilometres, easy. Maybe more.

Come Monday, we said to the bus people, 'It looks like we can open the road north tomorrow. So we want you to pack up but keep it quiet. Just tell people you're packing up to move site or to get things sorted a bit.'

Of course, as soon as the buses started packing up, word went around like wildfire. People soon got wind of it, which was always going to happen, and they all started packing. Before we knew it, everyone was packing.

At that stage, on the road north, the water was 0.8 metres deep at Carcoory Crossing, 80 kilometres from town. We had a helicopter going out to check the levels. That depth means the water is over the bonnet of a lot of vehicles so we probably should have kept the road closed. Fortunately, Carcoory has a cement bottom and we got council people there with machinery to pull cars through if they got stuck.

The commissioner said to Inspector Paul Biggin, 'It's really important, if you open the road, make sure they can get through. If someone drowns, we're in a world of hurt.'

We had that in the back of our minds. We had to make sure they could get through safely.

On Tuesday, 7 September, there was a big traffic jam going from Don's place, around the corner, past the pub, round the next corner and back past the caravan park. That's the only time there was a traffic jam in Birdsville.

At ten o'clock we opened the road and let the buses go first. Then, all jobs have their perks, so the inspector's girlfriend was in car number one, pole. Position number two was Don Rowlands' son. And position number three was my kids. After them, there was a general procession all day.

Most people leave Sunday so here's Monday, Tuesday, and we got them out Tuesday. Like I said it was 0.8 metres at Carcoory, over the bonnet of cars, but it was only in and out and we had people there ready to hook 'em up and pull 'em out if they got stuck. The water wasn't flowing either. It wasn't a current. It would be different if it was because it would have pushed them off.

The funny thing was that at three o'clock in the afternoon, South Australia opened the Birdsville Track. They were obviously waiting until most people left Birdsville before they opened their road. (Laughter) They're not stupid, those people.

Everyone left in an orderly manner. We opened the roads and let the cars go and off they went. They had to go north towards Bedourie. The buses had to go up to Winton and then to Longreach and back to Brisbane that way. They got home on Thursday. If you had a four-wheel drive, you could go up to Bedourie, then take the road from Bedourie to Windorah. Through that way, the detour was only about 200 kilometres

They all left that way, some never to return, no doubt. There were still cars all over town, belonging to people who had flown out because they had to get back to work or had other commitments.

While all that was happening, I also had people stranded out at Poeppels Corner. There'd been heavy rain out there as well and people were saying, 'Now what do we do?'

I worked out with them that they were just going to have to sit there until someone could get to them. I was monitoring them but I was looking at over 4000 people stuck in town. I wasn't going to send police out – they'd have had real trouble getting out there in any case – or go out myself. And Barnesy had to fix cars that were broken down, change tyres, and so on so we could get people on their way. It was a matter of prioritising 4000 people over a couple of cars stuck at Poeppels with water and food. They weren't in distress, they were just stuck.

I told them, 'Camp up. You might be there for two or three days.'

Most people are prepared for that.

In *Desert Yarns* the following month, I summed up some of the noteworthy aspects of having thousands 'Trapped in Birdsville!'

- On Tuesday morning, 1000 vehicles left travelling north on the only road open.
- Not one crime was reported during the racing carnival
- There was no record of an assault
- Not one traffic accident was reported
- No-one was charged with drink-driving
- Three people were evacuated by RFDS. All for illness.
- The heights of the creeks crossing the roads were up to 1.3 m.
- The 'Blow Before You Go' pre-emptive breath-test usually

conducted on Sunday prior to driving was cancelled. Not much use having a blow if you are not going anywhere.

- The mood of the crowd was one of 'we are all in this together, let's make the best of it'. The last police left on Thursday, four days later than planned.

In November, Inspector Paul Biggin gave me and the town a big rap in the *Police Bulletin*:

> Birdsville Officer-in-Charge, Senior Constable Neale McShane deserves special commendation. His efforts to work closely with officers on the ground, senior police and local government, while simultaneously dealing with an ever-increasing number of problems, were crucial to the operation's success.
>
> Not only that, the support from everyone in town was fantastic, too. Everyone was in that situation together, and the spirit of cooperation really reflected that.

Right through that September, rain and floods meant roads were opening and closing all the time. There were several instances of people travelling on closed roads. Then on 25 September, Search and Rescue Canberra called to say an EPIRB had been activated by a family of five near Haddon Corner, 277 kilometres east of Birdsville.

That was a rescue I won't forget. It was a Saturday and St Kilda were playing Collingwood in the AFL grand final. I was a long-time St Kilda supporter; I was at the MCG when they won their first (and only) premiership, beating Collingwood by a point in 1966. I was all set to watch the game. Day off. Then I got a phone call: 'SAR Canberra.' There goes the grand final.

So I headed off there with Barnesy and it was right at Haddon Corner. The family were bogged and had been for two or three days. They were badly bogged and couldn't get out.

They said they'd been scared about setting off the EPIRB but I said, 'No, set it off. One of the kids could have got asthma, or been bitten by snake, or if the rain continued, we couldn't get to you. If you can't get out, set it off.'

As it was, they'd been living rough for two or three days.

We pulled them out of the bog. They came back to Birdsville. By the time we got back, the footy game was over. It had been one of the most exciting grand final games in history. It was a draw. And I missed it.

The family we rescued were a nice family. Fortunately, they had an EPIRB because Haddon Corner isn't a popular spot. It's only the corner of Queensland and South Australia, whereas Cameron and Poeppels Corners are junctions of three states. So they could Not long after, one of my brothers, Simon, rang me from Melbourne and said, 'I've got tickets to the grand final replay. Do you want to come down?'

So I said, 'Sure. If the first game was a draw, this will be really competitive.'

I rang the inspector in Mount Isa and he said, 'Yeah, come up and fly from here.'

So Sandra came with me and we drove from Birdsville to Mount Isa, stayed in the police barracks, and flew Mount Isa–Brisbane, Brisbane–Melbourne on Friday. We got picked up by my brother's wife, Annette. Stayed at their place. Went to the footy on Saturday. We caught the tram in to watch the footy, so it was a fair trip: car, plane, tram.

And the Saints got towelled up in the first quarter. The game was finished by quarter time. Collingwood were three goals up or whatever. We got absolutely pumped. So that was going to Melbourne for the grand final. Unlike the week before.

The rain just kept coming. On 8 October 2010 it lead to two Dutch tourists getting bogged in the Diamantina Lakes National Park. They had a satphone, which they used to tell us they were bogged. They had a GPS, which they used to tell us where they were. What they didn't tell us was that they didn't know how to read the GPS.

The Diamantina Lakes Park Ranger went to the location they'd given and found no-one. Meanwhile, they were on their satphone saying that they were still bogged. They couldn't see or hear anyone nearby.

We then got a plane from one of the stations to do an air search for them. It didn't take long to find them. They were 10 kilometres from the position they'd given. The ranger then went and got them out.

Right through October people were getting stuck or running out of fuel as their vehicles battled through boggy conditions. It was just rain, rain, rain. If you look at how much rain fell that year, you'd be surprised. You wouldn't think it was the desert.

Roads were open for two or three days at a time. Then more rain. Then closed. Incredible. Out at Big Red, in front of Big Red, it was all flooded. You couldn't get to Big Red. You had to go on a detour down to the South Australian border, along the border, then back again. We had huge amounts of rain, not only in 2010, but in 2011 and 2012.

Your expectation is that you're going to live in the desert but I spent a lot of my time in Birdsville in a lifejacket. For three years, Lake Eyre was full of water. It was two-and-a-half years before it started to dry out. For Lake Eyre to fill you've got to have the Cooper running, the Diamantina and Eyre Creek and the Georgina running. And not just running, but really running.

A month later, with hotter months beginning, tourist numbers fell away and Birdsville once again started to revert to a quiet outback community. There wasn't much to do until 9 November 2010 when a stockman at Durrie Station fell from his horse and broke both his legs.

I drove out for that, and the ambulance went as well. He was treated at the scene by the station's staff, then the Flying Doctor landed at Durrie's dirt airstrip. It was better that he was flown out from there, rather than go through the ordeal of being brought back to Birdsville on 100 kilometres of unsealed road.

An incident like that doesn't normally require close investigation, unless there are special circumstances. If it's just a fall from a horse, police work isn't really necessary. You normally go out to things like that just to help the nurse. You keep your finger on the pulse so you can tell the inspector what happened. You get details in case you have to contact relatives. If property people don't have contact details for a staff member's next of kin, police have computer systems that can track people down all over Australia. So it's not the sort of thing I need to go out to, but I do.

After that it was pretty quiet until 28 December 2010. That was when an old bloke who was staying at the pub told the staff that he was going to walk out to Big Red. He was advised that at that time of year it might not be a good idea but he was determined to do it anyway. Off he went but he didn't get far, with temperatures well into the forties. Fortunately, someone picked him up and brought him back into town. Fortunately for me, that is, because I didn't have to go looking for him.

He was an old bloke. I thought that he was in his mid-sixties. Then on 5 January I found out he was seventy-one: he was listed as a missing person from South Australia who had left an aged-care facility.

He was listed as missing but he hadn't broken the law so I couldn't take him into custody. What I could do was find out what his situation was and contact his relatives or, in this case, the aged-care facility.

It turned out this guy had actually murdered his wife and spent a bit of time in jail. That was well before he came to Birdsville. Anyway, I decided he was a bit different but he wasn't going to do harm to himself or others, so I contacted the aged-care facility and left it at that.

He was walking around the country. He was travelling on foot and getting lifts. After a while, he turned up at Cordillo Downs Station. He was probably dropped off by someone who'd had enough of him after a couple of hundred kilometres. After that he disappeared off my radar.

CHAPTER 8

CYCLONE

Throughout January 2011 there was more rain, with more road closures. Then, at the end of the month, the town was warned to start preparing for the approach of the deteriorating Tropical Cyclone Yasi.

Heavy rain was already falling. It had been for months. Now Yasi was expected to hit the coast around Cairns and travel towards Mount Isa. As it weakened it would turn into a severe rain depression that would hit Birdsville.

We made sure the generators were full of fuel and that the relevant townspeople were well aware, especially Dusty, who runs the power station, the fire brigade and the SES. All the flood boats were serviced. I made sure all the police station radios and satphones worked. The police car was kept full of fuel. I had spare diesel in case of lost power. I made sure everyone had plenty of food and water. I had to make sure I had plenty of everything you need to handle an emergency.

I did phone hook-ups with senior police and council people, in case the severe rain depression came through and we were isolated for a significant period of time. Sure enough, after Yasi moved inland, the rain depression covered everywhere. We got 374 millimetres in one day. That's double our annual rainfall in one day.

What's surprising is that the town still remained dry. We took off in a helicopter and everything was covered in water, except Birdsville. The people who first settled in Birdsville were smart people because it remains dry. There's an Aboriginal ceremonial site on the edge of town, which suggests people have known that for a very long time. In modern times, the airstrip remains dry. It can become waterlogged, soaked, but it's still not under water.

Not only that, people here are used to floods. Being remote and isolated communities, they take it in their stride. It's something a city person would be stressed about but outback people aren't. City people have got a schedule to be somewhere. If they can't make it, it's a real big deal.

Where country people would say, 'I can't go, I won't go,' a city person would say, 'Well, I'm going.' That's why they drive through floodwaters, get washed away and die. They've gotta be home by five o'clock. Their husband wants their dinner by six and the kids have to be bathed. Outback people, even if it's a wedding, they say, 'The road's flooded, I can't go. Sorry.'

The Yasi flood event went on for a long time. Day after day after day I was checking river heights. The town was actually cut off for weeks. First it was cut off by local rain, then the run-off from all over Western Queensland kept the river levels high for quite a while after.

At times I had to wade through the floodwater to check the river height. To get accurate readings meant wading out to the flood marker, while watching out for snakes. Fortunately, I didn't see any when I was walking out to read the river heights, but there were plenty on the edge of the road, near the water.

Not surprisingly when the water comes up, all kinds of creatures retreat to dry land, including the snakes. When Birdsville becomes an island, you get to share it with the deadliest reptiles in the world, plus rats, mice, lizards, you name it. After the floods, vegetation becomes abundant and you can bank on a mouse or rat plague, which helps the population of snakes to flourish. Then there are the insects: flies, beetles, grasshoppers and, worst of all, sandflies. Their bite is worse than a mosquito and can itch for days after. The fishing is great though. Just ask the thousands of pelicans who follow the floods down. As the waters recede and the billabongs dry out, it's standing-room only around the edges. The pelicans all wait for an easy meal as the fish run out of the deep water that lets them escape to safety.

It was more than a month later, with the roads starting to open again, that I had to do a rescue 150 kilometres east of Birdsville. It was a German fella in a camper. How he got caught was, he was driving and it started raining, so he stopped. And it just kept raining. Raining and raining.

He didn't have a satphone or GPS but I knew he was there because I came across him on 3 March 2011. I was coming back from Betoota, while doing a regular patrol, and he'd pulled off the road. I said, 'Mate, you gotta get out of here. It's pourin' rain, you know. The road is going to close.'

He said he had plenty of food and plenty of water. He was always going to have plenty of water.

I said, 'No mate, you've gotta get going. Come on, let's go.'

And he refused. After trying to convince him for half an hour

I said, 'Oh well, you can stay here then. I'm going, otherwise you'll put me in jeopardy.'

I knew the road, and it was really torrential rain, so I said, 'I'm going.'

If I hadn't come across him then, I wouldn't have known he was missing.

I think he thought he'd only need to stay there one or two weeks. But he'd already been there four or five days when we decided to get him out.

First, I had to find him. The rain had closed the roads, so on 6 March 2011 we put a helicopter up. He wasn't where I thought he was. So on 8 March 2011 the Diamantina Council used their helicopter, which was doing flood relief. I tracked him down probably 10 kilometres west of Betoota.

When we landed the helicopter, on high ground nearby, we had to walk through floodwater to get to him. Then he wanted to carry all his gear onto the helicopter.

I said, 'No, just bring an overnight bag. Don't worry about the food. And get on.'

He wasn't that bright, old Hans, but he's thinking the water would go down and he'd be able to drive out. It was over a month before he could go out and get that vehicle. There's no way he had enough food for a month.

We pulled him out just on sundown and brought him back to Birdsville. I wish I'd made him come when I first came across him. I tried my best but he wouldn't budge. So what do you do? All I could do was monitor him and go through my usual list of enquires, in case he'd managed to continue on his travels.

Who do I contact for something like that? Everyone who may come across a traveller. So every roadhouse, every caravan park, every police station, every fuel stop, every outback property, oil rig and council depot. I contact everyone I can in an area larger than my jurisdiction, larger than Victoria. From Jundah in the east to Coober Pedy in the west, from Boulia in the north to south of Marree. Everywhere. I spread the net really wide hoping he'd turn up in one of those places.

People in the outback are really good. They take details. In a city they probably wouldn't, and if they did, they'd probably forget about it. In the outback, people are more helpful if you're looking for someone because they know what can happen if someone gets stuck. They know they can save an expensive search that may not be necessary.

With the town surrounded by water, in April 2011, I went on a boat patrol to Roseberth Station. What prompted the trip was a delivery of medical supplies but they'd also been isolated for a long time so I wanted to just have a yarn to them and give them a bit of company.

Gus from the pub was driving the SES flood boat. It probably takes the best part of forty minutes to get out to Roseberth. You're going up the river and you land at the base of that hill there, and walk up to the homestead.

Gus is pretty handy. He works as a barman but everyone in Birdsville has a few jobs. He's SES, fire brigade captain, and he came out in the helicopter when we were looking for that German fella.

Sandra came with us, for a run out of town. We had a bit of cake with the Mortons, had a cup of tea, dropped off the medical supplies and came back to Birdsville.

———

The following month, May 2011, the roads to Birdsville were open and the tourism season was starting to ramp up. Unfortunately, there was still no direct access to Big Red. A huge flood had gone down west of the town. People still had to detour right down to the South Australian border, 10 or 12 kilometres down, then drive along the fence line, then back over a sand dune, then come up the western side of Big Red. That was the only way you could get to Big Red.

I had scouted the bypass with Don, put the track in with him. We got it approved by Nell and David, because it's over one of their properties, Adria Downs. That was done so tourists could get to Big Red, and we were able to get there as well, if we needed to get out there. It more than doubled the distance to Big Red, from about 35 kilometres to around 70 kilometres. It was also a lot rougher track.

The lake in front of Big Red stayed there for two or three years. Doing the weather, including the evaporation tank, has given me some idea of how much evaporation there can be in the hot desert sun. For an ephemeral lake to stay for three years means there was a huge amount of water there to begin with. The evaporation rate in Birdsville is one of the highest in the country (around 3 metres per year).

On 16 May 2011, the police service sent me on a four-wheel drive course for four days. You'd think it was a little late for that – I'd been four-wheel driving constantly on either sandhills or flooded roads for the last five years, and had been in some epic rescues that tested the four-wheel driving skills of everyone involved.

Nevertheless, everyone had to be trained in four-wheel driving, so I went up to do the course in Mount Isa. You can always pick up something, even if you've got heaps of four-wheel driving experience. The course is not just four-wheel driving. It's using winches, recovery gear and so on. So that was quite handy. I got a bit out of it.

Things come up, things change. It's like firing a firearm. In the police force you've got to do it twice a year to keep your skills up. And the people teaching the course might have learned a few things from me. Yeah, I taught them a few things. (Laughter)

Not long after, in May 2011 a couple staying in a cabin at the Birdsville Caravan Park did a tour to Big Red to take in the sunset. They had expensive camera equipment. They returned to Birdsville and, because it was getting late, the manager of the caravan park said he'd drop them off at the Birdsville Hotel for dinner and place their camera gear in their room. They told him they were staying in Cabin 1. Unfortunately, they were staying in Cabin 5. They were in Cabin 1 the previous evening, at a different place. Another couple was staying in Cabin 1 and they weren't present when the camera gear was dropped off.

Sometimes a small change or mistake can start a chain of events that can escalate with monumental consequences.

The first couple returned to Cabin 5 after a good night at the Birdsville Hotel and retired for the night. In the morning, they noticed their camera equipment wasn't there and spoke to the manager. That's when the mistake was realised.

The couple staying in Cabin 1 had already departed. The camera equipment was no longer in Cabin 1. It hadn't been handed in to the caravan park office. The matter was reported to me.

As an outback cop, you're able to dedicate a large amount of time to an investigation, as in all day or even all week. (Laughter) Police in urban areas don't have that luxury. With a stealing complaint, a report is usually just taken and investigated at a later time.

I did an immediate patrol trying to locate this second couple, took statements and then put the net up. As in, I contacted neighbouring police stations at Marree, Bedourie and Windorah. The second couple were towing a caravan and had only stayed in the cabin for a bit more space and comfort, so I knew they wouldn't be going over the desert. I had all areas covered. All police at these stations were on the lookout. They also alerted the service stations, caravan parks, hotels, information centres and general stores in their area.

In the afternoon, the second couple were located by Sergeant Jim Beck of Jundah Police, who was also looking after Windorah. Jim is a tenacious police officer. You would want him investigating a crime if you're the victim but not if you're the offender. The couple denied seeing or taking the camera gear and accompanied Jim back to the station 'to help police with their enquiries'. That's police speak for, *We have the offender(s), we now just have to prove it.*

Jim rang me and I said, 'Give 'em an out. Say to them perhaps one of you picked the gear up by mistake in the rush to leave, thinking it was the property of the other person.'

Sometimes it's better just to get the gear back for the victims with all their precious photos of their travels. Offenders will sometimes cooperate if they know they won't be charged. They both continued to deny the offence so Jim told them he was going to search their caravan.

The male said, 'Not unless you have a search warrant.'

A little knowledge is dangerous. In Queensland, police have the power to conduct an emergent search if they suspect stolen property or drugs are in a particular place and the evidence would be lost if the search was delayed while they obtained a search warrant. Police then have to make application as soon as practicable after the search for a magistrate to authorise the search.

Caravan searched. Guess what? Stolen camera gear located in caravan. Now there were no more deals available. The male person admitted stealing said gear. Then the nasty things that happen when you're charged by police started: fingerprints, mug shot, DNA sample, charge sheet, court appearance, paying for a lawyer to represent you, the expense of returning to outback Queensland for court, fronting the beak and explaining why you stole someone else's property, name and court result in local press, hopefully not national press but that's possible, explaining to family and friends and, worst of all, a criminal record. All for camera gear they probably wouldn't use. The photos in this book and photos of rescues that were in major newspapers and news reports were mostly taken with a cheap $150 camera or camera phone. Both people were charged but only the male, who admitted stealing the gear, was prosecuted.

If expensive gear suddenly appears before you, don't think a kind benefactor has decided you need better camera equipment. The world isn't like that. Hand it in to police. It will save you a lot of grief. Also, if no-one claims it in three months, it's yours legally.

Two months later, fame beckoned. In mid-July 2011 the BBC came to Birdsville to make a documentary on the dust storm in 2009.

John White was there, the fella who rolled his vehicle out at Poeppels Corner. He and I went out for a day of filming with the BBC crew.

They said, 'Right, drive over the sandhill . . . Drive over a bit faster . . . Drive over looking concerned . . . Get out and have a look, like you're looking for someone.'

After doing that for a day the doco came out and I ended up on the cutting-room floor. (Laughter) So that was my media appearance for the BBC. John White is in it, but I didn't make it.

CHAPTER 9

DANCES WITH DINGOES

Every year, in the lead-up to the Birdsville Races the town gets steadily busier. In 2011, it was no different. If anything, it was busier than ever.

On 27 August I got called down to the town common. A dog belonging to someone camped there had bitten a passer-by.

I went down and found the dog's owner, who was camped just past the billabong with 'the accused'. I had a talk with him then went back to the station and did some checks on his vehicle. The person who owned the vehicle came up with a huge history for drugs.

I'd also received some other information about this guy so I did a search and found sticks of marijuana and drug paraphernalia. He was charged, fronted court and was given a reasonable fine for his trouble.

The dog gave him away. Drug dealers have big barking dogs for protection against being robbed but the dog also drew attention from police. Especially after it bit someone. The trouble was, I went down and saw him. Then I received certain information, so I went back. So maybe there were more drugs there than what I found. They may have been hidden.

A few days later, there was a report of a bad motorcycle accident up near Bedourie, on the Bedourie–Windorah Road, 200 kilometres north of Birdsville, involving a woman and her partner. The woman had a broken nose, a broken sternum, a collapsed lung and was briefly unconscious. The passenger on the bike was also injured.

She and her husband were actually a couple of ambulance officers. They were on the same bike and there was real concern for both of them. I didn't go out for that accident. Police from Mount Isa and the Traffic Branch who were down for the races went out because they were worried about it being a fatal accident, or a serious accident. I stayed in Birdsville and the police officer helping me went up with a Traffic Branch car. The injured were evacuated from Bedourie.

The accident wasn't so much about speed or a difficult corner, it was just that they were trying to keep the bike upright in deep gravel on an unsealed road. The tyre marks for 100 metres before the bike crashed showed it was all over the road, and then it went in, and over she went. It was a big heavy BMW. You get into the death dance, the old devil dance, problems, ay.

You see that quite often out here, especially with older riders. They watch a movie, old people riding across America, and they think, I'll do that. Then they ride across the Simpson Desert. But they're not as young as they used to be, they haven't got the experience on desert roads, and they write a cheque their body can't cash. A lot haven't ridden bikes for ages, they carry too much gear, and you often find out later that they fell off three or four times before the bad one. And there's always going to be a bad one. Almost always, they needed to be doing something differently, like, slow down and don't have as much gear on the bike.

Compared to the lead-up to the 2011 races, the actual event went off without any major problems. Then, after the races, more dramas. On 5 September, four older people from Western Australia came to the police station and reported a motorcycle rider missing. They said they saw him on the Warburton Track and gave him water and fuel. He seemed 'disorientated' but stated that he was heading south to go to the Birdsville Track.

The Warburton Track to the Birdsville Track had been closed by floods for over two years. The track was under the Warburton Creek. No-one had been down there for two-and-a-half years and the motorcycle rider was told that three times.

He said, 'Nah, I'll go down.'

I think he told this group he was going to swim across or some crap.

They came in and they said, 'Has he reported here? He said he was going to report when he got here.'

I said, 'No.'

They said, 'Maybe he reported to other police who were here for the races.'

I said, 'No, it's really strongly emphasised: if anyone reports, I'm to be notified. So he hasn't come here. Highly unlikely.'

The motorcycle rider actually wrote his name in their diary and he wrote, on September 2, that he expected to get to the

Birdsville Track the following day. It was now September 5 and there was no sign of him. So we knew he was out in the desert.

He hadn't used his mobile phone. It hadn't been activated for some time. He had limited fuel. I think they'd given him five litres. So I commenced a major investigation to locate this bloke.

I contacted South Australian Police, because the Warburton Track is in South Australia. I spoke to this prick at Port Augusta – that's another way of describing a fellow officer (laughter) – and he wasn't interested at all. He started getting cranky with me and saying, 'Oh, you know, you need to get his name, details.'

I said, 'Mate, I know all that stuff. You know, I've been doin' this for years. I'm search and rescue trained. Co-ordinator.'

I said, 'He's out in the desert.'

And he said, 'Oh well, we've got to make enquiries'.

So I gave him details. And I'm talking to my inspector in Mount Isa and he said, 'What they doin'?'

I said, 'Oh, they're making enquiries.'

He said, 'Where?'

I said, 'Oh, they're doin' a doorknock with his neighbours, triangulating his mobile phone, and all this shit.'

He said, 'You're joking?'

I said, 'Oh, I know.'

Anyway, that was on 5 September. I did all those enquiries where you ring everyone up. Spread the net wide. No-one had seen hide nor hair of him and I knew why: he was somewhere down the Warburton Track. It was completely flooded. He had no way of getting across. We're talking kilometres of water. So he couldn't swim across. It's not a line on the map, just a little blue line you swim across. And he was on a big bike. So it went to the fifth, the sixth, and his father is ringing me saying, 'What's goin' on?'

I said, 'Look, South Australian Police have got carriage of it. I've done a missing person report. He's in South Australia.'

He said, 'Nothing's happening.'

I said, 'I know. Look, between you and me, if you don't make a noise about it, you're going to lose your son. He'll die. You're losing that window. It's closing. He's going to run out of food. He's going to run out of water. He's going to get completely lost. You have to start making a lot of noise about it.'

He said, 'How do I do that?'

I said, 'Well, I'd be ringin' the media for a start. If you want to get coppers moving, you ring the media.'

On 6 September it's been four days since he was last seen, and they're doing doorknocks on the neighbours in the middle of Adelaide.

Then this inspector from South Australia rings me. He says, 'This fuckin' dickhead, his father's gone to the media.'

And it went from a sergeant looking after it to an inspector. An assistant commissioner was involved. It went up high.

He said, 'This fuckin' dickhead, I've got people ringin' me, assistant commissioner's annoying the shit out of me, you know.'

I said, 'Oh, that's terrible.' (Laughter)

He said, 'Where'd he get the idea to go to the media?'

I said, 'Dunno.' (Laughter)

He says, 'We've got to find this bloke.'

And we came to an agreement. He said, 'How about if we put a plane up and you come out and do a ground search, and come from the top end?'

I said, 'Yeah, we'll do that.'

Barnesy and me had already had a talk about what was happening. We said, 'We've got to do something about this, or this bloke's going to die. He's going to die for sure because no-one's going down. No-one will be travelling down there. The road's closed.'

So Barnesy and me left about four in the morning on 7 September. We went out almost to Poeppels, then travelled down the Warburton Track.

We knew he wasn't going to die of thirst. The road was flooded. It was September, so he probably wasn't going to die from heat stress. However, if he ran out of fuel and tried to walk out, he'd get lost. And trying to find someone from the air if they're on foot is almost impossible. If they're lying in the shade of a tree, you'll never see them. If he tried to swim, he'd drown. If he just sits there, he'll eventually starve. On a bike, he'll have limited food anyway. This bloke had no EPIRB, no satphone, no radio, nothing.

So we went down there. Then Barnesy radioed that he'd found a motorbike track, and no other tracks. Barnesy travels a lot quicker than me, in his ute. He's a competitive desert rally driver, drives in the Finke Rally and stuff like that. So I was probably an hour behind him and I thought, What's the point of me going down there? I'll wait for him to come back.

It was really hard going, and wet, and by this time it was probably 11.30 in the morning. So I had a camp, and 20 minutes later Barnesy came up on the radio saying he'd found him, at a billabong full of fresh water. Just as the plane from South Australia flew over, Barnesy found him.

He was still with his motorbike. Barnesy put the bike on his ute and came back to where I was, which was probably halfway down the Warburton Track.

I spoke to the bloke and said, 'Why did you go down there?'

He said he was going to leave his bike, swim across the river, then get a lift into Birdsville, which was never gonna happen. You're talking kilometres of slush and mud before you get to the river. That would be flowing, kilometres wide, and you've still got 10 kilometres to the road, from the river. That's if you know where the road is, haven't been swept far downstream, and walked in a straight line to it.

He said he was drinking his own piss.

I said, 'What about all the water down there?'

He didn't really have an answer for that. He said he was swimming in a billabong and this dingo came down and swam next to him.

I said, 'Yeah, I've seen *Dancing With Wolves*, too. That's a good movie.'

Then he said this pink iridescent snake came up next to him, and I found out from Don that there're no pink iridescent snakes in the desert. Probably none in Australia, probably none in the world. (*Cryptophis incredibilis*, also called the pink snake, is considered rare and only found on islands in the Torres Strait, in particular Prince Of Wales Island.)

My view is that he was either seeking media attention or attention from his wife, who he'd just separated from. I travelled back to Birdsville with him because I think Barnesy was sick of him by that stage. Actually, Barnesy said, 'Why don't you go in the police car?'

I thought, Oh thanks, Barnesy. I knew then. So we went back and he stayed in the barracks, too.

Sandra said to him, 'Oh, I'll get you a drink of water.'

He said, 'Well, I prefer bottled water.'

So Sandra gave him bottled water. We keep some in the fridge.

This is someone who's been drinking his own piss for three or four days.

Another thing is, he went down to see Barnesy and the bike was there and Barnesy said, 'The bill's $3500.'

That's for Barnesy to go out and get him and come back.

He says, 'I can give you $200. That's all I've got. If I win Lotto on Saturday, I'll give you the rest.'

Barnesy rang me, and I rang his father, and said, 'Look, it was Barnesy who said we've gotta go get him. He's rescued him, he's gotten up at four in the morning, didn't get back till probably six that night.'

His father said, 'It's alright, I'll fix it up.'

He rang up and paid by credit card. Barnesy rang me back and said, 'That worked.'

The fella stayed in the barracks and then a day or two later he rode down the Birdsville Track.

I don't think he'd been drinking his own piss. I think he had food. He was wondering if the media had been contacted. I said, 'No, I certainly didn't contact them.'

He ended up riding off and I heard he got back with his wife. So maybe it worked out for him. Probably a few weeks later she'd have worked out he was still an idiot. We'll never know.

That was a rescue where I think he went missing on purpose, but he still could have died. It was lucky for him that Barnesy and I were pushing to get things happening. And if you have carriage of that matter, and he ends up dying because South Australian Police were following standard procedure, you don't want that on your conscience. If you knew he was out there, you knew he was alive, and then a week later he died, you'd know you could have gone out and got him.

I sent a report on the incident to Port Augusta Police on 19 September. It concluded:

> [The motorbike rider] does not seem to appreciate the extensive and expensive search undertaken by South Australian and Queensland Police. He did the exact opposite of what a person should do and carry when travelling through the desert.
>
> Why a person would travel by himself with insufficient fuel, water, food, no communication equipment of any kind, not notify anyone of his travel plans and dates through the Simpson Desert and travel down a closed road (closed for two years) beggars belief.

There were more dramas on 14 September 2011 and beyond. I arrested a bloke who had blown into town during the races. He had false plates on his car. His car was unregistered, so he'd stolen plates and put them on his car. He was hoping the plates would help him travel under the radar. It turned out he was wanted on a warrant for drink-driving plus he had traffic offences. He'd been disqualified from driving, and he was uninsured. There may have been criminal charges as well.

This guy had been married to a woman from a very wealthy family. He was a pilot. He used to wear the white pants, the boots, the tweed jacket. Then, according to rumour, he was caught with a nanny and that was the end of him. He went from being extremely wealthy to being extremely broke. He was an alcoholic and he used to drink himself unconscious. He ended up living out of his car and bludging meals and accommodation off people.

He got arrested and taken to Mount Isa. Then he was released on probation. He came back to Bedourie. He was there a week or two and committed more offences there: running through gates of properties, stealing stuff from a council depot, drink-driving, false plates, all that stuff.

On 16 September 2011 this individual sent a death threat. He sent this bloke a text saying, 'You're fuckin' dead.' Something like that. He sent it from his phone. Clearly traceable.

What happened was, he'd befriended this bloke and stayed with him during the races. He's one of those people who latches onto someone, and this bloke got sick of him and had to get the coppers who were at the races to come along and throw him out. The police who did that didn't check him on the computer and find out about him but this guy didn't know that. He thought that this bloke involving the police was the thing that led to him being discovered, which was always going to happen. He thought this bloke had dobbed him, but he hadn't. That was someone else. (Laughter)

In September 2011 National Parks reopened Munga-Thirri (Simpson Desert) National Park, which had been closed by floods for months and months. Up until then, rain had been coming from all directions. Unfortunately, all that rain meant that there was masses of vegetation. In late September, the desert caught fire. Soon it was burning on a 90-kilometre front. So the desert went from being closed for flood to closed for fire within the space of about a month. It was a real Dorothea Mackellar moment, droughts and flooding rains.

There had been a bike rally and footrace across the desert planned for September, and that was cancelled. They had it all planned, then they said no, because of the fire. A few months earlier, runners in an ultra-marathon had been badly badly burnt in a bushfire. We didn't want a repeat of that. And rightly so, too. If you look at those girls, horrific injuries. Now, for any race, organisers have to consider the fire risk. That's mandatory throughout Australia.

During that time, two vehicles popped up that we were concerned about. They were near the outbreak, near the Hay River, and we were having to monitor them.

What can you do for them? Try and get them to a place where there's no fuel for the fire, or limited fuel. Or if they couldn't get to somewhere safe, get them to at least clear any fuel away from their camp. Sand won't burn, rocks won't burn, a saltpan won't burn. If they could get somewhere safe, they could just wait the fire out. Once the desert has burned, you're right.

In a situation like that, if you can, stay with your car, because that's your way out. That's your transport. And communication, too.

Fortunately, everyone got through that safely and after a couple of weeks, when the fires had burned out, the desert reopened.

A week before Christmas 2011 I got called out to a vehicle that was bogged near Big Red. It was bogged between Big Red and Little Red. They couldn't go any further and set off an EPIRB. Robbie and I went out and it was all wet between Nemesis Dune (the name you and I have for the big dune right after Big Red, that can be harder to get over) and Big Red.

There might be a point where you say, 'Look, you really should be able to deal with this.' However, a lot of travellers are old, or older, and they get tired and knocked up. As I've often said, you're better to go to a rescue early, or they're better to set off the EPIRB early, if they can't go any further and they think they're in a bad position. If they wait a couple of days they can get sick, or hurt, or try and walk or something. I'd rather they set it off early and we get out there, pull them out and let them get on their way.

That's what we did.

Grey nomads are a much-maligned group of travellers but I've got a lot of time for them. They're regularly accused of not spending a cracker in country towns and stealing toilet paper and soap from outback fuel stops, caravan parks, visitor centres and other places. There are stories of them stocking up with biscuits, chocolates, tea and coffee at free driver-reviver sites. I've heard of a woman going around with a cordless drill so she can steal toilet paper from the dispensers. She must have a lot of it as I have heard this story from heaps of locations in outback Australia. An urban myth, no doubt.

My view is the vast majority of grey nomads are decent Australians enjoying the retirement years they worked so hard for.

In almost a decade at Birdsville I could count the number of calls for service from grey nomads on one hand. They're usually very savvy. They watch the sun go down while enjoying a drink and nibblies, instead of dodging kangaroos, stock, wild pigs, emus and what have you. They're properly prepared and their vehicles are invariably modern and in good condition. They're honest, polite and always make enquiries regarding road conditions and places to go. They also do their bit for road safety by slowing the traffic down. (Laughter)

Sometimes, they're too well prepared. They come into the police station with their itinerary, properly set out with bold headings, different fonts and highlight colours. I tell them to throw it in the bin and say, 'If you like a place, stay. If you don't, move on.' They've lived their lives to schedules. Why do it in your retirement?

That said, outback Australia also needs younger people. And there's plenty of opportunity for them out here as well. There's zero unemployment in Birdsville and country towns nearby. Most Australians don't want to live in outback communities but they're missing out on great experiences and excellent career opportunities. If you live in the western suburbs of Sydney, Melbourne or any other high youth unemployment areas around the country, do yourself a favour, reboot your life and move.

I remember a young male came to Birdsville, a couch hopper. He'd stay at someone's house for a week or two, sleeping on their couch until he out wore his welcome, and then move to someone's else's place. At Birdsville he got a job with a local contractor, Nigel Gilby. Nigel is like everyone's favourite uncle. Soon this bloke was making good money and learning new skills. My daughter Lauren, who was doing QGAP at the time, helped him get a Medicare card, tax file number and other essential documents we all need to survive in a modern world.

After a few weeks he told me he was leaving. He felt isolated. I tried to talk him out of it, as did Nigel. He left and I found out later he got into trouble with the law. What a waste. He missed out on a golden opportunity to get established, get new skills, money in the bank and so on.

Another time, a French backpacker travelled to Birdsville from Innamincka when the road was closed. Locals told me he then wanted to travel across the desert. It was January and the desert was closed as well. I went and saw him, told him he wasn't crossing the desert and then got him a job with Nigel Gilby.

He loved Birdsville so much he worked for Nigel for six months, later left Australia, went back to France and has now returned to work with Nigel. Nigel is sponsoring his citizenship application.

Most people who move to the outback make really good friends for life and love the experience. Like you, Evan, and Michelle. You hear of women crying as they move to an outback town and then crying when they leave. Kids can ride their bikes and walk around town like we used to in the sixties. All the locals look out for them and it's so much safer from a crime perspective.

Older Australians, if they're not ready to retire, find it easier to get back into the work force in the outback. Brian Mooney and his partner Barb retired when Brian turned 65. After a year, he was sick of retirement. Both got jobs with the Diamantina Council: Brian as Tourism Officer and Barb in the information centre. They had a council-supplied house and car and travelled by plane regularly to events around the country representing the council at travel shows, tourism awards and so on.

When it comes to staying in touch, most country towns now have mobile phone coverage and the internet speed is improving all the time, so you can keep in touch regularly with family and friends. So if you're looking for a start in life, for something different, or for a great way to end your career (which is what I did), the outback has plenty of opportunity. Of course, you need to do your research (internet, outback council websites, cattle station websites) before you set off, so you don't end up in a broken-down mining town, but there are still plenty of places where there are more jobs than people.

***

Another quick response was needed on 18 January 2012. The wife of Bedourie cop, Tim Farran, reported him missing. He was driving up the Birdsville Track in his own car with his three young children, all under the age of five. It was night when his wife rang, and she was worried that he'd rolled the car, he was trapped in the car, and the kids had wandered off.

I said, 'Oh, that probably hasn't happened.'

Nevertheless, it was dark, he was overdue, he hadn't been in contact, it's the middle of summer, very high temperatures. So we've got to find Timmy.

I rang Mungerannie, and he'd left Mungerannie, but he hadn't arrived in Birdsville and he should have by then. So I was starting to think something had happened. He'd broken down or something.

I contacted Clifton Hills and fortunately someone from Clifton Hills had been at Mungerannie. They'd driven from Mungerannie to Clifton Hills and didn't come across him. That's about 120 kilometres. So we knew he was between Birdsville and Clifton Hills, which is 200 kilometres.

I said to the inspector, 'I'll go for a drive.'

This is late in the evening. I said, 'He's either 20 kilometres down the road or he's 190 kilometres down the road.'

Sure enough, there he was at 160 kilometres down the road.

Two flat tyres.

He was well prepared. He had water, he had a tent, the kids were in the tent. He was just going to wait until someone came along.

So I put Tim, the kids and the flat tyres in the car, and left his car there. We came back to Birdsville and he stayed in the barracks. In the morning, Sandra looked after the kids. Tim and I got the tyres fixed, went down and put the tyres on the car. He drove back and I followed him.

Both tyres went almost at the same time. The heat, the rocks. It was ferociously hot, especially for young children. They saw a snake come through their camp, too. So they had that problem as well. Out there, it's not going to be a python. It's going to be something extremely venomous. I think it was a taipan, which is the most venomous snake on the planet.

Tim was experienced enough to know what to do. He had the tent set up under a tree. It wasn't a very big tree but he had a bit of extra shade. He'd driven on the flat tyres until he found a bit of a shady spot. The tyres were wrecked anyway. Then he set up camp. He had plenty of water, he had a bit of food for the kids and was just going to stay the night until someone came along the next day.

During a break in the rain, on 10 April 2012, I escorted the first woman to run across the Simpson Desert, Jane Trumper, into town.

For me, it was sort of a community assist. Police car, the lights flashing to make it look sort of a bit showy. Or ceremonial. They were keen for that to happen and I said, 'Yeah'. She got a police escort, even though she could have run into town without it.

She had a beer at the pub and got me to sign a form saying she was the first woman to run across the desert. She reckons she was the first. She was a nice girl.

People appreciate it when you do something like that. It's a bit of community policing. Help 'em out. Why not? Not much else to do in Birdsville at that time of year.

Mind you, when I got back to the station, there was a domestic violence incident unfolding in town. I got back, then I had to go out and do a DV where a bloke threatened to kill himself. That's the last thing you want to do after doing something positive.

The rain had returned by the beginning of June 2012. On 1 June we had three stranded groups on the Birdsville Track: one out of fuel, one waiting for road conditions to improve and one with a burnt-out clutch. They were all coming up the track and it was pouring with rain.

I found out about them because two old people came to Birdsville and they said, 'There's people stuck down the track.'

This was two old women. Everyone else had trouble but they made it up!

Anyway, off I went. Down past Pandie Pandie I came across a bloke on a motorbike who'd had enough of battling through mud. Then there was a car with a burnt-out clutch, then someone who ran out of fuel.

The person who ran out of fuel was towing a big caravan and he had a gauge on his car that told him his fuel consumption. The road was so boggy and the wheels were digging in so much that his four-wheel drive was using a litre of fuel a kilometre. So he was never going to make it the few hundred kilometres to Birdsville.

I said to them, 'Look, we've got to get out of here.'

The rain was really heavy.

I ended up with three in the front, five in the back seat, and a couple in the very back. We hightailed it back to Birdsville. The vehicles stayed where they were for two or three days. We couldn't get back to them until it dried out enough.

When I went back, I took down two jerry cans. The person with the caravan unhooked it and drove his car back to Birdsville to get more fuel, then went back for the caravan.

It was a couple of days later, while I was playing tennis with David, Nell and Sandra, that I got a call on my phone.

This bloke said, 'I'm 8 miles out of Birdsville and my motor's stopped.'

I said, 'No worries, we'll get someone to take you out some fuel.'

Trouble was, he was also several thousand feet above the ground, in an aeroplane, with two passengers onboard. He was trying to glide the rest of the way to the runway but didn't think he'd make it.

So it was all hands on deck again. I got hold of Gus, who drives the fire truck, and other volunteers. They'd landed before we got the rescue underway. So we were hoping they were still alive.

The bloke in the plane told me he was trying to land on the western end of the airstrip, the unmade airstrip. We went down there and they weren't there. No sign of them. We were hunting around, then we found out they'd landed short of the northern airstrip. They'd got to the unmade part prior to the airstrip starting. It was just dirt.

They did a bellyflop. Wrecked the plane. It was badly damaged, bouncing over rocks and through mud. The propeller was bent. The undercarriage was damaged from hitting rocks. Fortunately, they got out in one piece. They were in very soft, wet conditions. The mud pulled it up.

I said to the pilot and the passengers, 'What happened?'

They said, 'We were flying along and the engine started spluttering and suddenly just stopped.'

I said to the pilot, 'Did you run out of fuel, mate?'

And he goes, 'Nah, no.'

So the pilot went off to get checked by the nurse and I opened up the fuel tank in the wing.

Bone dry.

He flew from Alice Springs. He was only 3 kilometres short.

No-one was injured. I took photos of the plane. They ended up pulling the plane to little bits and taking it away to work out what they were going to do with it.

A month later, on 5 July 2012, an 80-year-old woman started having chest pains 60 kilometres west of Birdsville. She'd gone out there to scatter her husband's ashes in Eyre Creek, or on Eyre Creek, because (believe it or not) it was dry. Her husband was another person who loved the desert. They used to go across the desert all the time and that was why they were scattering his ashes there.

The people with her activated an EPIRB and we got the call that she'd had a heart attack so I went out there. The ambulance also went out with the nurse, Sharon. An 80-year-old with chest pains makes you move more quickly.

Then we couldn't get the ambulance over Nemesis Dune, so I put Sharon in the police car with all her gear, resuscitation unit and all that, and we went ahead. I can travel a lot faster than the ambulance, which has a lot of gear and is top heavy. While I was driving, I was trying to organise help to get the ambulance to us.

Normally the ambulance can get over Nemesis but I think the sand was really soft. I really struggled to get over it in the police car. I knew the ambulance would have trouble. The sand can be a lot softer depending on the weather conditions. We could have hooked up the ambulance and pulled it over but it was more important to get to the patient with the nurse.

I called some guys on Big Red, the hot dogs up there (testosterone-fuelled males in flash four-wheel drives just going up and down Big Red), to help get the ambulance across Nemesis, which they did. Then they escorted the ambulance to Eyre Creek. We were probably out there twenty minutes before the ambulance turned up. Even that amount of time can make a lot of difference.

The woman was in a bad way. Her friends were right about her having a heart attack. We gave her first aid, oxygen and everything else. The ambulance arrived, we put her in and conveyed her back to Birdsville, then onto the Flying Doctor. So that was a good rescue. She survived.

Later in July 2012 there was a big celebration in Birdsville for the fifty-year anniversary of the first Nissan vehicle crossing the Simpson Desert. It was a big event. The children of the first person to drive across, geologist Reg Spriggs, were there. They'd done the original trip with him when he was exploring for oil.

So all the Nissans were there. They had the latest Nissan released in the country. There was a concert at the racecourse with James Reyne and Daryl Braithwaite. It was a big event and it all went well. All the locals were invited to the concert. Everyone went. Everyone except the Land Cruiser people. They weren't invited. They weren't welcome. (Laughter)

On 4 August 2012, I got a call that a motorbike rider west of Poeppels Corner had caught his foot in a tree root and broken his leg. His foot was twisted entirely around. It was a horrifically broken leg. He was in extreme pain. We needed to get to him as soon as we could so he could be given some pain relief.

We left at eight-thirty at night. Sam Barnes, Barnesy's son, was driving the ambulance. I was by myself in the police car. We were in satphone contact with the rider's support crew. They had him on the back of a ute, on a mattress, trying to get him closer to help, as in, pain relief.

We said, 'Just take your time. And drive slowly.'

They were 30 kilometres west of Poeppels. Although it wasn't good for the injured rider to be driven over the sandhills, it made sense for them to drive to cut down the distance between him and us.

I said, 'Just drive to the turn-off, the salt lake east of Poeppels, where you turn right to go on to Birdsville. We'll meet you there.'

We drove the 160 kilometres from Birdsville and they still hadn't reached the turn-off when we got there. It was after two in the morning. They said on the phone that they weren't far away. By then, we were pretty tired, so we had a camp there while we waited for them to arrive.

They arrived soon after and the patient was treated by the nurse.

I said to the bloke, 'Get as much morphine into you as you can because it's going to be a long, slow trip back to Birdsville. When the pain gets bad, just ask for more morphine. Don't worry about it. Just get it into you, mate.'

His leg was badly broken. Just twisted around. He was in a lot of pain. Heaps of pain.

Normally, you wouldn't drive through the desert at night if you didn't have to. However, this bloke was in excruciating pain and his mates were so happy when they knew that we were com-ing out, that help was on the way. There was talk of waiting for a helicopter in the morning, but what happens if the helicopter breaks down or the weather closes in? Then you're back to square one. So we decided to go out there and meet him. A lot of times that's what people want to hear; that someone cares about them and they're coming out to meet them.

We got to him and were able to administer morphine at about two-thirty in the morning. If he had to wait for a helicopter, it wouldn't have been until daylight before it took off from wherever it was, flew to Birdsville, then flew out there. You're looking at probably another seven hours.

When you're in pain, with a badly broken, twisted leg, that extra seven hours is going to be absolutely terrible.

We got back to Birdsville about 8.30 a.m. The Flying Doctor was waiting to take the rider to hospital.

On the way back I had to stop for a sleep because the sun was coming up and I was incredibly tired. I stopped and had a powernap for about half an hour. Just to revive. Get that sleep out of your eyes. Then I got going.

It was fairly exhausting, that rescue. You do a full day's work. Then, at 8.30 at night, you go for an eight-hour drive in the desert. And you're concentrating the whole time as well, negotiating sand dunes.

Three days later, we had to close the desert for a camel cull by the National Parks Service. That involves clearing the desert of people, then closing the roads at each end.

Tim Farran, the Bedourie Cop, came out to help me. He was on the eastern end, with park rangers. Ranger Don Rowlands and I were on the western end, at the Queensland–Northern Territory border. We did a run through the desert, making sure nobody was there. Then we set up a roadblock on the western end.

Apparently there are more than a million wild camels in Australia, and they wanted to cull them because the population doubles every eight years. It creates a lot of pressure on the environment that isn't adapted to such large introduced species. They devour vegetation and consume water supplies that native species depend on. When the desert dries out, the camels starve in their thousands. They become so desperate that some have been known to start eating each other. Others move onto cattle stations, destroying fences as they go. Culling animals is controversial but doing nothing has an impact as well. The camel cullers kill clean. They shoot them once, then shoot them again to make sure.

This was a Queensland cull. Northern Territory was running their own program. South Australia was doing theirs. All were funded with federal government money. They shot 17 000 over on the West Australian–Northern Territory border. In the Simpson Desert there weren't that many but there are some big herds out there. They didn't shoot them all but they shot a few of them. Over the last few years, since 2009 when the culling program began, it's brought numbers down by about a third.

A week later, on 12 August 2012, I performed another novel official function: veryifing an attempt to set the record for the longest line of swags. They were all snaking back and forth in front of the pub, all the way up to the corner. I went along the rows of swags with a measuring wheel and announced that the official recording was 533.8 metres: a world record. It probably was because no-one had thought of doing it before.

That was for a charity bash. That's not regular police work but you do it all the time. You don't expect it, but you do it every other week. And if the Birdsville cop puts his stamp of approval on it, it's fact. (Laughter) I don't think that went into the Guinness Book of Records. They'd have had their own people.

Not long after that, I was told that a vehicle near Cordillo Downs had been run off the road by another vehicle. Then a gun was pointed at them.

The people in the vehicle were a film crew. They made the complaint to someone, who then told me. Apparently they had it on film as well. What better evidence could you have? The film crew filmed the person with a gun.

While I was waiting for the people to report what happened, I got onto South Australian Police. We had the name of the person, the rego number and all that. He was an unsavoury character who'd been shooting dingoes on Cordillo Downs. He was a bushy type, like Milat, or Murdoch, or the bloke who ended up shooting the copper in the Northern Territory.

Unfortunately, the film crew never reported the incident. Police in South Australia tried to chase them up but they didn't want to get involved. So, if they didn't care, we couldn't do much.

I was looking for the vehicle in case it came into Queensland, as were the neighbouring stations. Anthony Brook, the manager of Cordillo Downs, was looking for it, too, because the incident had happened on his property and he didn't want this person there. South Australian Police put out a BOLF (Be On the Lookout For) statewide. They took it very seriously.

Unfortunately, the person went to ground. He didn't stick to known tracks and disappeared. He would have known someone would report it to police. So he'd have gone to ground somewhere for a couple of weeks until the heat died down. In the end the matter just petered out to nothing.

Whatever was going on, the reality is that it could have been much worse. And it gives you cause for pause. If someone's out there doing that sort of thing, what else have they done? They should be held to account for what they do.

As it was, this bloke was shooting dingoes but he didn't have permission to shoot on Cordillo. There's no bounty for dingoes in South Australia. You get paid for them in Queensland. But you can shoot them in South Australia and hand them in in Queensland, which is why we contacted all the stations, to check if this bloke had handed in any dingo scalps.

If we could find him and charge him with even a minor offence, it meant we could have taken his firearms licence off him for a start. It means they're not a fit and proper person. And we all know how important that is. And if you get charged with an offence in Queensland you get fingerprinted, you get photographed, you give DNA. You have to have that done. If you don't, you stay in custody until you decide to have it done.

Just before the Birdsville Races, people were starting to arrive when I got a call for help finding the brother of an SAS soldier who had been killed (with two others) in a chopper crash in Afghanistan. It was a mechanical fault or something. It wasn't a result of being shot down or anything like that. We got a call from the army because the brother of one of those killed was coming to the Birdsville Races.

The brother was actually a police officer from Western Australia. The inspector rang up and he's describing him to me – height, weight, colour of eyes.

I said, 'Stop. There'll be two cars here from Western Australia. We'll find him.'

This brother was in the first WA car we found. By that stage, mobile phones had come to Birdsville, and he already knew. It was really sad. The soldier who was killed had done three tours to Afghanistan before he lost his life.

The brother came down to the police station and used the landline because, with the sudden influx of people, the mobile network was totally overloaded. You have a phone system that normally handles one hundred people. Suddenly you have 6000 people in town. People are taking photos, using Facebook, down-loading stuff and the system just shuts down. The media were saying they were getting up at three o'clock in the morning to get their stories away by four because once the sun came up, the phone system became overloaded.

The whole races I don't get a single mobile phone call. Then come Sunday morning, after everyone leaves, I get all these calls: someone's setting off fireworks, someone's drunk outside the pub, disturbance at the caravan park. Delete, delete, delete. During the races, if people want us, they come and get us or use the radio. We use UHF radio to converse with the clinic, the fire brigade, the caravan park, the pub, stuff like that. So there's a way around things. Locals can also use their landlines.

Anyway, the brother came down to the police station, and we're trying to get him a flight out. The superintendent was really good. He said, 'Look, if we can't get you out, we'll get police to take you up to Mount Isa to fly you out of there.'

Sandra helped him. She rang up because we couldn't book a flight on the computer (the internet uses the overloaded mobile network) and got him a flight out, to get to his family.

That's one of the jobs you expect when you've got 6000 people in town. You're going to have many more occasions where a relative has died or is very sick and people need to be contacted.

The other thing about it was, it's the Birdsville Races, outback Queensland. The war in Afghanistan is a long way away in every sense. Yet it still manages to be felt in a tiny country town.

At the end of September 2012 the body of Noodle the Camel was found, shot dead, at Durrie Station. Only the body was found. No head. Noodle had been decapitated.

Noodle was called Noodle because he had a taste for dried noodles. His owner, who was using him to pull a cart on a trip across Australia, just had to shake the plastic bag of noodles and Noodle would come over for a treat. He'd been popular at the races that year and lots of people got their photo taken with Noodle outside the bakery.

Noodle's owner had left him at Durrie because he had a sore leg. He left him there to get better and he was coming back to pick him up.

I was away on holiday when Noodle met his demise. The police officer relieving took the report, then when I came back I continued the investigation.

What happened was that a person or persons unknown pulled 150 metres off the road at the front of Durrie Station. There was a fenced horse paddock where Noodle was being spelled before continuing his journey across the country. It would have been obvious Noodle was a pet camel because he came over to whoever was at the fence. He also had a peg in his nose. Noodle probably wanted a scratch but his assailant shot him at point blank range instead, then souvenired his head.

The investigation into what happened was hampered by the fact that it was some time before Noodle was found. The surrounding country was very sandy and the wind had erased any tracks that might have helped identify a vehicle.

A lot of people liked poor old Noodle. The townspeople ended up putting up a reward for Noodle's killer. It was a decent reward package. Dusty from the bakery put up $1000, which he later increased to $2000. Barnesy put up fuel. The pub put up accommodation and meals for two nights. Don and I put up a tour out to Poeppels. Sandra put up a star show.

We got a few phone calls on the case but nothing ever concrete. Noodle's killer remains at large. I think Noodle's head will be on the wall of some den somewhere or on some big white hunter's bar.

Did Noodle have any enemies? Not that we know of.

The shooting got national and international attention. A French journalist came out and did a story on Noodle at the next races. I took her out to Durrie, where Noodle bit the dust. There was a lot of media attention within Australia. The ABC and radio stations in the capital cities did a story. There were lots of interviews.

I don't know how a story like that gets up and running. I think it was first on the ABC – there were a couple of good photos of Noodle outside the pub and the bakery, and it was an animal story. People were appalled at the way he was shot. It was like if you came home and your much-loved family pet was lying there with its head cut off. It was devastating for the bloke who owned Noodle.

It was an opportunistic crime but it wasn't discovered for a few days so any physical evidence was gone. It's one of my cold cases, but it's not closed. Not in my book. As I said to the journalist from France, 'Truth never lies; justice never dies.'

There were some other cold cases that predated my time in Birdsville. Two of them involved missing persons. The first dates back to 1992. On 28 October of that year, a person was seen leaving Birdsville. On 1 November, his abandoned vehicle was located 71 kilometres north of the town. There was a message that read 'Broken down, headed north'. In October 1993, at Poeppels Corner, 171 kilometres west of Birdsville and 200 kilometres from where the car was abandoned, property belonging to the missing person was located. Nothing of the person has been seen or found since.

More recently, in August 2004, a 59-year-old male was sighted in a yellow Ford Laser sedan near Big Red. Some six months later, on 2 February 2005, the vehicle was spotted from the air by David Brook, who was checking on cattle 8 to 9 kilometres from Big Red. The vehicle was partially obscured from view by branches. The number plates had been removed. Despite a search and extensive enquiries in Australia and overseas, the missing person was not located. The vehicle is still at the Birdsville Police Station.

By October 2012 the weather was starting to get very hot and dry. Once again, fire broke out in the desert. This time four travellers in vehicles near the Hay River were threatened. Their location was really remote. I didn't go out there but I spoke to them many times.

I said, 'Just keep going. When you sleep, sleep in shifts so you can keep an eye on the fire. If it's starting to come towards you, hightail it out of there.'

I was monitoring them for the whole time until they got away from the fire.

Most of the time, you couldn't imagine fire being able to be sustained in the desert. There's too little vegetation. At that time, though, the desert was just full of fuel. We'd had rain going back to 2010, which meant everything had been growing. When the vegetation dried out in the sun, the place was just a tinderbox.

Back then, sometimes you were going through scrub and it would be higher than the roof of the car. Imagine if that got going. You just need a breeze and away it goes. Now, if you go out there, virtually nothing will burn – it's all died off because it's so hot and there's been no rain.

CHAPTER 10

THE WRONG CHOICE

Melbourne Cup Day, 6 November 2012, was one of the worst days in the job out here.

The day before it had been 47 degrees. Out on Ethabuka Reserve, three staff and contractors were recovering after a bit of a party the night before. In the morning, two of them went to check a bore. Then they decided to take the long way around to get back to the homestead. They got stuck on a sand dune. There were two of them in the car. The other bloke was asleep back at the homestead.

Ethabuka is 200 kilometres north of Birdsville, then you go about 120 kilometres west. It's almost on the Northern Territory border. It's a former cattle station that's now a wildlife refuge owned by Bush Heritage Australia. So the bore water animals like kangaroos, emus and so on, that have lived in this country for thousands of years without needing a bore.

These fellas were stuck. They had a winch on the vehicle but nothing but sand to hook onto. They had no shovel so they couldn't bury a spare tyre and hook onto that. They had no Max

Trax to put under the car. They had a spare tyre but they didn't use it or know how to use it. One or the other, but they had no shovel to dig it in.

They had a litre bottle of water each.

The car was full of fuel. We checked that. So they could have sat in there all day, in the air conditioning. Imagine, in a car with dual fuel tanks, with the motor just idling, and sitting in air conditioning, how long could they have stayed there? Ages. They could have turned it off when the sun started to go down, then turned it on again when it got hot the next day. Plus you'd get a cup or a couple of cups of water out of what comes out of the air conditioner. The windscreen washer bottle was full. So there was a couple of litres there.

Unfortunately, they made the wrong choice. They thought they'd walk back to the homestead. They were about 15 kilometres from the station. They got 7 kilometres. They never got halfway. Just too hot. Stinking hot: 47 degrees. The radiant heat off the sand would have been a lot hotter, too.

We found out by their tracks that they'd sat under a tree. They sat there for a while, then started walking again. Instead of continuing towards the homestead, they walked back towards the vehicle. Just disorientated, fatigued, dehydrated.

Mo Pieterse, aged twenty-five, passed away.

By the time they were reported missing, it was all hands on deck from the local properties. They all conducted a search. As it is with a lot of these cases, the car was found before the people. If they'd stayed with the car, they would have been found. That day.

There was a UHF radio in the car, too. If they'd kept calling, eventually they'd have got someone. The other bloke was sound asleep back at the homestead. He didn't hear them call, if they had called, but I'd say they would have.

Sometimes, you're just in the wrong place at the wrong time. It was bad luck for them but it was completely preventable. If they'd had a shovel, Max Trax or water. If they stayed with the vehicle, if they had a satphone, if they had an EPIRB, if they had a sand anchor. Not all of them. Just one of them. They would have survived. They had none of them.

They had this great big fridge in the car. Bone dry. Nothing in it. They didn't have a jerry can full of water. If that was in the car, they'd have had heaps of water.

Mo's body was found by one of the people from a property nearby. His mate was found not far away, barely alive. He ended up in hospital suffering severe dehydration. Tim Farran from Bedourie was the first police officer there. I got there early the next morning. That day it was 15 degrees cooler and drizzling rain.

It hit the community very hard. Mo was well loved.

Mo's family came out some time later and I took them out to Ethabuka. I showed them where the car was bogged, where the car was found, where Mo was found, where his hat was found. He dropped his hat. I showed them all those places.

They were lovely people, South African, and they were very conservation-minded. As was Mo. It was very sad. Husband and wife, mother and father and daughter, and they were very happy with the way police conducted the search but angry with the Heritage mob, that the car wasn't properly prepared and so on. And they weren't properly trained.

Unfortunately, Mo just made a poor decision, which a lot of people make, but he paid the ultimate price. He didn't have the right equipment or the people who own that property didn't have the right equipment in the car. They should have had procedures in place where you write on the board where you're going. That accident shouldn't have happened. It happened because the vehicle wasn't properly equipped for such a remote area.

You look at the police car: two satphones, sat radio, two UHF radios, EPIRB, a well-stocked fridge, two shovels, snatch straps, a winch on the car, two sets of Max Trax, and a 20-litre jerry can of water. Also, if I go out in the desert, I have to tell Communications in Mount Isa where I'm going and when I'm due back. And if I'm not back by that time, it might be an hour or two hours go past, then they start ramping things up and start looking for me. Really quickly. And they'll do it at three in the morning. Go early, once again, particularly when it's 47 degrees.

It's like that bloke down the Warburton Track. Start things happening early because you've got that window, and it starts to close in the desert real quick because of the heat and the isolation. If you make poor decisions, when you're fatigued, when you're dehydrated, they'll come back to hit you. With other rescues I've done, people were lost for days, but at this time of year, Mo was dead within a day, within hours. Only one wrong decision can cost you.

Only a few days later, on 12 November 2012, but for the prompt action of other members of the outback community, there could have been another tragedy. Two miners from Zimbabwe, each with a two-wheel drive, got flat tyres on the Arrabury Road, 250 kilometres south-east of Birdsville. They'd been misguided by their GPS. They were going from Perth to Mount Isa, and it took them to Adelaide, to Broken Hill, to Innamincka, then up the Arrabury Road.

They had two flat tyres on one car and this fella from an oil rig in the area came across them. And they said, 'Nah, it's alright. We'll leave the car here and head off in our other car.'

The oil fella put the word out. He contacted the Birdsville pub and said, 'If they're not there by a certain time, contact the police.'

Sure enough, they never arrived at the pub. The pub contacted me and I started ramping things up. They're not in a four-wheel drive, they just had a street car. Two-wheel drive. And the local area had just had bitter experience of what can happen when things go wrong.

It wasn't as hot as when Mo died but it was in the low forties. And once it gets past 40 degrees, it's just hot.

I got onto the oil crews. They started looking for these people, and fortunately they found them the next morning. They'd got another two flat tyres on their other car. By the time someone found them, they were out of water. They were out of food. They were thinking of walking off. They were taken to the drilling rig and put in an air-conditioned office. The oil people fed them and gave them water.

They called me and Tim Farran and I went over there. Tim had already come down to help with the search. We picked them and their four flat tyres up, brought them back to Birdsville, then Barnesy went out and put the tyres on the cars and brought them back to Birdsville.

I sent the oil workers a letter commending their actions. From Neale McShane to the Manager Bardrill Ltd:

The actions of Juan Berrio, James McWaters, Adam Powell
and their crews in locating, monitoring, taking details,

advising police and later rescuing and assisting the two males
not only prevented a tragedy but also saved an extensive and
expensive search involving aircraft.

Only the previous week a fatality occurred near
Birdsville where a person had left his vehicle and tried to
walk to get help and perished.

The actions of all Bardrill employees involved in this
rescue should be commended.

There was another potentially dangerous breakdown in mid-January 2013. Two workers were reported missing on the treacherous Walkers Crossing Road, 200 kilometres south of Birdsville. The community once again swung into action quickly. No-one wanted to see anyone else lose their life. These guys were found shortly after they were reported missing. Ironically, it turned out they were refrigeration workers.

In March 2013 I got a call at three in the morning. There was a bad accident in Bedourie. Two people were trapped in the car. Tim Farran was away at the time and there was no-one relieving, so I had to go up.

En route I was talking to the SES, council people and the nurse via satphone (hands-free, of course). They were already at the scene trying to get the two people out. I told them to be very careful of overhead powerlines. Check for that first before they went near the car. I didn't want someone to die while trying to help someone.

By the time I arrived, the occupants had been freed and taken to the Bedourie Clinic. The Flying Doctor was on the way. I ascertained the male driver was in a bad condition. His passenger, the owner of the car, had a broken arm and a broken thumb. Both were affected by alcohol to a large degree. As in, pissed.

The Flying Doctor arrived. He was busy on both patients. He told me the driver would never walk again. And he was right. That's the case so far, three years down the track.

The owner of the car was drunk. He was on the floor with a broken arm and when he found out he was going to Mount Isa, he said to the doctor, 'Hey mate, can you book me a ticket back to Birdsville tomorrow?'

The doctor said, 'It's the least of your worries, mate.'

I wanted to get blood from both of them. At that stage, I wasn't sure who had been driving. The doctor said yeah but then the driver's blood pressure dropped to almost zero and the doctor said, 'Can't do it, we've got to get him out of here.'

So it was a mad rush to get him into the ambulance and his mate onto the back of a ute (the town only has one ambulance), then down to the plane. When we lifted the driver's stretcher up, we found out that the line had jammed. So his blood pressure was actually fine. Anyway blood was taken in Mount Isa, so that wasn't an issue, but that's part of the procedure we have to go through when investigating a serious accident.

After they were flown out, I continued my investigation. I ascertained that they'd been drinking at the Bedourie Pub until ten o'clock, closing time. They then got takeaways and stayed drinking out the front of the pub until two o'clock in the morning.

They then walked to the owner of the car's parents' place, demanded the keys to his car, which was a V8, high-powered utility. His mother tried to stop him driving but he was too drunk, too pig-headed not to. He drove off and he was going to drive his mate home to the industrial estate north of town.

When they got to the industrial estate, his mate wanted to have a drive of the car. So the owner let him drive back into town. The owner later said that as they went round the sweeping bend opposite the garage, he looked at the speedo, which had a digital readout: 145 kilometres an hour. It was a 50 kilometre per hour speed zone at that time.

The car lost control, went through a fence, then rolled over into a yard that stores tyres, steel and so on. It was extensively damaged. Fortunately for the owner, it landed on a tyre. He didn't have a seatbelt on, and ended up half out of the car, half in the car. If that tyre wasn't there the car would have crushed him and killed him. There'd have been 1.5 tonnes of weight on him.

Instead, he got flown to Townsville, where they operated on his arm. He spent a couple of weeks in hospital.

Neither of them were wearing seatbelts. The airbags deployed and the vehicle's cabin was intact. Nothing was crushed. The doctor said to me, 'If they were wearing their seatbelts, all they'd have got apart from a few bumps and bruises, was a blood nose from the airbag going off.'

The owner of the car had been done for drink-driving before so was supposed to have an interlock device fitted to the car. An interlock detects alcohol levels in your breath and only allows your car to start if you register zero. The owner had to pay for it to be fitted in his car but he hadn't done so. It's a condition of his licence that he can only drive a car with an interlock device fitted. So he had broken the law by driving under the influence, and by driving a vehicle without an interlock device.

The car they'd been driving was a high-powered V8. Laws have been enacted around Australia to stop young people driving high-powered vehicles, wrapping themselves around trees and killing themselves and their passengers. (In Queensland they apply to P1 and P2 provisional licence drivers under the age of twenty-five). The owner, who was twenty-one at the time, shouldn't have been driving that high-powered car, even if he was sober, even if the interlock device had nothing to do with it.

Unfortunately, he'd been smooth-talked by a fast-talking sales-man in Mount Isa into buying a car that was totally inappropriate for Birdsville, totally inappropriate for him. A high-powered vehicle has a clearance of only so much, so it was totally inappro-priate for Birdsville. And illegal for him to drive. The salesman probably would have known that. They just took advantage of him. Like a lot of young fellas, they see this flash ute. He went up to buy a Toyota four-wheel drive which is high-clearance, perfect for Birdsville, travelling on dirt roads, the mud. He shouldn't have been sold that vehicle.

Many people said, 'He'll wrap himself around a tree.' He didn't do that but it was the same outcome.

He'd had the vehicle for a while but he'd been charged for driving it, and not having an interlock device prior. He had it up at Bedourie, so I hadn't seen it for a while. I think he was going up there and driving it. Police had charged him, he was told not to drive it, and he was actually going to sell the car the next day. He wanted to take it for one final burn. Which he did.

Everything about that night was an accident waiting to happen. The only thing they didn't do was text while they were driving along. And that's because there's no mobile coverage up there, or they probably would have been doing that, too.

The owner of the car got out of it pretty well. He went to court in Birdsville, he pleaded guilty to all charges, was fined $3500 and got disqualified from driving for eighteen months. On top of that, his car, which was almost brand-new, wasn't covered by insurance because of all the offences they'd committed. Just one of them voided his insurance. So his family is now burdened with an $80 000 bill for a car that's a heap of junk, not worth anything.

The other person, the one who was driving, was a big, strong, strapping young fella. He'll never walk again. He pleaded guilty to similar charges at Birdsville Court. I was the prosecutor for both matters.

We worked out a plea because of the huge price he'd paid in that he'd never walk again. He was convicted but not punished further. There was no further fine imposed but he had the mandatory driving disqualification. Twelve months or whatever it was. At least he didn't have a fine to pay, but that was neither here nor there. So that was that.

CHAPTER 11

THE DIAMANTINA CROCODILE

In May 2013 Don and I were having smoko in the police station. That's one of the few times Don's been in the police station having a cup of tea. (Laughter) A tourist came in and said, 'There's a crocodile in the Diamantina River.'

Don's words were: 'Bullshit.'

There was a photo but it was like a shot of the Loch Ness monster. iPhone photo. Just ripples in the water. So Don and I went down. We didn't see anything, but crocs spend most of their time underwater anyway.

Anyway, I asked Gaffney. He's lived in Birdsville all his life. Brookie. He's lived in Birdsville all his life. Don, who's lived in Birdsville all his life. All said, 'Complete and utter bullshit. It's a goanna, a snake or a water rat.'

In *Desert Yarns* I copied Don's line: 'Snake, goanna or water rat. Definitely not a crocodile.'

And no sooner had the ink dried than a freshwater crocodile (*Crocodylus johnstoni*) turned up in the Diamantina River. (Laughter)

The crocodile was reported on 16 May, and on 23 May the sighting was confirmed. Sandra and I went down and there it was. On a log. A crocodile. Not a goanna. Not a snake. No water rat, he. Or she. Sandra took a photo and it ended up on the ABC website.

It became a bit of a tourist attraction. We'd go down there and watch the croc while it was sunning itself on the riverbank. When our kids came to town, we took them down and showed them the croc. All the tourists would have a look. You'd go down and there'd be a whole group of locals with cameras looking or waiting for it to come up.

On 23 May, Inspector Biggin was advised. He thought it was funny. I'd told him about it previously and he said, 'Nah, wouldn't be a croc.' Then I told him and he goes, 'Ah, croc.' What do you do? Senior police didn't offer any advice or guidance. They thought it was the ranger's problem. Don's got carriage unless it bites someone.

Not long after, we had another accident and rescue. The Warburton Track was no longer flooded, and therefore open, as was the Birdsville Inside Track, for the first time in years. So a group of motorcyclists went down there and one of them came off his bike. He couldn't ride his bike so his mates, so-called, put him in his swag. Then they rode into Birdsville.

They went and saw Barnesy and said, 'Oh, can you go down and pick up a bike? And while you're there, pick up our mate, too.'

Barnesy said, 'Oh, what's he doin'?'

They said, 'Oh, he's hurt himself.'

So Barnesy rang me and by this time I'd got wind of it. On the high-frequency radio network, there was talk that people were waiting for the riders at the northern end of the Warburton Track or on the Rig Road, and they never came. So one of the radio network people reported that the riders were overdue. When some of the riders turned up in Birdsville, I put two and two together, and I went around and saw them.

I took Prue the nurse with me to get a better picture of their friend's injuries. They were in a room at the Birdsville Hotel, lying back on the bed. They hadn't reported anything to police. This is a mate who's got an injury.

The nurse said, 'Why didn't you dink him to Clifton Hills?'

They said, 'He's too crook for that.'

I said, 'Well, why didn't one of you stay with him?'

They said, 'Oh well, we thought we'd come up here.'

It felt all-too familiar. Not thinking. Wrong choices.

So we decided we'd better go down and get him. There and then. That night. He'd been there a while. We still didn't have a clear idea of his injuries. They'd said that he'd fallen off the bike. So he had some kind of injury. He wasn't just crook from a bloody headache.

Barnesy went down in his car. I went down in the police car. And John White, who was in that rescue in the dust storm, drove the ambulance with Prue the nurse.

We went down the Inside Track, 171 kilometres to where the Warburton Track is, then up there about 80 kilometres, where we found him in a swag. And we passed so many dingoes on the way. We were thinking, Oh gee, wonder if this bloke's going to still be alive? Instead of being torn to shreds, limb from limb.

Fortunately, he was, but he was in a really bad way. He had

broken ribs and a punctured lung. So Prue administered first aid, gave him painkillers and put him in the ambulance. Then we drove to Clifton Hills Station, where we'd arranged for the Flying Doctor to evacuate him. By the time we got there it was six in the morning. Still dark.

The people on Clifton Hills gave us quarters to stay in so we could have a sleep. I had a sleep. John had a sleep. Barnesy took the bike back to Birdsville. Prue stayed up with the patient the whole time, in the ambulance, monitoring his condition.

At about seven o'clock Prue woke me up. It was pouring rain.

She said, 'The Flying Doctor can't land, it's a dirt strip. We'll need to go back to Birdsville.'

So we headed up to Birdsville, which has an all-weather landing strip. By the time we got going, and with the deteriorating road conditions, we didn't get back until about one in the afternoon. And this poor guy wasn't evacuated until three. He was flown from there to Adelaide.

The accident happened in the early afternoon the day before, so it was over twenty-four hours before he got proper medical treatment. He had a punctured lung, broken ribs, and his mates just left him high and dry. I couldn't understand their attitude.

Plus the support vehicle sat there for twelve hours and didn't go and look for these guys. How do I feel about that? It's poor decision-making. And a lot of it is basic stuff. They're coming up this way. They're late. Why don't we drive down?

Was I tempted to grab this guy's mates and give them a bit of Birdsville bad cop treatment? No. Instead you just go, Ah geez, what where they thinking? A lot of people from the city are just not used to the bush. They're out of their league. They make dumb decisions and then make dumber and dumber decisions.

It just snowballs. There are times when you can make dumb decisions and it doesn't matter. Other times you've gotta make smart, strong, decisive decisions. With a lot of these rescues, they weren't made.

With these guys, the judgement came from others. In the *Network News* newsletter, the HF Base Coordinator, Robert Wright (2500), detailed how HF radio operators assisted with communications regarding the accident, then with the rescue effort by me and others. Robert concluded: 'In this case VKS-737 personnel, police, RFDS and Birdsville medical staff worked to ensure the best possible outcome for the abandoned injured rider. Why his companions abandoned him when he was injured and in distress beggars belief.'

July 2013 got off to a bad start. I had to shoot a pet Labrador that had been mauled by a dingo on the common. It had been dis-embowelled and had to be destroyed. It's one of those things that you don't enjoy doing but if the owner had to take the dog to a vet in Mount Isa to be put down, it would be in pain for a day. If I do it, it's the same result but instantaneous. Whether you're giving a dog the green dream or shooting it, it's out of pain straight away. It's common sense to put the dog out of its misery as soon as possible. And a lot of people here are not on high wages so the expense of getting to Mount Isa – fuel, accommodation, seeing the vet – is big money to them. So I'm the town vet but I've only got one trick in my kit bag. Kaboom.

On a brighter note, a few days later, Birdsville hosted the first Big Red Run event. The Big Red Run is a series of running events held in mid-June, with runs from Birdsville and around Big Red.

You can do 20 kilometres or a big long run.

The first event culminated in a concert on top of Big Red where John Williamson performed all his hits. People were up there with their chairs, wine and their nibblies. It was a lovely night. All the community were invited free; everyone who lived in the Diamantina Shire. That first year there were the competitors, a few support staff, tourists from town, and so on. There were a couple of hundred people at the concert, if that. In later years, it grew until the event attracts thousands.

In mid-August 2013 the Diamantina crocodile was still at large. Then these crocodile catchers, who called themselves wildlife warriors, turned up and told us they were on a mission: Get Snappy.

They stayed at the courthouse. I put 'em up there, and we soon worked out they weren't as good as they said they were. This one bloke pulled out a knife about the same size Crocodile Dundee had in his film and ran down this steep bank. Don is yelling 'Put the knife away!' and he kept it out. If he'd slipped it would have gone straight through him. It would have killed him.

There were two blokes and a girl and their go was to catch the crocodile. They had this great big net but they didn't know much about what they were doing.

They had a dog in the car, a German Shepherd, and this was August. They left the dog in the car with the air conditioner going all day. Apparently the dog didn't like the heat.

They used to buy steak every night from the Birdsville Hotel for the dog. Dusty at the bakery and Bronwynne (Barnesy's wife) at the roadhouse didn't like them until they started spending big there, on pies, drinks and such. Then they changed their tune.

It made me wonder. Was some old dear giving money to protect some poor endangered species or wildlife and it's going on pies and keeping a German shepherd cool and giving it a steak every night when a can of Chum would have done? Maybe they were using their own money but maybe it was money donated to a wildlife cause.

They put a net across the river and the crocodile jumped over the net. It was like the crocodile was playing with them. And this went on for days.

The only reason they caught Snappy in the end was Don told them what to do. It took ten days to catch this croc in a bit of water that's 500 metres long. What they did was just keep moving the net up until it ran out of water. Don told them that. That was possibly Birdsville's biggest ever collar and I wasn't in on it. Don was, though.

So they caught the croc on 24 August, and Dusty, Bronwynne and the pub made a lot of money out of 'em. I think the crocodile ended up at Dreamworld. Relocated.

Just before the Birdsville Races of 2013, the police station and courthouse were repainted. There was crap everywhere and the painters were going flat out to get it done before the races. At the same time, there was a federal election about to be held, and in the midst of everything, on 25 August 2013, this woman turned up and wanted to leave the ballot papers at the police station.

The election was going to be held on the Saturday of the races, which meant we had to have ballot papers for every electorate in Australia. A bloody ton of them. She had a ute full.

She said, 'I've got ballot papers here.'

I said, 'Nah, we can't take 'em. We're gettin' the police station painted. The council is lookin' after that. Go round and see them.'

She said, 'I've seen 'em. You people don't know what's going on.'

I said, 'I know what's goin' on. You're not leavin' 'em here.'

So she abuses me.

So I said, 'Give 'em to the council. Go deliver 'em round there. That's where the polling's going to be done. At the sports centre.'

Her husband's in the driver's seat of the car, abusing me, too. They're both getting up me. He never got out of the car. I worked out later why. Anyway, she got back in the car. They drove off to the end of the street, where the courthouse is, and did a U-turn. They came back and as he's driving past the police station, he's talking on his mobile phone. And still abusing me.

He's yelling out, 'Where's the tip, mate, so I can dump all these off?'

So I yell out, 'Don't talk on the mobile phone.'

He was breaking the law.

Off he went, so I went off after him. Gave him a ticket for talking on a mobile phone while driving.

That's the closest I've come to Birdsville bad cop.

He got a ticket and I found out later he couldn't get out of the car because he's in a wheelchair. He still shouldn't have been doing it.

He got a ticket, the first ticket I'd issued in ages, and he contested it. So I said, 'That's alright.'

It ended up not going to court, so he got fined the ticket plus extra money.

So that was him. The lesson: don't be rude to the Birdsville cop.

Two: don't talk on a mobile while driving. This is a police station, not a polling station. She just wanted to drop the stuff and go. Then it's my problem. But the ute was fully loaded with ballot papers.

One of the highlights of the 2013 Birdsville Races was the conclusion of a walk from Brisbane to Birdsville by a group call the Wandering Warriors. They were soldiers who had been wounded in action and they'd walked in relays, each walking part of the way, from Brisbane to Birdsville. Most of them had been wounded in recent conflicts. Some of them were quite old so they might have been wounded in Vietnam.

At the end of their journey they all walked into town together. All the people were clapping them, I escorted them in the police car, lights going, all that sort of stuff, so it brings attention to them. They stopped at the hotel and the mayor, Geoff Morton, made a speech. They made a speech and everyone applauded them, and it was a big deal: walk from Brisbane to Birdsville.

I think they were raising money for soldiers with post-traumatic stress.

The other thing that was notable about September 2013 was that there were three rollovers in three weeks. Rollovers tend to congregate around the races, mainly because people aren't used to driving on dirt roads.

There was a girl who rolled her car out near Durrie. A young woman, a race-club coordinator, was the first to arrive at the scene and she was too scared to get out of her car because of what she might find in the badly damaged vehicle. She steeled herself and got out of the car and helped the girl out. She was just so scared because you don't know what's inside the car. She was thinking people might be dead or really badly injured.

Rollovers are usually due to the inexperience of people driving on dirt and driving too fast for the conditions. They get into a slide, they hit the brake, and over they go. It's very hard when you slide to stop that foot going out.

I do a lot of driving on dirt roads but I don't have many moments like that. With jobs it's really important that you get there. It's no help if you lose control because you're going too fast and roll as well. Then they've got whatever the emergency was and then they've got you.

A couple of times I've gone into slides and I just take my foot off the brake and off the accelerator and wash off speed that way. One time, years ago, I was going along the road to Lake Machattie and I came up to a bend and the gravel was a lot softer than what I thought. I didn't know the road, there was a bit of a bend, and the vehicle started to slide. So instead of trying to stay on the road, I just went straight ahead. It's all flat. No trees. If I'd tried to stay on the road, I might have rolled the car. You've got to be careful, ay.

I stopped in a paddock, reversed up and, Oh yeah, there's the road there. A lot of people wouldn't have done what I did. It's in your brain to stay on the road. So you try to turn and bad things happen.

Often, the rolled vehicle is on the inside of the bend, rather than the outside, which suggests the bend wasn't the problem. Sometimes it's just on a straight road, too.

At the end of September 2013, a motorbike rider added to the accident count. He was a Queensland police inspector and he crashed near Betoota. He ended up with three fractured ribs.

He'd actually rung me and was going to stay in the courthouse with his mates. He had this big BMW bike and he fell off a couple of times before he had his bad accident. Once again, a few little ones before the big one. Once again, station people picked him up and took him to Betoota. By the time I got there the Flying Doctor had landed.

There are photos of him being loaded. He looked alright but a lot of times people are walking around but they're really badly injured. If people are walking around the accident scene, especially with rollovers, usually they're the worst injured of everyone.

This fella had fractured ribs and ended up spending a bit of time in hospital. The road conditions were pretty bad out there, it was like travelling on marbles. That may have contributed to the rollovers in the weeks previously.

The inspector ended up alright. He even sent me an email:

> Just a quick note to again thank you for your support at the time of my accident and the hospitality you subsequently extended to Graham, Brynley and Gary.
>
> They're all back home in Brisbane now and expressed their appreciation and gratitude for the hospitality you extended to them while they were in town. You've left a very positive impression on the guys throughout the whole episode and I thank you sincerely for your support.
>
> I'm mending albeit slowly and looking forward to getting the bike / wreck sorted so we can plan the next 'adventure' – I'll stay out of your Division next time :)

> *All the best and please, pass on my gratitude to the folks*
> *at the clinic / ambulance.*

Not surprisingly, road safety was the main theme for my next column in *Desert Yarns*:

> Over the past month police have attended three rollover
> accidents involving motor vehicles and one motorbike accident.
> Three were on the Birdsville/Windorah Road and one on the
> road to Big Red. Fortunately, no-one was seriously injured. The
> main reason being the occupants of the motor vehicles were
> wearing properly adjusted and fastened seatbelts. If they were
> not wearing seatbelts, I can guarantee there would have been
> fatalities or serious injuries at the very least.

Three weeks later, on 24 October 2013, Dusty and Therese from the bakery woke up at three o'clock in the morning to the sound of Therese's dog, Pepper, howling in excruciating pain. They looked after her for an hour and then she passed away.

They put it down to natural causes: age, illness or something like that. It didn't occur to them that she'd been baited. Pepper was much loved. Therese used to walk Pepper and Dusty's son Adrian's dog, Milo, around the town every night.

A week later, almost to the day, almost at the same time, Milo, who was a lot younger, woke them up with the same symptoms. He was howling for an hour and then Milo died. It was then that the possibility they'd been baited was raised.

The first thing I did was try and work out why anyone would start baiting. They were both quiet dogs. They didn't bark all night. They were much loved by their owners. Then you look at Dusty, Therese and Adrian. They're very community minded. Dusty and Adrian built the bar at Kevie's shed, out at the bronco branding yards. They were all well liked in town

Don Rowlands conducted extensive enquiries, as did I. I contacted Winton, because a lot of dogs had been baited up there. People were telling me there were a lot of dead crows in town. I enquired about that and was told no, if a dog ate a crow that had been baited, it wouldn't get poisoned. Poison's not transferrable that way.

So the dogs had to eat the poison. Going for a walk, maybe they picked it up. They're not on a lead, they're just walking. I looked at that. Then I looked at who was new in town as this sort of thing hadn't happened before.

I had my suspicions but it was one of those times where I couldn't prove anything. There was no evidence at all. People pointed out a person who could have been involved but there was no evidence pointing towards him. So it was left at that. A lot of times with suspicions, they're eventually found to be completely misguided. You can't just blame someone. So I kept an open mind, hoping something else would come to light. Unfortunately, it never has. Not yet, anyway.

In *Desert Yarns* the next month, I wrote about the poisoning of the dogs:

> The deaths of both dogs, particularly the way they died, has caused untold stress, heartache and misery to Therese, Dusty and Adrian.
>
> While we have no direct evidence of baiting the symptoms of the two dogs strongly point to the possibility. The laying of baits within town limits has serious public health and

welfare implications particularly for small children. It is strictly controlled under council by-laws and government legislation.

Unlawful use of baits or harmful substances carries a maximum penalty of $22,500 or imprisonment for one year. Poisoning an animal is an offence of cruelty under the Animal Care and Protection Act 2001 which has a maximum penalty of $75,000 or two years' imprisonment.

A few months later, in March 2014, another dog was poisoned, just a few houses from where the other dogs died. I worked out it had to be someone new to town as it hadn't happened in the six years that I'd been there. Don couldn't remember any other dog being poisoned in town. So it was a local, but someone new to town. That didn't rule out the subject of my previous suspicions.

The summer of 2013/14 started out quietly in Birdsville. Sandra and I went on holidays at the beginning of summer, on a cruise in the Pacific. When I got back, over Christmas I was sent to relieve at Dajarra, a small town between Mount Isa and Birdsville. Birdsville is pretty quiet at that time of year and my station could be covered by the Bedourie Sheriff.

At eleven-thirty at night on Boxing Day, I was told that a female had been stabbed at Urandangi. That's an even smaller town, almost on the Northern Territory border, north-west of Dajarra. No police station.

Myself and another police officer, Matt Proctor, started gearing up to go out there, then I got another phone call to say the female was deceased. Now it was a murder investigation. I got hold of the inspector, contacted CIB, did all that sort of stuff. Then Matt and I went out there.

It had been raining so the roads were very wet. Dirt roads. There were cattle on the road, so we had to watch that. It took us until about two o'clock to get there. It was still drizzling rain when we got there. A person waved us down and told us what had happened. We went around and there was a deceased female outside the park, and her partner was holding her, or beside her. We worked out he'd stabbed her.

We were there by ourselves when we received information that some vehicles had high-tailed it back to Alpurrurulam, where the deceased came from. Alpurrurulam is an Aboriginal settlement on Lake Nash Station, on the Northern Territory side of the border. So we quickly got onto Alpurrurulam police and asked them to set up a roadblock to stop people coming out. People might come out for retribution on the person who committed the murder. The family.

We also asked police in Mount Isa to send more officers down in case people took other roads to get around the roadblock. There's dirt tracks everywhere there. Alpurrurulam police then told us they'd got onto the person who runs the garage there and they weren't going to open the garage until 10 or 11 o'clock in the morning so no-one could get fuel. A lot of people needed fuel before they could get to Urandangi. It's a fair drive.

So we dealt with that and the offender was given all his warnings. All those warnings were recorded on tape. He made admissions to stabbing her. We found the murder weapon, a knife, across the road under a bush. We found out he did it because he told her to go to the toilet in the hotel and she wanted to go to the toilet in the park. That's why he stabbed her. If you can believe that.

He was placed in the police vehicle. Urandangi is a community with no electricity apart from generators. It's very dark there. No streetlights. Pam, who runs the pub and is in the SES, was really good. All the people there were good. Not that there are many people there. It's just a pub and a few houses.

Eventually, other police arrived. The CIB arrived. The offender was taken from the scene back to Mount Isa. We didn't want him there in case anyone turned up. There was going to be trouble. We stayed there while Crime Scene did all the investigation that happens with any murder in Australia.

After the deceased was removed, other police stayed in Urandangi. TAC Crime from Mount Isa came to provide law and order in the town. They made sure there was no trouble. We left probably later that morning, ten or eleven.

The offender was charged with murder and in October 2014 I went to the Supreme Court in Mount Isa for the trial. There, the admissions that he made to me at the time were ruled inadmissible by the judge because he was affected by alcohol. Fortunately, he made a lot of admissions to Pam, the local publican, which were admissible. Even so, the charge of murder was dismissed. He was convicted of manslaughter. I think he's out now actually.

Ridiculous. You kill someone because they went to the wrong toilet. He was filled with grief, absolutely overwhelmed with grief. There's his partner, his lifetime partner, lying dead, and he was the cause of her death for something so minor.

The sad thing at the trial was, apart from the jury, the defence, the prosecution, the judge and his associate, the only people in court were the police officer monitoring the defendant, the reporter from Mount Isa's *North West Star*, and whatever witness was giving evidence in the box (police, forensics, whatever).

No-one cared. There was no family there. No-one. It was a murder trial and the whole public gallery was empty. You were giving evidence to an empty room. You look at the murder trials in capital cities; they're packed with people. But no-one was there. No-one cared.

Back in sleepy outback Birdsville, the only incident over that summer was a bloke who did a petrol drive-off from Windorah in mid-January. The police officer there put out an alert and I picked up the person involved as soon as he drove into Birdsville. It turned out there was a warrant out on him and he was driving while disqualified. Once again, all the businesses in town were on the lookout and spotted him very quickly. At least he didn't have to pay for petrol to get to Mount Isa. He was taken straight to the watchhouse courtesy of the Queensland Police Service.

CHAPTER 12

DUMB AND DUMBER

Just before the desert reopened after the summer, Don the ranger and I spotted tracks heading out there. That was on 14 March 2014, only a couple of days before it opened. Whoever it was, they shouldn't have gone out there. We followed the tracks to Poeppels Corner. Once we got there, Don and I thought, you could spend a week out there searching all the tracks before you found anyone. And we still had a town to take care of back at Birdsville. Not only that, beyond Poeppels, they've left Queensland. If they made it that far, they probably made it across. So we gave up. We contacted Mount Dare and asked them to keep a lookout but they didn't see anyone.

Two days later the desert opened. Now people could get lost without being fined. Which they soon did.

On 27 April 2014 an EPIRB was activated in the late afternoon. The call came from Search and Rescue Canberra tasking me to respond. The location was 80 kilometres past Poeppels Corner, 250 kilometres west of Birdsville.

It was too late to put a plane up because by the time it got there it would have been dark. So there was some to-ing and fro-ing as to who to take. Barnesy? The nurse? Why have they set off an EPIRB? They might be bogged. Their car might have broken down. Out of chardonnay. Or someone could be badly injured, maybe bitten by a snake.

With an EPIRB you generally expect it's going to be something serious. Then, after some enquiries, we worked out it was three guys on bikes and one was an asthmatic. An asthma attack might have been why they'd activated the EPIRB. We ruled out mechanical problems because if one of the bikes broke down, you've still got two other bikes.

We decided to take the ambulance with us, even though that meant leaving Birdsville without a nurse for the best part of twenty-four hours. And the hierarchy in Queensland Health didn't want the nurse to be out if it was just a flat tyre or something like that. Fair enough, too. You're going out to one person and there're a hundred in Birdsville, plus whoever's in the caravan park. As it turned out, this rescue was twenty-four hours plus seven more.

While we devised our plan, SAR Canberra tasked a Dornier aircraft to fly over the scene. It was too late to put a regular plane up but this Dornier had night vision, thermal imaging, all the good stuff, but it had to come from Melbourne. It was a RAAF plane.

So the go was, we'd go out (me in the police vehicle and the nurse in the ambulance with Padraic driving). The Dornier was due to get there at midnight. It had survival packs it could drop and in those there was a satellite phone and radio. So they'd drop one of them, the people would pick up the radio, then tell the crew what was going on and the crew would tell SAR.

We'd find out exactly what was happening.

So, we're driving out there, and I get a satphone call just after midnight saying the plane flew over and they could see on the thermal imaging that there were three people there. One guy's in a tent but he's alive. They can tell he's alive by the heat.

They dropped a survival pack, circled and watched via thermal imaging. This survival pack has flashing lights all over it, it's got a siren on it and it's got orange smoke. It stands out like a dog's hind leg.

So these two guys walked over to the survival pack, had a look at it, then left it and walked back to camp.

'Oh shit. That's no good.'

So the plane dropped another survival pack.

Same thing.

The plane did another lap, watching the thermal imaging, and they dropped a third survival pack. They wrote on it, OPEN ME. They didn't even go and have a look at that one.

So we get this message. We go, Oh no. Fuck. How can they . . . ?

The plane circled for a while, hoping that the penny would drop. Unfortunately, the penny never dropped. The one thing the plane lacked was a loudspeaker so they could tell the people on the ground, 'Open the survival packs, you idiots.'

Eventually the plane ran low on fuel so they had to fly to Alice Springs and overnight there. There wasn't enough fuel for it to get back to Melbourne.

Anyway, we at least knew we've got one person in a tent and two walking around. We could assume the one in the tent is injured. He's not well. So we kept going.

We got there about eighty-thirty, nine in the morning or something. It was a fair hike out there. We came across the three bikes.

Scattered around them were these three packages. Lights still flashing. One of them with OPEN ME written on it.

I said, 'Boys, why didn't you go and open them?'

They said, 'We thought they were just marking the camp, so they knew where we are.'

I said, 'Mate, you're in the middle of nowhere. You set off an EPIRB. The plane found you and flew around you several times. We knew where you were.'

They go, 'Oh, yeah. Maybe we should have.'

Not only that, there was 4 litres of water in each package, which they had none of. There was food in each package, which they had none of. There's a satphone, which they had none of. A radio, which they had none of.

When we got to them, they were pretty thirsty. One bloke drank 2 litres straight up. Just downed it. All their water bottles were empty.

What had happened to them was, the guy who was injured had come off and hurt his back. Then he continued riding but it was just too bad. He was in a lot of pain. So they stopped and set off the EPIRB. The only reason they had an EPIRB was a neighbour of one of them suggested at the last minute, 'Boys you should take an EPIRB. Borrow mine.'

They had no support vehicles, they were overloaded, and their plan for that morning was, come ten o'clock, the two well people were going to ride off and leave their mate. They were almost out of fuel so they'd drained the fuel out of his bike to put in their bikes. That gave them a bit more but they didn't have enough to get out of the desert.

Fortunately, we got there prior to Plan B being acted on because then we'd have had two searches. We'd have had him, then we'd have had another search, trying to find these two knuckleheads.

After we'd filled their water bottles, we got a helicopter in because the injured man was in too much pain to be driven out. He could walk around but he was just doubled over in pain. So back injury, muscle, something like that.

The two boys packed up their camp. We arranged for Dave from Mount Dare to pick up the bike. Then these two boys said they were going to continue their ride.

I said, 'No. You're not. You're coming back with us.'

They wanted to ride across the desert to Mount Dare.

Their EPIRB was almost out of batteries. They had only the water that we gave them. Well, they had three containers full of water, food, radios, satphones and such. I said, 'Look, it's gone from bad to worse. We don't want to go on any more desert adventures today. You're coming back with us.'

I've really got no power to do that. If they had said, 'No, we're goin',' what can you do?

I said, 'No boys, you're coming with us.'

And they said, 'Oh, okay.' (Laughter)

They were faster on the bikes so they rode on ahead of us. I said, 'We'll meet you at the corner of the Knolls Track. Then we'll meet you at Poeppels Corner. We'll have lunch there.'

We get to Poeppels, and it's a stinking hot day by this stage. And they're sitting out in the sun in the middle of the day, on their bikes.

I said, 'Boys, you've gotta get shade when you're out here. On a hot bike, you'll get dehydrated.'

Even city people understand the concept of shade. I said, 'You've gotta think smarter, you know.'

So we got them into shade, gave them food, then off we drove across the saltpans and the sand dunes, back towards Birdsville. I'd already got a flat tyre on the Knolls Track, which Padraic helped me change. Then I got another on the QAA Line. So we changed that, and by that stage we were buggered.

So I said, 'You guys go ahead and we'll see you in Birdsville.'

We propped almost on the Northern Territory–Queensland border and went to sleep for a few hours. We were just too tired. By this time we'd been going since four-thirty the previous day. We had a sleep and then we headed back into Birdsville. The boys reported to Sandra at the police station so we knew they made it back.

Padraic thought the photos of that rescue were funny. I put some photos in *Desert Yarns* with Prue the nurse talking on the satphone while Padraic is standing with his hands on his hips and this bloke's using my jerry can to fill his water bottle. I wrote, 'Nurse Prue busy on satphone and Padraic supervising the filling of the water bottles.' (Laughter) There were three pictures and all he's doing in them is standing with his hands on his hips. The thing is, Padraic worked hardest of anyone. He's a guy who can do anything and he's really handy on a rescue. It was sort of tongue-in-cheek because when you need to change a tyre, Padraic's there, front and centre.

Padraic's wife Olivia thought it was funny. Well, she said she thought it was funny but I don't know if she really did. Ah well. It was a good line: Nurse busy, Padraic supervising.

The Dornier cost taxpayers $50 000 and my inspector suggested it was time to comment on people travelling through the desert not properly prepared. He said, 'A girl's going to ring you from the media, just put it out there that people need to be properly prepared. Unlike these knuckleheads.'

I spoke to a girl from some paper in Brisbane. It wasn't a local paper, but not one of the main ones, either. So I thought, Give 'em a burn, it's only in the bloody local paper. Well, the burn went round Australia. (Laughter) *The Australian,* the *Age, Sydney Morning Herald,* radio, you name it.

So many people made comments. Should have left 'em out there, and all this stuff. One phrase that I used got picked up and repeated: dumb tourists. I was a bit tired when I got back, I probably went a bit far but . . . I probably shouldn't have done what I did, but I did. So, you know . . .

Anyway, it was a lot of money to spend when we didn't need to. It was silly that they didn't open those containers so we could find out what was going on. If we'd known he was walking around but had a sore back, we could have just sent the helicopter in the morning. And they were going to head off at ten o'clock the next morning. Even after the plane had come and 'marked' their location, in triplicate.

Meanwhile, all these survival packs were in the back of the police car, lights still flashing. I probably could have worked out how to turn them off but I couldn't be bothered. I was bloody tired so I just threw 'em in the back. I get home and Sandra goes, 'What's all those flashing lights in the back of the police car?'

They're still going. A day later.

Everything they needed was in those containers. And they were there, eight or nine hours, flashing away.

OPEN ME . . . you dimwits. (Laughter)

I wasn't very surprised when these guys took offence at being described as dumb tourists. I suppose anyone would but they said they thought it was just going to be a pleasant ride through the desert, an easy trip. They said they were very experienced and well prepared. Then they added that next time they'd carry a satphone, more water, more food, and not take as much gear. As in, they'd be better prepared.

After years of floods the country was in drought again by mid-2014. On 16 May 2014 a drought relief concert was held on the oval. That was a good night. The Busby Marou duo came out and entertained Birdsville. Everyone had a good time. It was a typical Birdsville event: no violence or bad behaviour.

As for the drought, it was just getting drier and drier. By 2013 the Inside Track had opened for the first time in years. Goyder's Lagoon was dry. And after 2013 there was no rain anywhere. Virtually none. A lot of the properties destocked. I don't think it was a question of cattle starving or dying of thirst, because they'd seen the dry conditions coming and made plans to reduce their cattle numbers. There was enough feed for what they had left but things were getting increasingly difficult. And there's a point where you're no longer running a cattle station, you're just trying to hang on until conditions improve.

In July I was told by other travellers that a large four-wheel drive vehicle was travelling across the desert without spare tyres. It had had spares but they were all punctured. This was one of those big vehicles, like a monster truck, with a family in it, that was too big for the tracks. It was going over plants either side of the tracks and getting flat tyres, staking them on mulga roots.

I went out to Poeppels with my daughter, Lauren, and her husband, Damien. We went out because people were concerned that these people had no more spare tyres. And it was a family from

Germany travelling by themselves. So we went out to Poeppels (I'd always promised Lauren I'd take her but never had), down the Warburton Track, then up the Birdsville Track. We located them on the Birdsville Track. It turned out that they were fine but I asked them to report to me when they got in to Birdsville. Which they did.

A few years earlier I might not have bothered but my instincts told me it was safer to go out. I combined it with a desert patrol as well.

On 9 July 2014, the second Big Red Run was held. The previous year the crowds numbered a few hundred. This time there were a thousand people for the concert at Big Red, which this year was held down below, at the foot of Big Red instead of on it. The performers included James Reyne, Daryl Braithwaite, Kasey Chambers, Ross Wilson, John Williamson and Joe Camilleri. It was bigger than the one before and the next one was even bigger. It's getting to the stage where it rivals the Birdsville Races.

There were a lot of people eating and drinking but there wasn't any misbehaviour. It was a second schoolies for over-fifties. Everyone had a good time. No-one did anything silly.

A week later I went out on a joint patrol with my new counterpart from South Australia, Tom Christley. We went to Poeppels, across the desert to Dalhousie, then down to Oodnadatta and Maree. There's a famous pub at Oodnadatta, the Pink Roadhouse. There's a photo of us outside.

That was a good little joint patrol with Tom. He hadn't been across the desert so that was a first for him. I quite like doing joint patrols. It's always good to go across with someone, whether it's Don the ranger, or Tom.

By that stage I'd spent eight years policing the Birdsville area. I was in a position to share my knowledge with people. I've learned a lot from Don and added to that by being out there so much. Driving over sandhills was daunting the first couple of times but like anything else, if you do it for a while, you get better. You get to know the desert, you know what you've got to do to get over sandhills. If there's a problem, you know how to work it out.

It's a good thing to meet people you work with and I get along particularly well with Tom. He's a lot younger than me but we still get on really well. He's a good police officer, too. Decent person. Fun to be with. He's what you expect police to be: friendly, helpful, but when he needs to be tough, he is. He gets on well with everyone but when a firm hand is needed, he can show people where they've erred.

On joint patrols, when we meet travellers, we just talk to them and see how they're going. We don't search their car or anything. Most people you come across are pretty well prepared. You just ask them how they're going. Any issues. Anything like that. They're happy to see you.

When we're on a joint patrol, Tom's in his khaki South Australian uniform and I'm in my blue Queensland one. The difference really stands out. A lot of times people see police and they just see an Aussie police officer. They don't see the badge where he's from. So they know one's South Australia, one's Queensland. They think, Oh yeah, that's good, doing a joint patrol. There's a fair bit of surprise, coming across police in the middle of nowhere.

It often ends up in a photo op. Everyone gets out. Heaps of photos taken.

A few days before the Birdsville Races, I received a call regarding a person behaving erratically in the main street of Birdsville. As it happened, Superintendent Russell Miller was already in town. We'd been down to a conference together in Port Augusta.

This bloke, who'd come to Birdsville for the races, was lying on the road and cars were having to drive around him to get past. He was doing other strange things as well. So we went down to see him. It was immediately clear that he had a lot of mental health issues.

We took him to the clinic and the nurse got what's called in Queensland an Emergency Examination Order. We could virtually hold him there until we could get him assessed by a doctor.

At the clinic he was being really aggressive to the nurse, saying, 'Come on, give me some tablets.'

So the nurse gave him a tablet and he spat it out. I thought, This is going to be good. He's not going to take anything.

The nurse got another tablet and after a few minutes, he said, 'Alright, give it to me.'

So he ate it, swallowed it, and said, 'That's nothin'. That won't do nothin' to me.'

The nurse said, 'I want to give you an injection.'

He's really aggressive, swearing at me and the superintendent, carrying on. So the nurse gave him a needle and he's going, 'Come on, gimme more. Come on. That's done nothin'.'

So the nurse gave him another needle. After half an hour, he's still calling us names the whole time, and the superintendent is just standing there with his phone by his side, just filming him. I thought, That's clever.

He's still saying, 'Come on, gimme more, gimme more.'

So the nurse gave him a third needle. And it was like watching an Energizer Bunny ad. He just got slower and slower. He's abusing us, then stop, then abusing us. In the end he was sleeping on the floor.

Then the Flying Doctor arrived. Now, if he goes berserk in the plane between Birdsville and Charleville, it's major problems. And by now it was night. So they put him in one of those stretchers with a kilometre of velcro around him. They had a cannula in his arm, with a big injection all ready to go.

The doctor said, 'It'll be enough to stop a horse. If he plays up, we'll just hit him with it. Straight into his bloodstream.'

You've got to be careful. If something goes wrong in the air, where do you put the plane down? Australian outback. Pitch black. So they had him lined up and they had this needle ready to go. The slightest hint of him coming to? The Flying Doctor said, 'He won't wake up for a week.'

Off he went, fortunately, because he would have caused us a lot of trouble in the lead-up to the races. He had severe anger management and mental health issues. He came from Brisbane. He saw the races were on and decided to come. He got dropped off by someone. I'm still trying to work out who. (Laughter)

After that, the 2014 Birdsville Races ran as smoothly as they do most years. As the *Police Bulletin* quoted me the following month: 'The races were a huge success with no assaults, brawls, traffic crashes or criminal offences, apart from two nitwits setting off fireworks – one at an unmarked police vehicle – and two people with white powder in their possession.'

In September 2014 there was a group of people, aged sixty-up, who were riding postie bikes around the outback, raising money for the Flying Doctor. On the leg from Windorah to Birdsville, one fella came off at Durrie Station, 100 kilometres east of Birdsville. When he fell, the handlebars went into his stomach and he was pissing blood.

We said, 'Yep, no worries. We'll get the ambulance to you. Stay put.'

I rang Durrie Station. Unfortunately, they were away. That was a shame because they'd have gone to the accident and done things a lot differently and a lot better. Instead, while I was getting everyone ready to go, we got another call saying, 'It's okay. We're bringing him into town. We've put him in a four-wheel drive.'

That's a no-no. He's got internal injuries.

Then, in between him coming in and the rest of the group arriving, another old bloke fell off his bike and hit his head. He had repetitive amnesia. That's where you keep repeating yourself. That was about 30 kilometres out. So you've got two injured people, and two evacuations, in one night.

Then the rest of the crew were in the pub, yahooing, until one o'clock in the morning. You could hear them from outside, having a good time. There was probably about a dozen of them. Well, there were two less at that stage. They stayed till stumps and for people riding postie bikes, maybe they should have pulled the pin a bit early.

They left early in the morning, and I had to go up to Mount Isa that day, for training or something. I left, and then I found out that another person had come off about 100 kilometres south of Birdsville, in South Australia. This person who'd come off his bike had head injuries.

The nurse from Birdsville, being the closest, went down. He took people with him, to help out.

247

This nurse was just new to Birdsville and he received information that Clifton Hills Station had an airstrip that was 37 kilometres south of the accident scene. That turned out to be totally wrong. He got to the 38-kilometre mark and kept going; Clifton Hills was close to 100 kilometres down the Track.

If they'd returned to Birdsville, you've got a fully stocked medical clinic with drugs and instruments so you can tell how your patient is going. Then you've got an all-weather airstrip. If it rains, Clifton Hills is a dirt strip that becomes useless.

Then you've got the problem: what happens if no-one is there?

Anyway, they went down there and he got flown out but died about a week later from his injuries.

Apparently he was a big bloke. He was about 130 kilograms. Maximum weight for a postie bike is 100 kilograms. And what's a postie bike designed for? Travelling on footpaths at very low speed, putting letters in letterboxes. It's not designed for one of the remotest and toughest roads in Australia, if not the world.

That's why three got injured and got flown out by the Flying Doctor. Unfortunately, one of them died.

They were raising money for the Flying Doctor but with those three evacuations, you're talking $8000 per flight. I don't think the Flying Doctor made any money out of that fundraiser. In fact, the opposite.

At the beginning of October 2014, Birdsville's shoe tree was set on fire.

The shoe tree was owned by local property owner (and the mayor at the time) Geoff Morton. Years ago, he'd said to someone, 'I'll put a pair of shoes up on a post so you know where to turn off to get to some cattle yards.'

That was at a side track from the Eyre Developmental Road between Birdsville and Bedourie. Since then it flourished, with people putting more shoes on it. There were scores and scores of shoes. Then, it all went up in smoke.

I went out with Don. We ascertained that someone had put a tyre at the base of the shoe tree, and lit that. That burnt everything. I made enquiries but I only got a couple of clues. It turned out there had only been one car travelling north that day, a council person, a really reputable person, who wouldn't have done it. It was one of those cases in the outback where, if something happens, unless someone passes soon after, and sees a car travelling, it's hard to work out who was responsible.

Did Geoff have any enemies? None who would burn the shoe tree. It was more a tourist attraction. He just owned the signpost. That was destroyed as well.

Now, someone has put another sign up and put bars across so even more shoes can be hung there. There's probably more shoes there now than before. The tradition continues. That's another of my cold cases. The culprits are still at large but my enquiries are continuing.

A couple of days later, 3 October 2014, the federal court sat in Birdsville to deliver its decision on a major land rights application affecting much of the region surrounding the town. They actually sat at Pelican Point, down on the billabong. All the wigs and gowns were there. Aboriginal people came from all over the outback, including as far away as Alice Springs, and a huge area of land covering the north of South Australia and the country around Birdsville was handed back to them.

The court sat in Birdsville so Aboriginal people could see that the land was actually handed back. They could actually hear it, instead of reading some long-winded legal note. The hand-back meant Aboriginal people have to be consulted for any development. That covers public land and leasehold areas, too.

Don was there, and all the elders, then there was a community event at the hall. Sandra and I went. It was very well received. Everyone was there, all the community, all the people of the town. Everyone was really happy. It was a really good event.

On 22 October 2014, I got a satphone call from someone 40 kilometres east of Poeppels Corner, about 130 kilometres west of Birdsville. They couldn't get over a sandhill.

I asked, 'Have you dropped your tyre pressure?'

This fella said, 'Yeah but I just can't get over.'

They'd tried repeatedly the previous day to get over the sand dune. They couldn't do it. So they set up camp and rang us in the morning.

At nine-thirty in the morning, I headed out there with Don.

When we got out there, Don let the tyre pressure down. They (an older couple) had dropped the tyre pressure but they hadn't dropped it enough. Then Don put the fella in the car, gave him some lessons in sand driving.

He drove straight over.

And over the next dune, and the next, all the way back to Birdsville. We got back around eight that night. So, it took ten-and-a-half hours to let someone's tyres down.

I wouldn't say that rescue falls into the dumb tourist category.

They'd come up the Warburton Track to Poeppels. Then they'd gone along the saltpans, which are pretty easy. They only hit trouble when they got to the dunes. They were pretty well prepared. They had plenty of water, plenty of food. And they had a satphone.

You could hear in this bloke's voice that he was having a problem. After eight years of doing rescues, I could hear when I needed to go. If you say, 'Try this, then ring me back', what happens if the satphone goes flat? Then they think, The coppers don't care about me. We'll go back the other way. Then they run out of fuel. Or if you don't hear back, they're now under the vehicle.

It was hot, too. Very hot. The flies were horrific. I remember that. So I said, 'Just stay in the shade. Just makes yourselves comfortable. We'll see you in a few hours.'

They knew someone was coming out. They were glad to see us. We followed them back and they were happily going over every dune. Another pleasant drive in the bush.

All sorted. No-one had to die that day. Everyone's happy. And once again, someone is touched by the way Birdsville helped them. And they've been coming back ever since. They came out and stayed four days at the courthouse. Had a barbeque. Don and Lyn came down. They got to know Birdsville. Got to know us. They were nice people.

It wasn't so happy four days later, on 26 October 2014. I got a call to a disturbance at the community hall at about three in the morning.

There was a seventieth birthday party for Spinny Lonergan, an old stockman. The problem started when the girlfriend of the fella who ended up a paraplegic a year earlier was dancing with some other guy. He cracked the shits. He got really jealous.

I think that's when the penny dropped. He's in a wheelchair because of his car accident, she's up dancing. I think his girlfriend was coming to the realisation that the relationship was over. She'd stood by him for nearly a year. I think he knew that and it all came to a head, and he got very aggressive. A window was broken.

He started yelling and screaming. People started yelling at him, calling him a cripple, which certainly didn't help the situation.

When I got called down there, he was in the middle of the street in his wheelchair, in a very agitated state. Fortunately, I was able to talk to him. I called the nurse down. She was a relieving nurse, a young woman, and she struck up a really good rapport with him. So she sat talking to him for probably an hour.

People tried to get involved but they weren't of any benefit at all. We had to send them away because they were just getting him upset. They meant well but they weren't doing well. Eventually we arranged for him to be taken home by a friend.

By the time he left, he'd settled down a lot. He was in a better frame of mind but he said he was leaving Birdsville. The friend stayed the night, then the nurse went round in the morning to see how he was going. She monitored him. She also gave him something to help him sleep that night.

Later in the week I went around and saw him and said, 'Look, you're probably better off going where you've got family.'

He's of Islander descent. He'd been living at Windorah, then he moved to Bedourie and was working there. After his accident, he moved to Birdsville because there was a house that was suitable for him. It had a bathroom with wheelchair access. It had all the rails to hang onto.

The nurse would go round to visit him every day. Make sure

he was travelling okay. And so on.

He originally comes from Sarina, near Mackay. It's a big town. Mackay's a big town. There are people there who are also disabled, in similar situations. He'd be able to play sport with them, instead of being stuck on his own in Birdsville. Here, the temperature is 40 degrees every day. There's no social outlet at all for him, or virtually none.

He was pretty much housebound. He had to pay people to go up and get him a can of Coke, and a lot of them were taking advantage of him. Like, they'd also get a can of Coke, and other things as well, like a pack of cigarettes.

I suggested to him it would be best if he went home, which was something he wanted to do anyway. And he's been there since then. By all accounts, he's doing alright. He's training as a weightlifter. There're gyms up there he can train at. It's a better place for him. I've heard he can bench press 180 kilograms. That's a lot of weight.

Another young Birdsville local had problems on 8 November 2014. A young woman, Kelly Theobald, got a flat tyre 80 kilometres south of Birdsville. She couldn't change it, couldn't get the nut off. So she panicked a bit and tried to drive back to Birdsville. She was too far out and eventually the tyre was shredded, then the rim went, then she couldn't go any further. She spent the night out on the Birdsville Track.

She was going down to Innamincka to meet her boyfriend. He was at the pub there. She left at four in the afternoon. So you'd think if she wasn't there by ten, he'd start to get worried. By eleven, he'd start back-tracking along the Walkers Crossing Road, and he would have found her. He never did that, for reasons unknown.

She was found by people from Birdsville. They conveyed her and the car back to Birdsville. As they were loading the car on the truck, the boyfriend turned up and said he had been driving down all the mining lease roads, looking for her, worried.

Kelly Theobald had come to town in 2011. She was a young girl. She worked in the pub, behind the bar, serving meals, stuff like that. She was very well liked in town, a very smart girl. I'd describe her as an over-achiever. She had two degrees. She was a journalist. She wrote articles for *Outback Magazine, 4WD Magazine*. She was an accomplished photographer as well. She had a blog where she used to write all the time.

When she first came to Birdsville, she got in a relationship with Sam Barnes, son of the local mechanic and Bronwynne Barnes. They lived together for two to three years. She also wrote a children's book about her Volkswagen travelling through the desert. The book was called *Onslo*, which was the name of her car. She and Sam travelled across the desert in their Volkswagen, which was quite a feat.

Eventually, she and Sam broke up. She came down to the police station looking for a community house. That's Sandra's role, to fill in the application and get them a house.

I said to her, 'Look, you're a pretty girl. You're clever. Why don't you leave Birdsville? Go back home, go to a big city.'

She started crying and said, 'I love Birdsville.'

I said, 'Oh, sorry.'

So we went round to find accommodation for her in the short term. She ended up staying with Jenna Brook in her house. Then she left there and moved in with Jody Barr, a council worker, and his girlfriend, Francie, a German backpacker who lived in Birdsville for a few years. She stayed there for a while and eventually Sandra got her a house in Gibber Court, opposite where you used to live, Evan.

By this time, she was working at the information centre for the Diamantina Shire Council as the tourism officer. She used to write articles and was editor of *Desert Yarns*, the community newsletter, which was right up her alley, being a journalist. She worked really well at that job. She wasn't just serving people at the counter. She was dealing with people coming to town, coordinating events for the races and so on.

She ended up leaving Birdsville with Wade Gilby and they went up and managed a property at Charters Towers. That didn't work out so they took up contract mustering, then she returned to Birdsville. She was another person for whom Birdsville, whatever the attraction is, was the place for her. She just loved it.

Her mother told me the family travelled through Birdsville when she was a little girl, like ten or eleven. And she said, 'I love this place. I'm going to come and live here.' And her mother dismissed it, just a little kid talking, and sure enough, when a job came up, she applied for it and lived at Birdsville. She was here for the best part of four years.

Late in 2013, when Kelly was twenty-six, *The Australian* featured her in an article on young people in the outback. She'd actually enrolled to do a Masters degree in human rights in Paris. She'd been working in Birdsville to save enough money to do her degree. When she had enough money, though, she couldn't leave.

On 13 November 2014, a young French couple arrived in town, planning to drive across the desert, just before it was due to close.

The temperature at the time was 44 degrees. They were staying at the pub, where the staff were trying to talk them out of it. When the pub couldn't convince them it wasn't a good idea, they called me.

I completely agreed with the people at the pub. So I got this couple to come down to the police station. I told them the dangers of the desert. It was a very hot day. Dusty. The car they were driving was an old dilapidated four-wheel drive that they'd obviously bought from some other backpacker at Cottesloe or Bondi Beach or St Kilda. But they were determined to cross the desert.

I said, 'I tell you what. I'll take you out. I'll go out in the police car. You follow me, and I'll show you what it's like.'

So we went out to Little Red. They went up. They got bogged. They got to the top, but as they went down, they got bogged in the dip on the other side. So I had to get them out. I showed them how to put Max Trax under the car, and they got out. And then the next sand dune, Nemesis Dune, they really struggled. They couldn't make it up.

They were digging the car out and I was letting them get the experience. I said, 'Listen, you've got to dig all the sand out so you can get the Max Trax under.'

They didn't have their own Max Trax. They'd borrowed mine. They were digging and digging, and as they're digging, the sand's falling back in, it's 44 degrees, the flies were driving them nuts. Then the penny dropped. It wasn't a good idea to cross the desert. Eventually they got the car out and they said, 'Nuh, not gonna do this.'

I sort of said, 'This sand dune is small compared to some of them out there in the desert.' Which they weren't. (Laughter) Sometimes you've gotta do that. Mind you, some of the dunes around Poeppels give Big Red (claimed to the biggest in the Simpson Desert) a run for its money. If they're not that big, they're not far off it.

Then we went back over Big Red and I gave them some other options. They wanted to go to Alice Springs. So I suggested they go down to Marree and up through Oodnadatta, which is a good drive. You go past Lake Eyre and William Creek, then up to Oodnadatta or across to Coober Pedy. Or you can go up to Boulia and along the Plenty Highway.

I think they were happy to take my advice. They wanted to cross the desert but they also had to get to Alice Springs. That way they'd get to Alice Springs and still see a fair bit of the out-back as well.

It was a bit of job taking them out but it was either half a day doing that or two days trying to rescue them, in the middle of the desert, when they're half dead. It's 30 kilometres instead of 130 kilometres, or 230.

CHAPTER 13

NO COUNTRY FOR OLD MEN

On 18 April 2015, the ABC's Josh Bavas did a story on *Australia Wide* about how I was due to retire when I turned sixty in November. Being the Birdsville cop gives you a certain amount of media exposure but nothing could prepare me for the response to Josh's story.

The following day, the premier of Queensland, Annastacia Palaszczuk, commented on Facebook, 'Thanks Neale for your dedication and service to the Queensland Police Service and to the people of Birdsville over the past years. I join with the police minister, Jo-Ann Miller MP, in wishing you all the very best in your retirement. Thank you!' The story then got picked up by media all over the world. Within a few days, the story was run as far afield as the *Daily Mail* and the *Guardian* in the UK and the *New Zealand Herald*. The story also ran in Korea.

We got a sense of our media profile on 22 April 2015, when the then federal minister for communications (and soon-to-be prime minister), Malcolm Turnbull, came to town. He was accompanied by Bruce Scott, our local federal member for Maranoa. There was a function at the pub, a meet and greet, where everyone got to talk to Malcolm. He made a bit of a speech there. It was quite an event as there was a car rally in town at the same time.

In the morning, there was a breakfast at the Dingo Caves, for the rally, and Malcolm turned up for that. He offered to help cook and all that sort of stuff.

Then there was a function at the bakery, for all the locals. Malcolm made another speech there in relation to communications. There wasn't much mention of Birdsville not being on the National Broadband Network. (Laughter)

He was very personable, very easy to talk to. He spoke to all the locals. He wasn't distant or anything like that. He was very friendly and even kissed a baby. I introduced him to Sandra, because she wasn't at the pub the night before.

He said, 'Yeah, I remember seeing you on *Australia Wide* the other night.'

That was a bit of a surprise. Normally it's us recognising him, because he's a politician. Instead, it was him recognising us.

Meanwhile, my brothers were combing the internet for stories about me. In early May my brother Phil sent me an email:

> *Hey Sarge [my nickname, from when I was a prosecuting sergeant]*
>
> *You are trending big time on social media thesarge birdsvilleplod*
>
> *Great Sarge quote: 'I call Birdsville the land of plenty. Plenty of dust, plenty of insects and most of all, plenty of heat!'*
>
> *I see a blossoming career as a late night TV host beckoning.*

Then Phil found an article about me in China's *Epoch Times*. He wrote:

> *I particularly loved this quote:*
>
> 麥克夏恩說：「伯茲維爾和別的地方非常不一樣。我稱這個地方是多物之地。很多的塵土，很多的昆蟲，很多的熱量
>
> *They would have been rolling in the rice fields at that one!*

The manager of the Outback HF radio network, Steve Johnston, was also very complimentary in an article in the winter 2015 edition of *Network News*:

> During his time in Birdsville Neale has worked very closely with the VKS-737 Radio Network involving many recovery operations particularly in the Simpson Desert. If we needed assistance with a subscriber who was in trouble, Neale has always been on call to help.
>
> As the sole police officer in town Neale regularly has to call for assistance from Don Rowlands, the local National Park ranger, as well as the ambulance officer and the mechanic from Birdsville Auto.
>
> On behalf of the staff, committee, operators, volunteers and subscribers to the VKS-737 Radio Network, I would like to thank Neale for all his past assistance to the Network and wish him all the best for his future activities in his retirement.

It was good to get so much positive feedback but it wasn't about to go to my head. After reading about my exploits, the less-than-glamourous realities of the daily routine always put things in perspective: the weather at 6 a.m., then correspondence and station duties, then a patrol of the Birdsville township, the hotel, caravan park, service stations and surrounding areas. After lunch, more correspondence and station duties, then a patrol of the Birdsville township, the hotel, caravan park, service stations and surrounding areas. Day after day. Once a week, the routine varied slightly. After doing my correspondence and station duties, I'd clean and tidy the station, mow and whipper-snip the yard, remove the rubbish, then clean and wash the police car. Not many TV segments and newspaper articles went into detail about that. The norm wasn't as newsworthy as a phone call that meant all hands on deck.

There was another of those phone calls on 23 May 2015 while Sandra and I were on our afternoon walk. A motorbike rider in the desert had broken his leg. He was 80 kilometres west of town. I got the crew together. Don drove the ambulance with Andrew the nurse. Sandra and I were in the police car. Off we went, and we got there at about nine o'clock at night.

This fella's leg was badly broken. So we gave him first aid and pain relief and put him on a stretcher. Then, to get him to the ambulance, I had to lift and carry one end of the stretcher. It really took it out of me. He was a reasonably sized fella. And we were trying to move the stretcher on wheels through the sand. We were virtually dragging it. I was exhausted by the end.

He was placed in the ambulance and, because this fella's leg was so badly broken, Don suggested we travel south between the dunes until we met the Birdsville Inside Track, rather than go east and bounce him over the dunes. Then we could drive back up along the flood plain where there are nowhere near as many dunes. It's a much longer drive but the road is a lot smoother.

By the time we got to Birdsville, it was about one o'clock in the morning. I was exhausted. Really tired. The patient was loaded onto the Flying Doctor.

As it turned out, twelve hours later, I was loaded on to the same plane.

When I went to bed, I wasn't feeling at all well, but I hoped I'd be better in the morning. Instead, when I woke up, I had big trouble moving my right arm. I had pain in my right leg. I still felt really fatigued.

When I made Sandra a cup of tea and some toast, I found it really hard to butter the toast. I managed it, but it was a real struggle. I thought, Gee, what's wrong? I can't move my arm properly. Then I took the tea and toast in and I spilt half the tea.

Sandra said, 'What's wrong?'

She said I had a vacant look in my eyes. Then she used her first aid training. She thought I was having a stroke because whatever was happening to me was affecting the right side of my body. She did all these tests, made me hold out my arm, stand on one leg, blah, blah, blah. I passed all of them but I still didn't feel 100 per cent. Far from it.

So we went down to the clinic. The nurse did some tests on me. Then he rang the Flying Doctor.

The doctor said, 'No, gotta get 'im.'

My blood pressure was sky high. Really high. And I'd had good blood pressure when it was tested only a few weeks before.

I was given medication to drop my blood pressure, to thin my blood, because by now they were sure it was a stroke. It was affecting the right side of my body. Sandra said my face had dropped a bit as well, on the right side.

Yet I could still get up and walk to the toilet. When the Flying Doctor arrived, I walked to the ambulance, sat in the passenger seat, got driven out to the plane. I walked onto the plane, up the stairs. I lay down on the bed and they did further tests on me, in relation to this and that. Then we headed off.

We were originally going to Toowoomba, but they were monitoring my signs on the way. Halfway there I heard the doctor say to the pilot, 'No, we'll go straight to Brisbane.'

My heart sank.

Normally, if you're not too bad, you go to Charleville. If you're worse, you go to Toowoomba. If you're real bad, you go to Brisbane. That's what I tell people when they're flown out.

Again, in Brisbane, I walked off the plane. Except, when I first went to stand up, I fell back down.

The nurse said, 'Just rest for a while.'

Then I was able to walk down the stairs but they were watching me in case I fell. The ambulance was there. They laid me on a stretcher and put me in the back. They took me to the Princess Alexandra Hospital. Emergency.

They did all these tests on me. I spent the night in Emergency, and half the next day. Then I went to a short-term room where they monitored me. I was there for three days and during that time my condition deteriorated. It just got worse and worse. In the end I couldn't use my arm. I couldn't move my fingers. I had no movement in my arm at all. Same with my leg. I couldn't walk. I was being pushed around in a wheelchair. My mouth had dropped and I was just feeling so tired. Not feeling good at all. Specialists came and saw me. MRI. Scans. Cardiologists. You name it.

After four days, I went to the Geriatric and Rehabilitation

Unit (GARU Ward). I spent the rest of May there, all of June, and the first week of July.

When I got there, I was being pushed around. I couldn't shower by myself. I had to have my food cut up for me. I had to get lids taken off things because I didn't have the strength to hold the jar to unscrew them. Essentially, I only had the use of my left hand.

In rehab, though, they want you to move from day one. They want you to go down to the dining room rather than lie in bed feeling sorry for yourself. Get up and go down there. Good idea. They gave me a stick to walk with. I just couldn't do it. Too exhausted. Too far. And when you look at it, it's not that far at all. So I was pushed down in a wheelchair for about four or five days.

Then they said, 'No, you've gotta walk.'

At first they let me use a walking stick. Then the physio took the stick off me.

They said, 'No, you don't need the stick.'

If you keep using the stick, you'll end up relying on it all the time. They put a belt around me with velcro and hung onto me. I walked down to the dining room. That happened for three weeks or so. Everywhere I went, someone had to hold onto me. I couldn't go anywhere by myself. Toilet. Shower. Go for dinner. To physio. Wherever.

They started physio virtually straightaway. First they assess you, then you do minor things: moving something from there to there, or lifting your leg up. Then there was occupational therapy, which is on your hands. Like, square peg, round hole. Trying to write. I couldn't write at all. Then speech, because my mouth had dropped. Also, you lose some of your memory function. They'd have a sentence, 'chase brown dog cat', and you'd have to put 'brown dog chasing a cat'.

After a few days, I noticed I had a little bit of movement in my fingers. When my daughter, Lauren, put her finger in my hand, I could close my hand. If she didn't put her finger there, I couldn't close it.

Lauren, who is now a teacher, had come down from Atherton. My son Andrew lived in Brisbane, so he was there too. My son Robbie, he came down. The police service flew Sandra down from Birdsville. They got her on the plane with less than an hour before it was due to depart.

They said, 'Get to the airport. We'll get you out.'

Sandra stayed with Andrew, otherwise the police service would have got her accommodation. So all my family were around.

When I was first in hospital, after about a week, Robbie took me out in a wheelchair. We went round, outside the hospital. It was a beautiful day and just so good to get outside.

The police service was really good. The superintendent from Mount Isa visited me while I was in Emergency. He came back and visited me when I was in the GARU Ward. I got a phone call from the commissioner of police, flowers from the minister of police, a lot of police officers sent get-well cards and flowers. Assistant commissioners rang up to see how I was going. The Police Union came and saw me a few times to see if I needed anything.

The community of Birdsville were really good. They sent me a get-well card, a photo of the town that said, 'A whole town wishes you a speedy recovery.' It was signed by the whole community.

It really buoyed my spirits, all that.

Don the ranger rang or sent me a text every day, to see how I was going or to tell me a few jokes. He sent a picture of his dog, Koopah, with a note: 'Koopah misses ya.' Barry and Narelle Gaffney sent me flowers. Nell and David, too. It made me feel a lot better having so many people care about me.

I had a visit from a stroke survivor, Old Joe. He was a volunteer. He came in, and the poor old bugger, lovely bloke, was in a wheelchair with his hands up there, drooling out the side of his mouth, and he told all the recent stroke victims, 'This is what happens. You've got to keep working to get better.'

I said to him after, 'When did you have your stroke, Joe?'

He said, 'Seven years ago.'

So it was a bit . . . I was hoping the volunteer would come in doing cartwheels. Jump up and click his heels together. However, he was a lovely bloke and it was good talking to him.

There was also a Neighbourhood Police Beat (a police station) at the hospital. When I went through Emergency, they came to see me. I saw there was a police officer there and thought, Oh some poor bugger's been shot or knifed or bashed or been in a bad car accident. It turned out this police officer was there waiting for me.

He said, 'We're here to help you. Need anything, sing out, we'll come and see ya.'

He and the other police there came and saw me on a regular basis, to see how I was going. When I got a bit better they'd pick me up in the police car and take me down to their office, which was in the hospital grounds, because I couldn't walk that far. I'd go in there and send emails, even though I could only use one finger, because I couldn't move my right arm. They'd talk to me, have a coffee with me, and it was like I wasn't sick. It was like I was back at work. Talking about work and stuff like that.

When it was time to go back, they'd say, 'Nah, we'll take you back.'

Then they'd take me for a drive around the area. It was good just to get out, get a bit of fresh air.

Not long after my stroke, I managed to get to my mother's ninetieth birthday. She turned ninety on 21 June and I was really keen to go down to Melbourne for it. The specialist said, 'You can go, but only if you go in a wheelchair from the car to the plane and then when you get off the plane to the car.'

I said to him, 'Yeah, no worries.'

I said to myself, 'Tough nuts, no way.'

I walked onto the plane and walked off. It took me a while but I did it. I went to my mother's birthday. Fortunately, it was during the day. She was glad to see me. She was worried about me, too. As were my brothers. It was good to catch up with them.

I went to the party and I lasted about two hours or so. Then I said to Sandra, 'I've gotta go home. Just too buggered.'

I was buggered about an hour into it but I hung on for another hour.

My mother said, 'Good of you to come anyway.'

Sandra drove me home and my ninety-year-old mother outlasted me. Double. Five hours. And she was drinking and I wasn't drinking.

The specialist had said, 'You can have one glass of wine but make sure it's a good one.'

So I had one glass of wine. It was good to go down. It was good emotionally, too, to get out and go down and see my mother and brothers.

After six weeks of treatment and rehab, I left hospital on 9 July 2015. I stayed in Brisbane, continuing rehab, until 24 August. I lived in an apartment near the hospital provided by the Police Helping Hand Fund. All police make a donation to the fund, a couple of bucks a week, and the money is used to provide accommodation for police in situations like mine.

I had rehab every day, or most days. It was either physio, occupational therapy, speech or a combination of all three.

The quality of care from the medical staff was magnificent. The specialist, the doctors, the nurses, the physios, the occupational therapists were all working together so that I could make the best recovery. You hear all these stories about the public health system but I couldn't fault it.

A lot of Australians don't realise how good our public health system is, compared to other countries. I've got private health insurance but I was in Emergency for four days, then I went to rehab. At the time I didn't know whether I was Arthur or Martha, so I just went with the flow. Then I thought, I've got private health, and I spoke to the social worker and she said, 'Don't change. You've got the specialist, he's got a handle on what your situation is, you've got the occupational therapists and the physios. Just leave it.'

So I did. The best thing I did.

The social worker also said, 'Look, we're here to look after you. How much sick leave have you got? We can look at social security.'

I said, 'I've got twelve months' sick leave and I've got six months to go until I retire.'

They said, 'What about somewhere for your wife to stay?'

I said, 'No, that's good. She's staying at our son's now and when I get out of hospital the Police Fund has given us an apartment. So that's all covered.'

She said, 'What about cost?'

I said, 'It's all free.'

She mentioned a couple of other things, too, and I said, 'It's all taken care of.'

'What about your house?'

'Lyn's watering the garden.'

She said, 'Well, you're well looked after.'

Even Craig Shepherd, the senior sergeant in Mount Isa in charge of looking after me, had said, 'Don't worry about anything. Work things, it'll all be sorted. You just worry about getting better.'

I can't thank the police enough. And the Police Union. They came around and visited me and said, 'Don't worry, we'll look after you.'

While all this was going on, there was one person who was by my side through all of it. Sandra. She got flown down, she came in every day, came by train, sometimes twice a day. Brought me in a paper, or a chocolate, or a cup of coffee. She visited me all the time.

She coped pretty well but it can't have been easy. You don't know how it will go. Will I get better? Am I going to be disabled for the rest of my life? Strokes affect people in different ways: emotionally, physically, all of that stuff. You can lose your memory or you may have bouts of anger. So she had all of that to worry about as well.

As it was, I was lucky in a lot of ways. My stroke didn't affect things like memory or sight. I can remember dates and times and places pretty well. It affected other things, like I get emotional easily. My successful recovery wasn't because I worked hard, it was because I was lucky and I got excellent medical treatment.

While I was in hospital I encountered other stroke patients who were in much worse situations than mine. Some had lost their memory completely. They couldn't spell dog. They had to go back to Grade 1, to learn how to write and how to spell. They had to be taught how to sound words and stuff like that. Other people couldn't use one of their arms at all. And they're going to be like that forever.

I'll never forget an experience that I had early on, when I was in rehab. They had an outdoor area where you could go out and sit. I was out there, feeling sorry for myself, and this young guy came out. He would have been in his thirties or younger. He had no legs. I got talking to him and he had a positive outlook on things and I thought, Gee. And there were people there with MS. It's a downward spiral for them, and they're in their thirties. The best they can do is try to reduce the rate of decline.

Even though I was doing heaps of scheduled physio, I started doing extra. I was doing physio in bed, squeezing balls and stuff. At night time, after dinner when the physios had gone home, there was a flight of stairs like a fire escape. Concrete stairs. And I'd go up and down those.

I started off going up and down once, and I'd be hanging on, with both hands on the rail, and I'd go step to step. One step, both feet on the same step. Then I could go step to step with one hand on the rail. Then it was normal step after step, and eventually just one hand hovering over the rail. Eventually I got to the stage, over a two or three week period, where I got to going up and down ten times. Two flights of stairs. It just proves, you do the hard work, it pays off.

At the end of June 2015, I sent an email to all my colleagues in the Mount Isa Police District. Among other things, I wrote:

> I don't know why I had a stroke as I had good blood
> pressure and don't smoke. I only had six months to
> retirement. Still, as John Lennon sang, 'Life is what happens
> when we're busy making other plans.'

I will be out of hospital next week then doing rehab for six weeks in Brisbane. My plan is to make the most of rehab and make the best recovery I can. I also intend to return to Birdsville for the races. I don't think I will be well enough to work but it would be good to say goodbye.

Both Sandra and I have received excellent treatment by the QPS and Police Union. They couldn't have done any more to assist in my recovery and provide every assistance to Sandra and me. I am extremely proud to be a member of both the QPS and Police Union.

I wanted to get back to Birdsville for my last races and I just managed it, by about a week. I got back on 24 August, three months to the day after my stroke. I finished at rehab but I was still on sick leave. My doctor was happy for me to go. He thought it would be good for me to go back, say goodbye to people, do the last race meeting, but not work. By then, of course, there was a relieving officer at the station: Kate Plant.

The people in town were glad to see me, but it was like I wasn't the officer in charge any more. There was another police officer there. They were going to her for things. So things were different but I knew that, because I'd been away since May. It was now the end of August. It wasn't like it was my station any more. Kate was the officer in charge. I was there as, like, a spare. I was on sick leave anyway. You know, the world goes on.

Sandra and I returned to our house in Birdsville. It's part of the deal. You don't pay any rent. You just pay rates. We moved back and Sandra returned to doing her QGAP job. She was on carer's leave while I was sick. Kate lived in the barracks.

We prepared for the races. Well, I didn't have to do any

preparation, the operation order or anything like that. It was more just being there. It was hard to stay away. As people came into town, I went and met them and all that.

I wore my uniform a few times. A lot of times it was for a particular reason. Like, the superintendent came down, he wanted a photo for police media, Facebook, and stuff like that. He gave me a long-service medal so I put the uniform on for that. There were a few other times I put it on just to go round with Kate.

The real preparation Sandra and I had to do was for visitors. My retirement had been announced in April, but it wasn't until November. So, between returning to Birdsville after my stroke and my retirement, family, friends and police came from everywhere.

A lot of police who weren't working came down to say goodbye to me. They knew they wouldn't be able to come down for my send-off so they came down for the races. A lot of friends came and stayed in the backyard.

All my brothers came a week before the races, not long after I got back. I got a great photo of all my brothers at the race track. It's in the starting stalls, and we're numbered one to five. One for the first born. Five for the last born. We had a barbeque at the courthouse. We went down to Dickeree Waterhole at sunset, drove up on the sandhill and had a drink up there.

My cousin, Les Dowe, and his wife, Wendy, came out and camped in the courthouse. My brothers stayed in the house. They left the Wednesday before the races but a lot of the stall holders were already set up and working. A few of the stall holders came around for a barbie at the courthouse: Johnno the pizza man, Kevie the t-shirt man and Salty the blacksmith. Then Johnno had a pizza night. We had them at the courthouse as well.

By the time the races started, the house and the courthouse

grounds were overflowing. There were people camped between the police station and the house, back past where the evaporative tank is, and then over the back fence as well. There were more in the police paddock where the old police trackers' hut is.

A lot of people came out. We were friends with the former Australian Ambassador to Hong Kong, Les Luck and his wife, Jenny. He's retired now. They came out. There were a couple of ex-police officers from Victoria, retired, police from Queensland, friends we've met over the years. Birdsville was a very social place during those races.

Police started arriving Wednesday and Thursday in the build-up to the races. On Friday I went to the corporate tent with Sandra, the superintendent and his wife, Vicki, and his son and daughter. His son's a police officer, too. I went to Brophy's on the Saturday, walked around, socialised with people. Sunday I assisted at Blow Before You Go, where people can check that they're under the alcohol limit before they drive. I didn't work the instrument. I just went up there.

I got the Birdsville Social Club, which was running a barbeque away from Blow Before You Go, right on the corner, to come down. They weren't doing much business. I said, 'Come down to Blow Before You Go. There's a heap of people there who've been drinking all night. If they smell sausages, they're going to buy one.'

They did. And they sold out.

Kate Plant came up with the idea that people should make a donation to the Flying Doctor when they have a blow. Good idea. We raised $880.

I enjoyed the last races. I had a good time. I didn't do much work. I did prosecute the court on the Saturday and Sunday.

There was a guy who'd belted Darren, the barman at the pub, because he was dancing with his girlfriend (now his ex-girlfriend). Darren got a punch in the mouth and smashed glasses. The bloke got fined $750, plus $750 compo. This was an affray prior to the races, heard at the court that's held during the races. Then there were some drink-drivers: four people who were dumb enough to drink and drive at the races.

After it was over, I went up to the pub on Sunday afternoon with a few off-duty police. I wasn't drinking, just having a soft drink, taking in the atmosphere of Sunday after races. That's when things start to wind down because everyone who can go on Sunday morning does. A few people stay on now; it's changed. They come earlier and stay later rather than eat dust from other cars all the way in and all the way out.

We had a barbeque that night at the courthouse. On Monday night the Traffic Branch had a function for me and Sandra, gave us presents, and thanked us for looking after them for the past nine years. Most of them had been there for a fair while. We had looked after them, provided the barbeque, cleaned up the courthouse, arranged the firewood, all that sort of stuff. So that was nice.

Some people don't have much nice to say about the Traffic Branch. Some say they come down to the Birdsville Races to revenue raise and pick on the poor motorists. I obviously have a very different view. All police who work at the Birdsville Races have a very important role to play and do an excellent job but I always appreciated the presence of the Traffic Branch from Mount Isa and Cloncurry and the Roadside Drug Testing Unit. They would set up roadside breath-testing and drug-testing on the roads leading into Birdsville prior to the races, during the races and at the completion.

The sergeant in charge of the Traffic Branch, Sergeant Shaun

English, attended all nine of the race meetings that I did so he knew the drill thoroughly and his team always hit the ground running. Officers would be out in the heat, dust and flies for hours, breath-testing and drug-testing drivers. This sent a clear message that drink- or drug-driving isn't tolerated, even in the remotest part of the state. Some 2500 breath-tests would be conducted over the four-odd days. The vast majority of drivers would have no alcohol or drugs in their system and the police would have a pleasant chat to them and the occupants of their vehicles and many times give advice on places to camp, Birdsville and the surrounding district. This was excellent PR for the police service.

Once, a person came up on the UHF radio and said, 'The mongrels are breath-testing outside the racecourse.' He was howled down by twenty other radio users with comments like, 'To stop idiots like you, they're doing a great job, pull your head in, they're making the races safer, leave 'em alone.'

Police on trailbikes patrolled the town common between Birdsville and the racecourse where the vast majority camped. Many times they apprehended drivers doing dangerous and/or stupid acts and took appropriate action. Word would spread that police on trailbikes were enforcing the traffic laws and it made camping a lot safer and pleasant for everyone.

A word of advice to people travelling to the races is: don't speed, drink- or drug-drive, use your mobile phone while driving, go without a seatbelt or do any stupid or dangerous act with a motor vehicle. What I also suggest is: fuel up when you first arrive (to beat the queues on the Sunday after the races), get any necessary supplies, find a camp and park up for the weekend. There are buses to and from the race track for a gold-coin donation to the Flying Doctor and everything is close in town. You don't have to worry about having a sober driver as you can walk everywhere.

If you drink on Saturday night, on Sunday morning there's Blow Before You Go outside the roadhouse, across the road from the caravan park, where you can have a pre-emptive breath-test before getting in a motor vehicle and driving home. It's free, unless you want to make a gold-coin donation to the Flying Doctor.

Despite the visible police presence, every year traffic police would charge drivers with drink-driving as they left the racecourse. This despite the fact that you could actually see the police in their high-vis vests and their cars with flashing blue-and-red lights from the racecourse parking area. From there to the road into town it's as flat as a tack and there's not a blade of grass. So it's not like the cops are hiding. Some people are just dumb.

There was plenty of breath-testing on Sunday as well, when most people leave town. One driver told me he got pulled up for a breath-test and said, 'I've been to Blow Before You Go.'

The traffic officer said, 'That's for fun, this is for real.'

He went zero again.

Proudly, I can say in my time at Birdsville, at nine race meetings, we didn't have a fatal or serious accident either in town or on the roads leading away from Birdsville. This is in large part due to the excellent job of the Traffic Branch and the RSDT Unit, as well as Blow Before You Go. The only accident I can remember on the Sunday after the races was in 2011, when a vehicle braked as a snake crossed the road and a bike collided with its rear. The rider broke his wrist and was flown out by the Flying Doctor. Not bad for nine race meetings and thousands of vehicles each year.

We also got a lot of support from the council and the ABC when it came to getting out messages about road safety. Chrissie Arthur, who has been a reporter with ABC North West for many years, deserves special mention. She's a great friend of the outback and of Birdsville. Whenever she interviewed me about the preparations for the races, she always threw me a question about road safety and off I'd go. The race club promoted Blow Before You Go and put out messages about wearing seatbelts. Everyone was onboard about promoting road safety.

On the Tuesday after the races, things had really wound down. Nearly everyone was gone. It felt sad that it was my last races, in some ways, for sure. I wasn't well enough to work, not completely. Looking back now, I wouldn't have been able to do a rescue. Not the way I used to do it. I'd struggle. If I had to drive out in the desert, I could do it, but if you've got to get out and dig, get off a sandhill, change a tyre in a dust storm and drive for thirty hours, I'd really struggle. I know that.

My health wasn't up to it. It wouldn't have been fair on the people I was rescuing. People, if they call the police, they expect you to be able to help them. If you can't, you shouldn't be there. People expect you to do your job.

It was sad, but I knew I was retiring anyway. The stroke probably didn't make it as sad because I knew I'd struggle. It's also nature's way of telling you it's time. Unfortunately, I still had one last job to do.

CHAPTER 14

HEARTBREAK CORNER

A month after the races, on 2 October 2015, I got a call at seven-thirty in the morning. Kate rang me and said there was a fatal accident 20 kilometres south of Birdsville.

I said, 'Oh, that's terrible. I'll come down and give you a hand.'

I'm a South Australian police officer. As soon as Kate crosses the border, she's a civilian. She's got no power to stop cars. If someone's drunk, she has no power to give them a breath-test. All those things you need when police investigate an accident: power to impound a vehicle, preserve the scene, block the road. So I put on a uniform and went down with her.

A car had rolled over but it was back on its wheels. I got there and I noticed Wade Gilby was lying on a doona with his mum. He was injured. He didn't have a shirt on but he had his jeans on.

Then we were told about a deceased female lying beside the car with her head facing towards the front of the car. She was covered by a blanket. A doona. I lifted it up and noticed it was Kelly Theobald.

Oh no.

278

She was obviously deceased. I checked her. She was dead but I called the nurse over and he checked as well. She was deceased.

This was someone that I'd known well and cared about. I was really. . . I had a job to do so I thought, There's not much you can do. She's deceased. Get on with the work that you're required to do.

We had to preserve the scene because you could clearly see the tyre marks on the Birdsville Track where the car had left the track and rolled over. We had to preserve those. We had to get Wade onto a stretcher and get him off to hospital because he was in a bad way, too.

We did that. Unfortunately, there was nothing we could do for Kelly. At least, at that time.

We were concerned as to who was actually driving the car. Even though Kelly was deceased out the driver's side seat, and her seat was forward, and his seat was back, there's times where people have moved seats forward and back to make out someone else was driving.

We were concerned about that, and we had to contact South Australia Police, because the accident was just over the South Australia border. They had to start preparing to come up to do the investigation. Then Kate went back to Birdsville. She followed the ambulance back a short time after, because South Australia wanted a blood test from Wade and wanted a version from him as to what happened.

I was left at the scene. Kevin Scott from the SES and council was with me, along with a few other council workers and SES volunteers. We preserved the scene, put vehicles around it.

I wanted to get Kelly out as soon as we could. You know, she's there lying in the dirt, but we couldn't get the ambulance back because the Flying Doctor was coming in. Then the Flying

Doctor needed the ambulance to convey Wade to the plane to get him out.

So it wasn't until one o'clock that the ambulance was able to return to the scene. During this time, we'd conversed with the investigators from South Australia and they told us they wanted certain photos taken, certain measurements taken, which we did. Kate Plant did those and I assisted her.

Then Kelly was placed on the stretcher and taken back to Birdsville to be lodged. Kate went back to do all that.

While this was happening, members of the community were on the scene, many of whom knew Kelly well. Everyone was sad but it didn't affect me that much because it was just like a job at that stage. It did later, but not at that time. Everyone said, 'Poor thing', and all that, but you're busy working, doing things. You're writing down details for your statement and taking photos for South Australian police.

We were worried, because of modern technology like Facebook, that Kelly's parents should be told as soon as possible rather than have them hear about it through social media. There were rumours getting around that it was Kelly. People knew it was her car, people who'd been at the scene knew it was her and they'd gone back into town. People were ringing Sandra and saying, 'Was it Kelly Theobald who was killed?'

And Sandra's going, 'I can't say.'

So we were really keen to get the relatives notified; the mother and father.

I said to Kevin Scott, 'It's going to be a day of sadness.'

They'd have been at home in Melbourne. A police officer would come to tell them, and they're going to tell Kelly's siblings, then the grandparents, then the immediate members of the family, extended members of the family. Friends. It was just going to be a day of sadness. Added to that, Kelly had been about to go back for her sister's wedding.

Kelly and Wade had been going to a rodeo at Tibooburra for the weekend. They were supposed to meet Donna Gilby, Wade's mother, on the corner where the station road from Pandie Pandie homestead (where Kelly was working) meets the Birdsville Track. However, at some time early in the morning, they'd travelled north to come into Birdsville.

We don't know why. Wade's lost his memory as to what happened. So we may never know what they were doing. They weren't getting petrol because everything was closed.

South Australia police arrived about two o'clock in the afternoon. They flew up a team of four and landed at the Pandie Pandie airstrip. Tom came up from Marree. He arrived there about the same time.

We could see the airstrip from where the accident was, just a short way away. They'd only travelled a kilometre from the turn-off to Pandie Pandie. If that. Wade's mother drove down and came across the accident. She was heading down there to meet them at the station turnoff. They should have been at the corner. They'd travelled beyond that, towards Birdsville.

The investigators came and did a complete investigation. They were there until about six o'clock at night. Then we came back into Birdsville. They continued their investigation at the police station. They went up to the morgue to view Kelly. I didn't go up. I didn't want to, obviously. So Kate went up with them.

They didn't leave until the next day. They conducted further enquiries during the course of the next morning, then left at about two o'clock in the afternoon.

Kelly was placed in the forward compartment of the plane that the police were in and flown out. Before the plane took off, most of the town gathered on the oval. We had placards with farewell messages on them and her little Volkswagen was there, too.

We were all there waving goodbye to her. So sad, ay. That's when I got really upset. I couldn't stop crying. There's tears coming down. It really hit me.

The day before, I was doing my job, that I'm trained to do. Then it really upset me. Mmm. Because she was in the prime of life, twenty-seven years of age. Young girl. Shouldn't have happened. The investigators aren't sure if she was wearing a seatbelt. That might have been why she died. If she was wearing one, she would have had a few bumps and bruises. We think Wade had his seatbelt on. That's why he only had injuries.

There are questions unanswered. He had a head injury and says he can't remember anything about it.

It was a rollover. Rolled right over and back on its wheels. In my time at Birdsville I've been to at least sixteen rollovers, if not more. That was the first fatal accident. And it turns out, no seatbelt, and she was a friend.

They had the funeral in Melbourne and then her mother, father, sister and brother transported her ashes back to Birdsville. She loved this place.

Her father said, 'She didn't want to be buried in some cemetery where people never go and visit her.'

They wanted her ashes to be scattered on Big Red, which she just loved. They had a ceremony at Big Red and we went there and again the whole town was there. Her brother wanted to drive up Big Red in Onslo the Volkswagen. The urn with Kelly's ashes was on the front seat. He tried and tried and tried and couldn't get up. He'd come back down, drop the tyre pressure, try it again. Couldn't get up there. Tried so many times. And everyone's willing him up. Then, eventually, he got up. And everyone's cheering. And that was good.

Then her ashes were scattered and people said a few words about Kelly. We had a few drinks up there, to her. Then we went back to the hotel and had a few more.

I'd been through a lot in the previous few months. I could probably blame the stroke a bit. It affects your emotions. But also, she was a young girl with a lot going for her. We had a fair bit to do with her. She used to come into the police station. She worked at the pub. We knew her from there. We knew her from the information centre. She used to compile *Desert Yarns*. I used to write my police column but she'd fine tune it a bit, make it a bit better to read. She helped Sandra with the star show. She did a big blog post on the star show. She was a really nice girl.

We knew her really well for four years. A long time. Sandra got her a house in Birdsville. We used to give her advice on certain things. She told us she was buying a car and we spoke to her about that. We registered Onslo for her, the blue Volkswagen.

She ran community events and so on. If she needed someone to talk at community events, she'd ask me and I'd say, 'Yeah. No worries. What do I say?' (Laughter)

I think, getting upset, I've been to a lot of accidents over forty-odd years and seen a lot of sad things, but knowing her and combining that with the way she died, and the stroke, and I was retiring . . . Last job. What a way to go out. Poor Kelly.

I said in an interview, 'She was born and bred in Melbourne, but her heart was in the Australian outback.'

Kelly had actually gone home to Melbourne in early August

but she'd said to her mum, 'I can't handle the traffic, the people, I'm going back to Birdsville. I'll come back for the wedding.'

It wasn't to be.

Between the races and my actual retirement, on my sixtieth birthday, on 21 November, I went back and forth for more tests in Brisbane and Mount Isa. On one visit Sandra and I attended our son Andrew's graduation as a firefighter, a long-time ambition of his. Sandra gave him a photo from when he was three with a big fireman's hat on, with the message, 'Some little boy's dreams do come true.'

I was still on sick leave but Sandra was back working, doing her QGAP duties. While she was doing that, she got a charming email on 17 October 2015 from a desert traveller, outlining his itinerary:

> *This is to let you know that same as this time last year I'll be going through the Simpson Desert. Also, my 50th birthday will happen on Sunday 18th of October at the corner of French Line and Knolls Track (I camped there last year as well, it's a nice place, just next to the 'dingo' tree stump). I invited all (241) of my Facebook friends to the party but I doubt anyone will show up, so in the end it will be just me. The party starts one hour after sunset and I'll keep it quiet and clean up the place. I will not continue driving next morning until I'm properly sober and all alcohol has left my bloodstream, I promise.*

Sandra and I didn't attend his party either but Sandra had been living in Birdsville for five years and had never been to the places this fella was describing. Usually, when I was out on a rescue she was holding the fort, answering phones, relaying messages, keeping track of where everyone was. I had always promised to take her out to the desert to show her Poeppels Corner but somehow I'd never got around to it. We were going to go right across the desert during the winter of 2015 but that didn't happen because I got sick.

So in early November, we went out with Paul Jackson, who was the Bedourie sherriff, and Shane Long, who was the relieving Birdsville police officer. We went to Poeppels, then down the Warburton Track (where I've done a lot of rescues), then back up the Birdsville Track (where I've done a lot of rescues, too). For me, it was a little victory lap, a final patrol, about two weeks before I retired.

It was good going back through that country I've been to so many times. I wasn't driving, other police were driving. It was good. As in, I don't have to come out here again. (Laughter) I didn't do it because I wanted to go. I did it to take Sandra because I promised I'd take her. We did it in one day. Long day.

That was the first time I went as a passenger and the first time I went out there and it wasn't a job. I didn't have to make sure I didn't crash or get bogged or lost.

It wasn't a case of good riddance. Like a lot of people who keep coming back, I love the desert. I love the colours. The sunsets are beautiful. You get up on a sandhill and you know there's no-one around for hundreds of kilometres.

It's a beautiful part of Australia: the colours of the sand, the way the wind shapes the sand, the ripples. The salt pans are beautiful. You think they're full of water when you first see them but when you get there you realise the white is the salt, not water. And it's just a vast expanse. You can see for as far as the eye can see.

Then when you get over to the furthest point you can see, you can see as far as the eye can see again. (Laughter)

As the date of my retirement approached, people started making arrangements for a special farewell function at the community centre. My birthday was on a Saturday, which meant the function was to be held on my very last day.

Even before then, messages started coming in. On 2 October 2015 I got a letter from the Australian Maritime Safety Authority, the Search and Rescue people in Canberra:

> *Dear Senior Constable McShane*
>
> *This letter is to note your imminent retirement from the Queensland Police Service and to offer you the thanks and appreciation of the Australian Maritime Safety Authority (AMSA) for the cooperative relationship we have experienced over the many years of your service at Birdsville.*
>
> *As you would know from your own experience, the Australian national search and rescue arrangements rely heavily on good working relationships between AMSA and the relevant police jurisdictions. Almost all search and rescue operations that we lead are essentially conducted jointly with police services that have the local knowledge, contacts and communications.*
>
> *Achieving rapid and successful rescues in the harsh conditions and poor communications of the remote Australian Outback is often challenging, and it is not made easier by the range of community issues that police need to deal with at the same time as a search and rescue operation.*

*We have the benefit of a single focus on search and rescue.
Police often do not.*

*On behalf of AMSA and JRCC Australia (Joint Rescue
Communications Centre), thank you for your contribution
to the Australian search and rescue arrangements and all the
best for the future.*

John Young
General Manager
Search and Rescue

The function at the community centre was a community event but
plenty of police and well-wishers came as well. The police jet with
a planeload of senior police came out from Brisbane. Colleagues
from around the Mount Isa District, Queensland, Victoria and
South Australia were also there.

The social club put on dinner for everybody and Don Rayment,
president of the social club and manager of Adria Downs, was
master of ceremonies. Jimmy Crombie and Henry Butler welcomed
everyone to country.

Dusty Miller, the Birdsville baker, said some nice things:

Tom Kruse and the movie *Back of Beyond*, the death of the
Page family and the success of the Birdsville Races have made
Birdsville into the iconic town that it is. Along with that we've
got the iconic Birdsville Hotel, and I think we're about to see the
end of the iconic outback cop, Neale McShane.

One of the reasons he is a bit iconic is because he's a bit of
a media man. I asked him to make out a bit of a list of the stuff
he's done over the years and he's had more media appearances
than the bloody Prime Minister.

He's been on Channel 7 *Sunrise* twice, Channel 9's *Today Show*, Channel 10's *The Project*, ABC *Countrywide*, ABC Radio many times. He's done live interviews on BBC radio (*World News*), half a dozen English newspapers, *New Zealand Herald*, just about every Australian newspaper and a radio station in every capital city in Australia. That's one hell of a record.

One of the reasons this cop is so well liked here: he's easygoing. He's tough when he's gotta be but he's an easygoing cop, well liked in town. We'll miss you and farewell.

The deputy commissioner of the Queensland Police Service, Mr Brett Pointing, was one of the senior police who flew out from Brisbane. Others included Assistant Commissioner Paul Taylor, Assistant Commissioner Mike Keating and Assistant Commissioner Clem O'Regan. The president of the Police Union, Ian Leavers, was also there.

Mr Pointing was very complimentary. He said:

> Neale, to have the community here speaks volumes for how well respected you are. Neale is a quintessential country copper. Very community based, good at his job, he didn't necessarily use the ticket book for everything but every now and then used a stern word depending on the circumstances. That's country policing and that's important. Thanks very much for the way you've represented us. You've been a great ambassador for us for twenty years, in one of the most remote policing posts anywhere in the world.

Mr Pointing had apparently heard that, as a sworn police officer in Queensland, South Australia and the Northern Territory, I'd tried to draw three wages. I'd often joked that if the Birdsville cop could do that, they'd never have any problems filling the position.

The deputy commissioner then presented me with the Queensland Police Meritorious Service Medal. He said:

> There's very few of these ever given out. This recognises all the selfless hours Neale has put in, the rescues, all that, but more importantly it represents Neale's service to regional and rural Queensland. It represents his service to the bush. We're finding it increasingly difficult to get police to leave the south-east corner and come into regional and remote Queensland. For Neale to do it for all his twenty years means a hell of a lot to us. It's so important to get people into remote communities that want to be here, that want to engage with the community and be part of it and take these communities forward.

The Member of the Legislative Assembly for Mount Isa, Robbie Katter, was one of several people who drove all the way down from Mount Isa to be at my farewell. I really appreciated the effort, and what he had to say:

> Every time your name came up, it was usually followed by, 'Geez he's a good bloke.' I wish, when I'm done, whatever I'm doing, that I'd be appreciated and have the calibre of people here flying in and driving all this way to make sure you knew how much they appreciated your effort. Having good police in a town is a huge thing for communities like this and you've done a superb job of it.

South Australian Police Inspector Ian Humpy presented me with a certificate from the South Australian Police Service that read:

A certificate of appreciation is awarded to Senior Constable Neale
McShane of the Queensland Police Service for his support to the
South Australian community while stationed at Birdsville Police
Station. Since his arrival at Birdsville in 2006 Neale has developed
significant working relationships and links with SAPOL officers.
He has also provided ongoing service to the South Australian
public by responding to events including sudden deaths, missing
persons, wanted offenders and has co-ordinated rescues, searches
and recoveries in the very remote and isolated north-east region
of South Australia. He has also attended and assisted with
the investigation of road crashes, including fatalities, in South
Australia. Due to the significant distances between Marree and the
Queensland border the time taken for SAPOL officers to attend
can be very significant. Birdsville on the other hand, being so much
closer, is often far more accessible and in some cases his response
has alleviated the need for one of our people to attend. So Neale's
contribution and support for the South Australian community is
acknowledged and appreciated by the South Australian Police.

Signed Bronwyn Killmier

Assistant Commissioner, State Operations Service

Ian then added:

We are so far away but you are not forgotten. The policing
service in Queensland is not forgotten. The work you do for us is
not forgotten. And the work of both Neale and Sandra, and I say
this with all sincerity, is not forgotten. You're a long way away
but we know you're here and we rely on you, depend on you and
vice versa. We support each other. Thank you and all the best.

Then it was the turn of the current Bedourie sherriff, Paul Jackson:

When I came out to Bedourie, basically, Mount Isa said, 'Any questions, just call Neale.' I did call him and he's a wealth of wisdom. I've been in Bedourie for three years now and he's the guy. For him, policing on the line is an art form. It's this bloody boundary that's not quite the same as policing on the coast. It's a little bit different out here. You have to engage the community and I'm sure all you from Birdsville know that he does that so well. He also has that line in the sand that people know: don't cross that bloody line or it's going to go pear-shaped very quickly. In the last few months the bosses have been sayin' to me, 'Take what you can from him. Milk his information. Get as much information as you can from Neale, because that information, that knowledge, you cannot replicate. The guy knows too much.'

Finally, Don and Lyn Rowlands spoke. Don didn't want to say too much, in case he got too emotional, but he said:

You've been a good mate, it's been great working with you. We've had some great fun. Sometimes it's been a bit difficult, when we've run out of tea, but it's been really good. You're now retired, so I can start to feel comfortable because I was starting to think you were getting to know the country better than I did. It was a bit of a challenge for me, mate.

Then Lyn said:

Neale has made many a great friendship over the past ten years. Now here we are, saying goodbye to our police officer and his family, who we've respected and worked with very closely in his work as the Birdsville policeman, respectfully serving this unique township with a firm but good-natured hand. So to Neale, Sandra and your family, our friends, sadly it's time for a new chapter in your lives. Another town, another city, but you will all remain in our hearts forever. We will miss you all dearly. On behalf of Don and myself, our family and the residents of Birdsville and the Diamantina Shire, all the best. Good luck and may the dust never settle.

When it was my turn to speak, I tried to keep it light. I said:

Thank you all for coming. Most of you have come a long way, except for the school teacher, who lives across the road.

Some people think sixty is a bit young for retirement but there comes a time to move on. If you don't believe me, just ask the last five prime ministers.

Reflecting on forty years as a police officer, twenty in Victoria, then twenty in Queensland, I said:

I've had a great career. I made the finishing line. I stumbled on the last hurdle but I got over it. A former police commissioner, Mick Miller, once said, 'Policing, you've got a front-row seat on the greatest show on earth, which is life.' You see some good things, some sad things, some happy things. Fortunately, in my career, there's been a lot more happy than sad. Fortunately, I didn't have to shoot anyone. More important, no-one shot me.

Sandra spoke, too. She said:

> You think that you lose your family when you travel remote.
> Well, you do miss family occasions. But you pick up the police
> family. And they are so precious. When Neale was sick, nothing
> was too much trouble. The police service organised everything.
> I'd like to thank every one of you very much.

The proceedings concluded with a presentation by Sergeant Major
Ian Haycock (retired). At sunset he had taken down, folded and
framed the Australian flag that was flown on my last day as the
officer-in-charge of the Birdsville Police Station.

The next day, most of the police headed home, the town settled down, and life pretty much returned to normal. That night,
we (Sandra and I, Evan and Michelle, Don and Lyn, Dusty,
Sergeant Major and Mick Molloy, the relieving cop) had one
more barbeque at the courthouse. It was a perfect evening, with a
beautiful desert sunset. And it was a bit cooler than the previous
couple of days of over 40 degrees.

If I hadn't felt a strong connection with the desert, I probably
wouldn't have lasted nine years in Birdsville. It is beautiful. And
there's never a dull moment. I look at all the jobs I've done over
nine years. It was a great place to work: you're in charge, you
weren't going around dealing with people affected by drugs or
people fighting or neighbourhood disputes and stuff like that.
That sometimes happened over nine years but it was the exception
rather than the rule.

There was always something exciting happening in town,

whether it was the races, the Big Red Run, a rally coming through or a politician coming to town. You're going out on patrol with Don and he's telling you about his land, his culture, his people. Sitting around a campfire having a cup of tea. He takes you to places and you're travelling through the desert, not even on a track. He's just driving but you know with Don, you've got full confidence he'll get you where he wants to take you. And get you back. He's a GPS on two legs, as I say. He's been great, Don.

There's different personalities in town, and they're all unique. The way the town clicks, the way the town operates, some people don't like each other but it doesn't affect community events or social events. They just don't talk to each other.

I really enjoyed the nine years. There's times when it's quiet. In summer the phone hardly ever rings. It's stinking hot and you can't go out but if you've been in England, it's freezing cold and you can't go out there either. You just deal with what you've got. You don't say, 'Gee, I wish it was 30 degrees cooler.' You just know it's going to be hot and you deal with it.

Running the races is a major event, for the town and for the state. So you do everything you can to make sure it's successful, not only by policing it but by making sure people who come there have a good time.

When you're doing rescues, you've got a good car, you make sure you've got it properly prepared. It's the old thing: proper preparation prevents piss-poor performance. You make sure everything's organised. You're paranoid about making sure that people who are overdue come back in. You know if they die it's going to be really bad for you, and worse for them.

Fortunately, almost always it was the opposite. I remember one rescue Don and I did where we were helping a fella bring back this big camper trailer. We stopped for the night and started getting dinner ready and this bloke says, 'No fellas, leave this to me.'

He was a big bloke, very well off, and his whole camper trailer was like a kitchen. He had a fry pan, gas and the whole works. He had Moet champagne. He had a coffee percolator. He made dinner and we were out there drinking champagne and Crown Lager beer, and eating the best steak you could get. We had a great night. Roughing it in the desert.

A pleasant day in the bush?

It was. (Laughter) Definitely.

AFTERWORD

Inspector Trevor Kidd Interview with Evan McHugh

The day after Neale's retirement, I spent some time with Inspector Trevor Kidd who, with Inspector Paul Biggin, has been Neale's boss for all of his time in Birdsville. He believes he may even have been on the selection panel when Neale applied for the job of Birdsville cop. Inspector Kidd has firsthand knowledge of almost all of Neale's exploits and achievements, and the occasional nervous moments along the way.

I first asked him about the challenges involved in having a police officer stationed in one of the most remote places in Australia.

'Headquarters for the district are based in Mount Isa, 700 kilometres from Birdsville. So a lot of it is telephone stuff. It takes a whole day for Neale to drive up to see us or for us to go and to see him.

'Neale is not the sort of guy who ever kicks up and gives you problems. If something's happened he'll say, "This is what's happened and this is what I'm going to do about it. This is what the plan is."

'So he comes back with a solution which, as a manager, that's what you want. He's always been like that. He's dead calm. I've never seen his pulse rate get up at all.

'One of the things is, behind the scenes, Sandra was always around to take calls and organise stuff. She virtually runs that station when he's out gallivanting around the countryside. She's the one that holds the fort. It can't be understated what an important role wives and partners play in remote policing. If we can't find Neale – comms are terrible out here, even a satphone can be terrible – she's the one who knows roughly where he is and what's going on.

'It's always a concern from our point of view that when we've got to rescue someone, we lose our rescuers when they go out there. They did one rescue that was sixteen hours just getting out there. One way. It took them forever. It just went on and on.'

What qualities does the police service look for in a police officer for a town like Birdsville?

'Strictly speaking selection is based on merit. You look at the best applicant for the job. You look for someone you think will fit in with the community. Have they got a family? It's not only the policing side; there's the HR side, the domestic side. It can be very difficult for single people, for instance, in really remote areas. Traditionally, you don't get that many applicants for jobs in these remote places. We kicked a goal when we got Neale. I've gotta admit we initially were going, "Prosecutor? And he wants to come out to Birdsville?" But you talk to 'em and you go, "Yeah, that might work. He's got the right look."

'My vision of Neale, as I say, he'll drive seven hours to come up here. He'll rock up into my office and he's got his uniform on but his shoes probably haven't seen polish for God knows how long. And sometimes I'm not sure how long since his shirt's been ironed. But he just walks in and says "g'day" and "how you goin'?" He's just a really laid-back, easygoing guy but he's absolutely reliable.

'If he says he's going to go sort out a rescue or a crash at the airport – usually it's the landing gear, thankfully, but there'll be instances like that – he'll give you the brief and no matter what's going on, "Yeah, the plane's come down, oh, undercarriage is gone. Yeah, yeah, no, they're alright." It's just the way he goes. Very cool.

'He's got a really good relationship with Australia's rescue authorities. He's one of their key people down here. Imagine, you've been out on some of these journeys with him, Evan, but that relationship that he's got with organisations like that – the South Australian Police and all the other organisations – he's held in really high regard.'

And he's the only person they can call on, isn't he?

'He's the only one. Bedourie's an hour-and-a-half up the road and we'll try and use Bedourie to back up Birdsville and vice versa.'

Do you ever consider the safety of the rescuers when the margin of their safety is so thin?

'We do. Ultimately you're responsible. That's why you need a good briefing from Neale and the people involved. What are the risks? Who have you got going with you? You've got Don, you've got Padraic. Have you got comms? We'll look at the options, too. Do we have access to a chopper? What's the best way to get to these people? Invariably they're out in the middle of nowhere. Even if there's an aircraft, you've still got to get a vehicle there.

'You've got to look at it but you can't go and lose your people or put them at unacceptable risk to go to some of these places. We have to take that into account. That's why we also talk to the rescue authorities, AMSA and all those sorts of places. Alright, what's the best way, a Dornier or something, drop off a package to them to start with until things settle down? You may not be able to get there that day or that night because of the conditions. So we'll try and see if the aircraft can do a drop.

'That's one of the things. Those three bike riders. When they were hurt and they activated their EPIRB, that's one that sticks in my mind the whole time. There's three people, they've activated the EPIRB, there's rescue aircraft costing a fortune going out there. The big drive. The packages are dropped down and they walk over and look at them and go back to their camp. And wait for someone to drive up in a car to them. Didn't check for water, radio comms or anything.

'It's always people doing silly things. People have gone off into the desert and generally speaking when they're getting rescued they've gone off with no water, no experience and Neale and the team from the community end up going out there and basically putting themselves at risk doing it.

'There are people who've had no preparation, no concept of what they're getting themselves into and that's one of the real frustrations with policing not only at the bottom end of our district, Birdsville, but we also go all the way up to Mornington Island and up there in the water, people in the Gulf of Carpentaria do the same thing. They don't prepare, they don't tell anybody, they wander off and do all these adventures and we end up having to rescue them.'

What was it like when you heard there was an emergency in Birdsville but it was Neale being flown out?

'We were devastated when he had the stroke. He'd gone out, done the rescue, came back and didn't feel well. Next thing we know we're getting phone calls. Sandra is talking to us. Everyone is briefing us. He's in the RFDS. We've gotta get him down to hospital and care. Certainly when we envisaged him down there, we're thinking, Life can be tricky sometimes. The fact that he's made the recovery he has is a testament to his character, really. He just plugged away. He's not an extroverted sort of guy but he's got strong willpower and a strong mind and determination. He works his way through it.'

Have there been moments of amazement at some of the things Neale has done?

'There are moments where you smile but there's a great sigh of relief that they've come back. That episode where they virtually drove for a whole day, sixteen hours or whatever it was, to do a rescue. And then you visualise what the country is like, in a couple of troopies, driving through the night and whatever it is and you just go . . . so many things could go wrong. It's what police officers and people supporting them in the community do but you do really have some nervous times when these jobs are going on. Trying to get information back because you don't know what's happening because your comms are so bad usually. It gets nervous waiting. We're really thankful when you do hear they're back and they're safe.

'They've driven out and picked people up and driven over sand dunes or been bogged and had to dig 'emselves out and had to keep going and dig 'emselves out again. He said once, Donnie was even shaking his head and wondering what they were going to do, and you think, They sail pretty close to the edge sometimes but that's policing in a place like this.

'I think I was on the phone when he said he found the Chinook. Neale's famous for saying I've just got this aircraft or this chopper or the army's in town or someone's in town and we're going to do this or that. And you go, holy heck, because in reality there's a lot of procedures and protocols for doing some of this sort of stuff. And again, he's down here, he's the man on the ground, you really have to take onboard what he has to say. If he's got the support of that stuff, we work our way through all the red tape and stuff later on. Everybody works together in these places, and that's what's good about it. No-one gets bogged down too much with things that aren't important at the time. Invariably you get people out. Invariably you can work things through.'

When he told you there was a crocodile in the Diamantina, did you think the remoteness and isolation might have finally gotten to him?

'You smile and have a laugh about it because . . . only in this part of the world. We have lots of things of that nature in our district. We're nearly a quarter of the state and nearly all of it is remote, so these oddball things happen. Then you end up thinking, What idiot brought that down with them? How'd they cart a croc, a freshwater croc, whatever distance, probably from up towards the top end of the state somewhere, and drop it down here? Do you see it getting washed down in a flood? It's not going to happen. So I've got a vision of some young blokes or someone thinkin', Wouldn't it be funny if we drop a croc down at Birdsville or something like that?'

'Then you think, Well that's going to get a lot of media attention. And Neale handles the media really well. Every four-wheel-drive magazine, every magazine in Australia, mentions Birdsville and Neale McShane. He's a part of the legend of the place. And again, Sandra and the family are in there with it. They're a team and without that team the thing doesn't work.'

APPENDIX 1

Useful Diamantina Radio Frequencies

Adria Downs	8 Duplex, UHF 14
Arrabury	1 Duplex, UHF 8
Clifton Hills	UHF 12
Cluny	UHF 9
Coorabulka	UHF 21
Cordillo Downs	UHF 6 and 2
Durrie	3 Duplex
Glengyle	UHF 4
Mooraberree	4 Duplex
Morney Plains	2 Duplex
Mount Leonard	8 Duplex
Pandie Pandie	8 Duplex
Roseberth	UHF 24
Desert frequency	UHF 10

Diamantina Shire vehicles are on UHF 39 and truckies and tourists are usually on UHF 40

Birdsville Police monitor UHF 39, 40 and 8

APPENDIX 2

Neale McShane Medals

Commonwealth Medals

1. Australian Police Medal, entitles Neale to use the Post Nominal APM
2. National Police Service Medal
3. National Medal with first and second clasp.

State Medals

1. Queensland Police Meritorious Service Medal
2. Queensland Police Service Medal with twenty-year clasp (for Diligent and Ethical Service)
3. Victorian Police Service Medal with fifteen-year clasp (for Diligent and Ethical Service)